THE
LIVING DESERTS
OF SOUTHERN AFRICA

Barry Lovegrove

Dedication

This book is dedicated to Jennifer Jarvis and Gideon Louw who introduced me as a student to the wonders of sociality in desert mammals and the physiology of desert organisms, respectively.

Published by Struik Nature
(an imprint of Penguin Random House South Africa (Pty) Ltd)
Reg. No. 1953/000441/07
The Estuaries No. 4, Oxbow Crescent, Century Avenue, Century City, 7441
PO Box 1144, Cape Town, 8000 South Africa

Visit **www.penguinrandomhouse.co.za** and join the Struik Nature Club for updates, news, events and special offers.

First published by Fernwood Press in 1993
Fully updated, revised and redesigned edition published by Struik Nature in 2021

1 3 5 7 9 10 8 6 4 2

Copyright © in text, 1993, 2021: Barry Lovegrove
Copyright © in photographs, 1993, 2021: Barry Lovegrove, unless otherwise indicated
Copyright © in line drawings, 1993, 2021: Loretta Chegwidden
Copyright © in maps and diagrams, 1993, 2021: Barry Lovegrove,
Penguin Random House South Africa (Pty) Ltd, unless otherwise indicated
Copyright © in published edition, 2021: Penguin Random House South Africa (Pty) Ltd

Publisher: Pippa Parker
Managing editor: Roelien Theron
Concept and cover design: Janice Evans
Designer: Neil Bester
Cartographer: Liezel Bohdanowicz
Picture researcher: Colette Stott
Proofreader: Colette Braudo
Indexer: Emsie du Plessis

Reproduction by Studio Repro
Printed and bound in China by C&C Offset Printing Co., Ltd

ISBN 978 1 77584 704 5 (Print)
ISBN 978 1 77584 705 2 (ePub)

Front cover: Namib web-footed gecko, Namib dune sea
Title page: Sossusvlei, Namib-Naukluft National Park
Opposite page: Ground pangolin, Tswalu Kalahari Reserve (Wendy Panaino)
Contents page: Ostriches, Kgalagadi Transfrontier Park
Spine: *Conophytum* species, Succulent Karoo (S Molteno / CC BY-SA 4.0, Wikimedia Commons)
Back cover: Gemsbok, Kuruman River Reserve; Author photograph (Val Adamson)

RESEARCH AND CONSERVATION

OPPENHEIMER

We are committed to leaving the world better than how we found it, and to building sustainable and prosperous societies. We will do this through focused engagement across the land, people and cultures we touch.

Contents

Acknowledgements

I would not have considered a revision of *The Living Deserts of Southern Africa*, from scratch, were it not for the persistent prompting of Duncan MacFadyen, Manager Research and Conservation at Oppenheimer Generations. Thank you, Duncan, for your encouragement. I would also not have been able to undertake the task without the generous sponsorship from Strilli and Nicky Oppenheimer. My heartfelt thanks to the Oppenheimer family and their staff.

During my photographic field trips, I was assisted in various ways by many enthusiastic people: Justin and Vreyni du Toit (Middelburg); Colin and Katya Lovegrove (Barrydale); Andrew McKechnie (University of Pretoria); Pieter and Verencia Bernade (NoHeep Farm, Kamieskroon); Pieter van Wyk (Ai-|Ais/Richtersveld Transfrontier Park); Arnold Meyer, L.W. van der Merwe, Dylan Smith, Gus van Dyk, Xolani Vundla, Wendy Panaino, Thilo Beck (Tswalu Kalahari Reserve); Tim Clutton-Brock, Walter Jubber, Natasha Evans, Léa Sueur, David Seager, Kate Thompson, Camilla Soravia, Nickolas Pattinson (Kuruman River Reserve); Kim Prochachka, Colin Attwood, Phil and Gill Cohen (Cape Town); Marika Raves (Maltahöhe Hotel); Nils Odendaal, Lee Tindall (NamibRand Nature Reserve); Gillian Maggs-Kölling, Eugene Marais (Gobabeb Namib Research Institute); Ed Barthorp, Andrea Pawel, Mwalonga (Zoe) (Oana Nature Reserve); Rynand and Rosie Mudge (Windhoek). Thank you.

Several specialists assisted in identifying plants and animals for me: Rolf Becker (euphorbias), Eugene Marais (insects), Alison Young (various plants), and Andrew Young (conophytums). Thank you.

Without the generosity of many biologists and photographers, this edition of *Living Deserts* would have been unaffordable. I am truly grateful to those who provided me with their photographs, either at no charge or at a reduced price: Chantelle Bosch, Andrew Young, Gert Krüger, Oliver Halsey, Peter Chadwick, Maria Oosthuizen, Ryno Kemp, Carsten Schradin, Galun Rathbun, Daryl Balfour, Peter Steyn, Andre Demlon, Gus Mills, Maxime Briola, Wendy Panaino, Mark Anderson, Trip Lamb, Stuart Nielsen, Timm Hoffman, Hana Petersen, Marinus de Jager, Michael Whitehead, Denis Hansen, Petra Wester, Steve Johnson, Timo van der Niet, Glen Pure, John Sibbick, Victoria Keding, Denis Hesemanse and Nils Odendaal. Thank you.

A special word of thanks must go to Val Adamson, for the author photograph on the back cover.

I am grateful to Tony Weaver for reviewing Chapter Ten.

At Penguin Random House I would like to thank Pippa Parker, publisher of Struik Nature, and the rest of her publishing team – Roelien Theron, Neil Bester and Colette Stott – for their diligence and their professional and creative guidance throughout the making of this book. Thanks, also, to Liezel Bohdanowicz for her superb maps and diagrams.

Lastly, I am very grateful to my partner, Christopher Duigan, for holding the fort on my long absences from home and for making it easy for me to work from home in my own office.

Opposite: The grass *Stipagrostis sabulicola* grows along the lower slopes of dunes in the Namib Desert, where the water content is the highest.

Preface

Twenty-eight years have passed since Fernwood Press published the first edition of *The Living Deserts of Southern Africa* in 1993. I was young and unemployed when I wrote the book, and my head was stuffed with the science behind how animals and plants have adapted to living in arid and desolate regions – a passion I wished to share with others who love deserts. Now I am older, wiser, retired, but no less fascinated by the remarkable deserts in our region.

As the first edition relied on design and printing technologies that are now dated, I was faced with the daunting task of starting from scratch, recreating the text and all the visual components that made up the earlier book – about 500 photographs, maps and diagrams. Understandably, I delayed this quest – very pleasant, as it turned out – until retirement. I undertook four photographic field trips in 2019 and 2020 and, wherever I travelled, in Namaqualand, the Kalahari and the Karoo, I was humbled to learn that in the intervening years *Living Deserts* had become the holy writ for many: tourist guides, reserve management staff, researchers, students and others. So, it gives me enormous pleasure to be able to offer a revised edition to those who have utilised and enjoyed my book for so long, and to those who have yet to discover the deserts of southern Africa.

Today I understand adaptations to desert environments in plants and animals so much better than before because our way of studying the subject has changed significantly during this time. When I wrote the first edition, I called myself an ecophysiologist – someone who studies animals' physiological adaptations to their environment. Physiologists are drawn to deserts, for it is in deserts more than any other terrestrial habitat that plants and animals suffer the most and endure the harshest physical conditions. It is in them that the most interesting and predominantly physiological adaptations occur.

But then I discovered that the term 'adaptation' was being severely abused. In the 1980s, and even before then, adaptation was the explanation given for every little trait difference between species in different habitats – an approach that the famous, and controversial, evolutionary biologist Stephen Jay Gould called the 'Adaptationist Programme'.

The question that gave rise to a new discourse, advocated by the population geneticist Joseph Felsenstein, was this: how much of the value of the trait that is being claimed to be adaptive is truly adaptive, and how much has been inherited unchanged from its ancestor? For a trait to be considered adaptive, its value would need to be different – to have evolved – from that of its common ancestor, indicating that the species had adapted to the modern environment. In the case of an inherited trait, its value might indeed have been adaptive in the common ancestor, long ago, but it is not necessarily adaptive in the descendant if the trait remains unchanged.

Answering this pivotal, novel question requires the construction of a family tree of the study species in order to discover how species in the group are related, who their common extinct ancestors are, and when new lineages appeared. For example, if you were studying humans (*Homo sapiens*), you would need to construct a family tree of anthropoid apes, or take it even further and include the monkeys, lorises, galagos, lemurs and so on. This approach is known as phylogenetics, and its inferences concerning adaptations apply to all disciplines of biology today, not just physiology.

Those physiologists who were previously indifferent to evolution were now obliged to think like Charles Darwin. Some balked at the prospect, but many embraced the new discipline of evolutionary physiology, and I, for one, willingly became one of its adherents. I have called myself an evolutionary physiologist for 20 years of my 25-year career and I have loved every moment of it.

The change in philosophical direction in animal and plant physiology did not mean that ecophysiology would become redundant – far from it. There was, and always will be, an important role for mechanistic physiology

---

Opposite: A meerkat, having climbed up a camel thorn tree, keeps a lookout for predators. Meerkats take turns to act as sentries so that the rest of the group can forage at ease.

to play in asking crucial 'how' questions. For example, we might want to know: how do plants or animals deal with heat and water fluxes? Evolutionary physiology, on the other hand, approaches the same subject with 'why' questions: why do heat and water fluxes differ between species in different habitat types? Of course, these two disciplines are not mutually independent. Evolutionary physiology remains dependent on mechanistic physiology for understanding physiological form and function in plants and animals.

If I were to expunge the term 'adaptation' from this edition in all cases where phylogenetics was not employed to verify adaptive processes, there would be nothing left to publish. In short, an enormous amount of verification is yet to be undertaken, and a mound of data still needs to be reworked and re-analysed from an evolutionary perspective. I emphasise this point because many traits that I attribute to adaptations in plants and animals may one day be found to be inherited. Time, ultimately, will allow us to distinguish between adaptation and inheritance.

Nevertheless, there are several instances in this new edition of how phylogenetics has been applied in concert with mechanistic physiology. A beautiful example is provided in Chapter Ten, in which the evolution of the extraordinary succulent Aizoaceae plants is discussed.

I share this perspective because it helps to explain my approach to the revision of the various chapters in this book. In particular, those chapters dealing with heat, water and metabolic adaptations are mostly mechanistic in nature, and so did not require much revision other than the addition of new data.

Chapter One has been extensively edited, made necessary by the publication of an updated vegetation map by the South African National Biodiversity Institute (SANBI) in 2018.[1] The computational methods to identify biomes, bioregions and vegetation units are more advanced nowadays and the new biomes map provides a much-improved description of the vegetation of the desert biomes.

I have added a new chapter on the palaeontological history of the Karoo. It was inspired by my frustration at the general lack of appreciation, certainly by South Africans, of the extraordinary animals that once roamed the Nama-Karoo millions of years ago. How can I discuss the Nama-Karoo without mentioning that, underfoot, carnivorous and herbivorous proto-mammals and dinosaurs lie fossilised in ecosystems that were very different to those of the modern Nama-Karoo? I needed to limit the chapter's contents, but if you wish to appreciate how phylogenetics has been used to bring these animals back to life, you might like to read my book *Fires of Life: Endothermy in Birds and Mammals.*[2]

The chapter that has been edited most extensively is Chapter Ten – The future of the deserts. This is for very good reason, as the chapter now incorporates new developments in conservation and climate change. When I wrote the first edition, very few biologists were aware of climate change. Moreover, very little was known about the climate monsters, El Niño and its wicked sister La Niña, which terrorise the world's climates today, especially in the Southern Hemisphere. Climate change, more than any other threat, will have and already has had the greatest impact on southern Africa's deserts. The rate at which change is occurring means that in a single lifetime these deserts will be significantly altered – never to be the same as when they were first enjoyed. On a positive note, though, it is pleasing to report that, with the exception of the Nama-Karoo, there has been a substantial increase in the size of land that has been set aside for conservation. This trend has been driven in part by the establishment of three large, privately owned reserves.

One of the biggest changes that I have made to the book is the manner in which most of the scientific information has been sourced and cited. I have added discrete endnote numbers that correspond with a list of publications at the back of the book. I have done this mostly to direct students and researchers in desert biology to the original information, and to provide interested readers with the opportunity to delve deeper into the subject. In addition, it also allowed me to reduce the number of graphs and diagrams that some readers of the first edition found to be too scientific.

Lastly, a comment on place names. I am a sentimental old man. The names 'Kalahari' and 'Acacia' pulse through my veins alongside those of Neil Young, Beethoven, Chopin and Robert Jacob Gordon. But for the sake of science, I needed to make some blood-thickening compromises. The former Kalahari Gemsbok Park has now been incorporated into the Kgalagadi Transfrontier Park. However, throughout the book I have retained the word 'Kalahari', except when referring to the park.

The same applies to the Orange River, which was given its name by the early explorer and commander of the Cape Garrison, Robert Jacob Gordon, in the eighteenth century. It is derived from the name of the royal Dutch dynasty, the House of Orange. Some publications, maps and organisations, however, refer to the river as the Gariep, an Afrikaans rendition of the Khoekhoe word !Garib.

My preference for the retention of the earlier names is based simply on the fact that they have been recognised internationally for a very long time, so foreign readers of the book are unlikely to get confused – and neither will Google Maps.

Those are easy compromises to make, and they do not involve science. But, by far the most jarring for me concerns the change of the name Acacia to either Vachellia or Senegalia. My favourite of all trees, the camel thorn, which I have always known as Acacia erioloba, I must now call Vachellia erioloba, if I possess any respect for science, which I do in buckets. With the advent of phylogenetics, the group of approximately 1,500 species of tree and shrub previously lumped into the genus Acacia has now been shown to have formed several distinct lineages. After a long and extremely emotional and acrimonious bun fight among botanists, final agreement was reached at the 17th International Botanical Congress in Melbourne in 2011.[3] The Australians got to keep the name Acacia for their acacias, and Africa's 'acacias' became either Vachellia or Senegalia. I have used the new names when referring to various trees formally, but I have employed the term 'acacia' or 'acacias' to refer to them informally. Science does not bother with informalities.

Apart from the demise of the African Acacia, there has been a surprisingly large number of name changes for plants and animals over the past several decades. Again, these changes can be attributed to the explosion of phylogenetic techniques. Some are again hard to accept, such as the change of the name Aloe to Aloidendron in some species, but others will hardly be noticed. I have double-checked all generic and species names, but if I have missed any, I take full blame.

BARRY LOVEGROVE
PIETERMARITZBURG

The deserts of southern Africa

Above: Two subadult meerkats, recorded in the Kuruman River Reserve, learn to scan the environment for danger.

Left: The Ai-IAis/Richtersveld Transfrontier Park in the Succulent Karoo – seen here after a nine-year drought – is a biodiversity hotspot, despite being one of the most arid regions in southern Africa.

The words 'living deserts' in the title of this book may seem contradictory to those who know that the term 'desert' is derived from the Latin *desertus*, meaning 'abandoned'. How 'living', one may ask, can an abandoned place be? The immediate image that comes to mind when most of us think of a desert is one of a desolate, scorching hot and dry place where very little seems to live or grow. And yet, while it is certainly true that deserts in general support less life than rain forests do, the deserts of southern Africa reveal the richest diversity of life of all the deserts of the world, if one only knows when and where to look.

There are, for example, 204 species of vertebrates that are known to occur in southern Africa's desert regions and nowhere else in the world: 121 are reptiles, five are frogs, 44 are birds and 34 are mammals. To add to this variety, there are many species – such as gemsbok, eland, rhino, elephant and lion – that occur even in the driest of desert regions, but also range more widely throughout the wetter African biomes, and therefore do not qualify as true desert vertebrates. This is also true for several bird species that move into and out of the desert regions in response to seasonal or unpredictable abundances of food. The fact that reptiles constitute the highest proportion of the desert vertebrates clearly illustrates the worldwide tendency for these cold-blooded (ectothermic) creatures to predominate in particularly arid climates. In southern Africa the species richness of reptiles is particularly impressive: in the Namib Desert, which is very small compared with other deserts of the world, there are no fewer than 23 endemic species.

Having mentioned species richness, though, it must be stressed that this book is not a field guide to all the organisms of the deserts of southern Africa. More than anything, its aim is to convince the interested naturalist or traveller that the 'stop-identify-tick-go' syndrome associated, quite understandably, with the profusion of excellent field guides in our bookshops can be so much more rewarding when supported by an understanding of the basic principles that allow desert organisms to eke out their existences. And that is what this book is about: how desert plants and animals are adapted to cope with the rigours of desert life. And rigours there are in abundance: scarcity of water; extremes of temperature; shortage of food and shade; and, in general, conditions that are variable and unpredictable.

Subsequent chapters discuss how desert organisms are adapted to these rigours in terms of their form and structure, their ecology and behaviour and, most importantly, their vital functions such as nutrition, respiration, excretion and reproduction. In this introductory chapter, however, let us first develop an adequate definition of a desert, and identify and describe the four distinct desert regions of southern Africa.

Towards a definition of a desert

There are several ways in which a desert may be defined. The simplest and most common modern definition classifies desert regions according to their mean (average) annual rainfall, recognising three categories: extremely arid deserts (up to 100 millimetres mean annual rainfall); arid deserts (100 to 250 millimetres); and semi-arid deserts (250 to 500 millimetres). If we were to accept this definition and take the 500-millimetre rainfall isohyet as the cut-off value

below which we could define southern Africa's deserts, irrespective of the degree of aridity, then our desert region would extend from southern Angola virtually to the foot of Table Mountain on the west coast and clear across the southern African subcontinent to within 230 kilometres of the Mozambique coastline in the east. Few people would question the inclusion of the Kalahari and Namib deserts in this conceptual zone and, at a stretch for some, Namaqualand and the Karoo. But we would inevitably encounter opposition if we incorporated the northern parts of South Africa (North West Province, Mpumalanga and Limpopo, including most of the Kruger National Park), southern Zimbabwe and western Mozambique. Yet these areas do fall within the 500-millimetre isohyet and thus would qualify as semi-arid deserts.

A major shortcoming of a definition of a desert based solely on the rainfall statistic is that it conveys absolutely no information to us – and certainly not to desert organisms – about how much rain falls in a single rainfall event in any given region. Nor does it tell us how frequently such rainfall events occur. This information is of paramount importance to inhabitants of desert regions, for although the total amount of annual rain is certainly crucial for ensuring successful life, the predictability and variability of the rainfall determine the type and function of such life. And that is the subject of much of this book: how desert organisms overcome the risks of simply not 'knowing' when it will rain next.

Rainfall events over most of the typical desert regions of southern Africa are notoriously infrequent, unpredictable and variable from year to year. In fact, the rainfall in the northwestern part of the subcontinent is about four times more variable than it is in the northeastern sector. The unpredictability of rainfall increases dramatically the further north one travels up the west coast from Cape Town, reaching its peak in the Namib Desert (see Chapter Ten for a discussion on El Niño effects). Here it is not uncommon for a number of consecutive years to pass with hardly a drop of rain, and then for one sudden storm to deliver two or three times the average annual rainfall in a matter of hours. So, although two regions may have an equal mean annual rainfall on paper, in real terms the reliability of the pattern of rainfall that each region receives may be markedly different.

Basing his definition on these criteria, Israeli botanist Imanuel Noy-Meir described a desert as being 'a water-controlled ecosystem with infrequent, discrete and largely unpredictable water inputs'.[1] While this working definition is a long way from presenting a complete picture of a

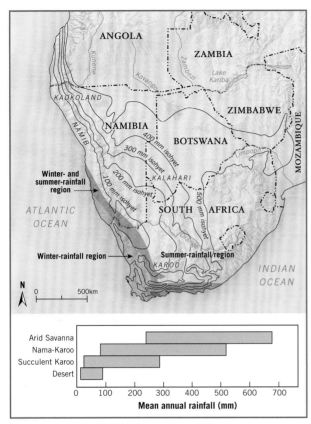

The mean annual rainfall in southern Africa. The subcontinent is subdivided into regions of winter rainfall, summer rainfall, and between them, both winter and summer rainfall. Sixty per cent of the annual rainfall occurs between April and September in the winter-rainfall zone, and between October and March in the summer-rainfall zone. The inset graph shows the mean annual rainfall of each of the desert biomes. (South African Weather Service)

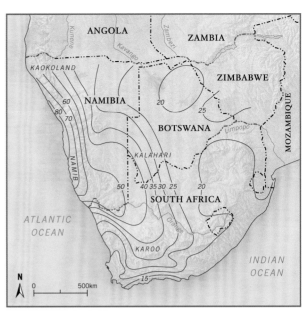

The relative variability (unpredictability) of annual rainfall in southern Africa. The figures represent the percentage of the variability of the mean annual rainfall. (South African Weather Service)

desert, let us accept it as a starting point from which to explore southern Africa's arid regions more thoroughly.

Quantity and predictability of rainfall are major factors, but another consideration that cannot be ignored is the rate at which moisture may be lost through evaporation. Even if two different regions were to receive a similar pattern and quantity of rain per year, this does not mean that equal amounts of water would be available to the organisms living there – the two areas may have entirely different rates of evaporation (see box, overleaf). The ratio of evaporation to precipitation can therefore also be used to define a desert. In this case, a desert can be classified as a region in which the annual evaporation from standard water pans exceeds the precipitation into the pans. Using this criterion, we can identify differences between the eastern part of the subcontinent and the western arid zones.

As shown by map F in the box on the evaporative power of desert air (page 17), the average rate of annual evaporation in the northeastern sector of our conceptual 500-millimetre isohyet desert zone is considerably lower than that in the west. Moreover, those parts of the western interior that do not benefit from daily doses of cool, moist oceanic air, for example the Kalahari Desert, have a much lower relative humidity (map C) and therefore a higher water vapour saturation deficit (map E) throughout the year. The saturation deficit determines the rate of evaporation. It is the difference in water vapour pressure between a body of air that is fully saturated (100 per cent relative humidity), such as that immediately above your skin, and one that is partially saturated, for example, air with 50 per cent relative humidity. The value gets large, of course, when the relative humidity of the air is low, and then the rate of evaporation is massive.

Climatic statistics alone cannot give a satisfactory definition of a desert. However, a study of climatic patterns, such those affecting water availability, which in turn affect the lives of plants and animals, leads to an alternative approach: to identify certain traits in plants and animals which might indicate whether some are better adapted to the rigours of desert life than others. Thus, we shift the focus of the definition from the environment to its inhabitants.

The evaporative power of desert air

A hot-air balloon drifts gently above the Pro-Namib in Namibia. In the distance the vast dune sea of the Desert Biome can be seen. The plains in the foreground host annual grasses vital to the survival of desert vertebrates and insects.

The immense evaporating power of desert air strongly increases the rate of water lost not only from the desert surface after rain, but also from plants and animals. Evaporation is higher in the northwestern parts of southern Africa than it is in the northeast because of differences in a number of interrelated climatic features.

In the first place, the west has the highest levels of incoming radiation (that is, thermal heat, measured as joules per square metre) from the sun in summer (map A). This is due mainly to the fact that the west has an average of 330 days with 50 per cent of maximum possible sunshine per year compared with 240 to 270 days in the east (map B). The relative humidity, or amount of water vapour in the air, in the interior of the west is about a third of that in the east because it is fed with descending dry air masses from the north, whereas the east receives air masses generated over the warm Mozambique Current (map C). Daytime relative humidity frequently remains below 20 per cent throughout the year in the northern Nama-Karoo and southern Kalahari Desert.

The clearer skies and lower relative humidity mean that there is little moisture in the air to impede the passage of the incoming radiation, and so high maximum summer temperatures occur in the west (map D).

If the relative humidity of the air is low, that is, there is not much water vapour in the air, then the water vapour pressure of the air is considerably less than that of the air over moist surfaces that are saturated with water vapour at the same temperature. The difference between vapour pressures, measured as the water vapour pressure saturation deficit, is a measure of the dryness of the air, and can be considered to be an indication of its evaporative power: low vapour pressure results in high saturation deficits, which generate high rates of evaporation, such as occur in the west (map E).

In association with the intense solar radiation, high temperatures, low relative humidity and high saturation deficits, the measured average annual evaporation from water pans in the western half of southern Africa is about twice as high as it is in the eastern half (map F).

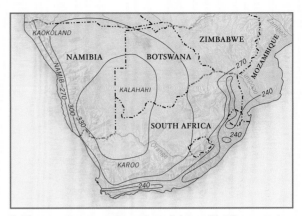

A: The incoming thermal radiation (megajoules per square metre per day) from the sun, measured in summer.[2]

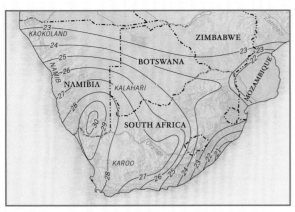

B: The average annual number of days with 50 per cent or more of the possible sunshine duration. (South African Weather Service)

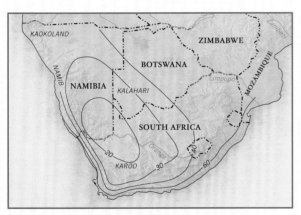

C: The mean monthly relative humidity (per cent) measured each day in January. (South African Weather Service)

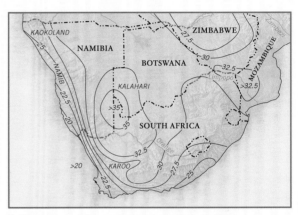

D: The mean daily maximum temperature (°C) for January.[3]

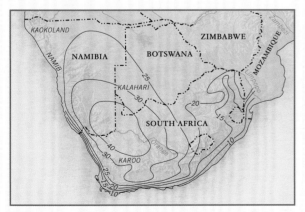

E: The mean water vapour pressure saturation deficit (WVPSD: millibars) at 14h00 each day in January. WVPSD is an index of the evaporating power of the air. (South African Weather Service)

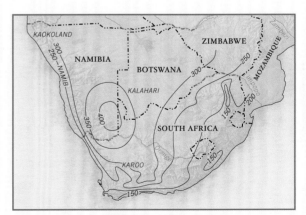

F: The average annual evaporation (centimetres) from evaporation pans. The strong west–east gradient is an outcome of a combination of the climatic effects depicted in the maps on this page. (South African Weather Service)

Kingdoms, biomes, bioregions and vegetation units

The most sensible place to start looking for adaptive traits in desert organisms is at the bottom of the food chain, in plants. As soon as mention is made of plant distributions in southern Africa, it is very important to emphasise the unique nature of the subcontinent's flora. It is a remarkable fact that the vegetation of southern Africa, especially that of the Cape Floristic Region, which spans the Western, Northern and Eastern Cape and contains about 9,000 species in 90,000 square kilometres, is comparable with the most florally diverse equatorial forests.[4-7] Moreover, 70 per cent of the species are endemic to the winter-rainfall region of the Cape Floristic Region, which is extremely unusual for continental plants – the patterns of endemism are more typical of plants on offshore islands.[8]

It was once believed that the vegetation type known as fynbos, on account of its high number of endemic families, was solely responsible for the high species richness in the Cape Floristic Region. Nevertheless, even when fynbos is excluded from analyses of plant species diversity in the Cape flora, southern Africa still boasts very high plant species diversity. Indeed, when averaged over the entire region, the number of plant species that grow in southern Africa is nearly twice the number that grow in Australia, a large continent that is comparable in many climatic respects. So where, then, is this non-fynbos diversity to be found? One need look no further than the deserts.[9]

In our attempt to define a desert, the important question to address is: are there obvious differences in plant adaptations that would allow us to separate one broad region with its representative plants from another? In many respects, the German philosopher, geographer and naturalist Alexander von Humboldt answered this question two centuries ago. While climbing the formidable Chimborazo Mountains in Ecuador in 1802, he realised that plant associations and adaptations could indeed be separated on the basis of climate and altitude.[10] In fact, attitudinal gradients frequently serve as good illustrations of climate-related adaptations in plants. Even in southern Africa observant travellers may note conspicuous boundaries geographically separating general vegetation types along an altitudinal gradient.

Some transitions between plant patterns are clear and abrupt, whereas others, with less obvious boundaries, are more difficult to distinguish. Nevertheless, southern Africa has been divided into nine major vegetation patterns, or biomes. Since the essence of biome classification is to identify geographically distinct plant associations that display obvious adaptations – for example, to their respective soils, topography or climates – for our purposes the biomes that define desert-adapted vegetation should suffice to define our desert vegetation types.

The concept of a biome has developed dramatically since the first edition of this book. Early studies defined a biome on the basis of the 'plant life-form' system of plant categorisation originally proposed by the Danish botanist Christen Raunkiaer in 1934.[11] Raunkiaer's argument was

The Fynbos Biome, to the south of the Succulent Karoo Biome, is famous for its biodiversity. It is also the habitat of the orange-breasted sunbird, a fynbos endemic.

The Cape sugarbird, seen atop a *Leucospermum*, is indigenous to the Fynbos Biome. It is one of two species in a family found only in southern Africa.

elegant and quite simple, and although there have been many attempts to modify his method, it still remains the 'quick and dirty' way to identify a biome. If you were to be dumped anywhere on Earth in a foreign habitat, it would take you a few minutes to define the surrounding biome using Raunkiaer's method. He proposed that the feature of the plant that defends it against the unfavourable season – in his case, the minimum temperatures of the European winter – would provide a good index of the plant's adaptation to its climate. The feature he chose was the height of the bud-bearing shoot of the plant relative to ground level. Since the air temperature always decreases sharply within the first few metres above ground, his logic was that plants that bore their buds high up must be better adapted to the worst extremes of the European winter. On this basis he proposed five different life-form classes: phanerophytes (trees), chamaephytes (shrubs), hemicryptophytes (grasses), cryptophytes (bulbous plants) and therophytes (annuals). These were the life forms that I discussed in the first edition of this book.

These are horrible words; they do not slip off the tongue easily and are not intuitive for a non-specialist. Fortunately, a new classification scheme uses the term 'growth form' instead of 'life form' (see box, page 20), and employs descriptive terms and qualifiers for each growth form that we can more easily understand: tree (small, tall, emergent, succulent, fern); shrub (low, tall, soft, geoxylic suffrutex, succulent, semiparasitic, semicarnivorous); climber (woody, woody succulent, herbaceous, herbaceous succulent); herb (herb, megaherb, geophytic, succulent, parasitic, carnivorous, aquatic); epiphyte (herb, succulent, shrub, parasitic herb, semiparasitic shrub); graminoid, or grass-like (graminoid, mega-graminoid, bamboo); and other (moss, liverwort, lichen, macroalgae).[12, 13] All these forms, except geoxylic suffrutices and geophytes, can easily be imagined: they grow above ground. A geoxylic suffrutex is a large, underground woody rhizome that usually imitates the plant's low shrub form above ground, and a geophyte is a plant with herbaceous underground storage organs such as rhizomes, corms, tubers and bulbs.

The concept of a biome is considerably more complex now than it was when *Living Deserts* was first published. The definition goes way beyond criteria based merely on the physiognomy of the vegetation. Ladislav Mucina at Murdoch University in Perth, Australia, reviewed the biome concept in 2018, describing it as follows: '[A] biome is a multiscale phenomenon, spanning several large-scale spatial levels, including global climatic zones, continents

The iconic quiver tree is endemic to the Desert, Succulent Karoo and parts of the Nama-Karoo biomes.

Four species of plant huddle together in a granite fissure in the coastal Sandveld of the Succulent Karoo.

and landscapes at subcontinental and supraregional scales. At all scales, they may show various vegetation-physiognomic aspects that could represent multiple stable states. The patches of biomes are linked by a common network of ecological processes that define the selective pressures as macroclimatic, soil-related, hydrological and natural large-scale disturbance factors and stressors. A biome at any large spatial scale is a tangible, ecological-evolutionary unit, carrying a legacy of deep evolutionary assembly processes. Depending on the extent of the spatial scale, we may be able to distinguish zonobiomes, subzonobiomes and continental/regional biomes. Biomes are basic building blocks that make up the biosphere.'[14]

Plant growth forms

A biome can loosely be defined as a large, naturally occurring community of vegetation and wildlife that has adapted to a specific climate. In addition to factors such as soil type, climate and topography, the combination of dominant plant growth forms serves as an important defining criterion. In the desert biomes, the most important forms are trees, shrubs, grasses and herbs (annuals). Climbers and epiphytes, such as lichens growing on other plants, occur too. Examples of these growth forms are given below.

Trees: Woody trees of any size, such as camel thorn trees (*Vachellia erioloba*), Arid Savanna Biome.

Shrubs: Some common shrubs are *Lampranthus* and *Ruschia*, Sandveld, Succulent Karoo Biome.

Grasses: Short plants with long, narrow leaves, such as *Themeda triandra*, a palatable grass for herbivores, Nama-Karoo Biome.

Herbs (annuals): Plants such as Namaqualand daisies (*Dimorphotheca*) that grow seasonally, mostly from seed, Succulent Karoo Biome.

Climbers: Rooted plants, such as *Microloma sagittatum,* that clamber up other plants for support, Succulent Karoo Biome.

Epiphytes: Plants, including *Teloschistes capensis* (seen here), that grow on other plants and derive nutrients from the air, rain or fog, Sandveld, Succulent Karoo Biome.

More than a hundred species of the small, button-like *Conophytum* genus are endemic to the Succulent Karoo.

Do not get too flustered by Mucina's wording. All we need to know is that, using the concept of the biome, and employing vegetation, geographical, soil type, climate, topographical and several other databases, computer models developed by the South African National Biodiversity Institute (SANBI) produced a comprehensive vegetation map of South Africa in 2006. The map, as well as descriptions of each biome's vegetation units, appears in *The Vegetation of South Africa, Lesotho and Swaziland*, edited by Ladislav Mucina and Mike Rutherford.[15] It is essential reading for anybody interested in South Africa's extraordinary flora. It is available online and is an extremely useful source of information when travelling because you can easily identify and read all about the surrounding vegetation units, as long as you know where you are! Although Mucina and Rutherford's biomes map has been updated (2018), only their earlier map and vegetation descriptions were available to the public at the time of publication.

Nine biomes were identified in South Africa, but only four of them can be considered to be desert biomes: the Nama-Karoo, Succulent Karoo, Desert and parts of the Savanna biomes. In addition to the nine biomes, 36 bioregions within the nine biomes were identified and mapped. A bioregion is a composite spatial terrestrial unit defined on the basis of similar biotic and physical features and processes as that of a biome, but at a regional scale. There are two bioregions recognised in the small southern distribution of the Desert Biome that occurs along the Orange River in South Africa: the Southern Namib Desert Bioregion and the Gariep Desert Bioregion. The main distribution of the Desert Biome is in Namibia. There are six bioregions within the Succulent Karoo: Richtersveld Bioregion, Namaqualand Hardeveld Bioregion, Namaqualand Sandveld Bioregion, Knersvlakte Bioregion, Trans-Escarpment Succulent Karoo Bioregion and Rainshadow Valley Karoo Bioregion. The Nama-Karoo hosts three bioregions: Bushmanland Bioregion, Upper Karoo Bioregion and Lower Karoo Bioregion. There are six Savanna biome bioregions; only two can be considered as desert bioregions based purely on their westernmost distributions and climatic criteria. These regions are the Eastern Kalahari Bushveld Bioregion and the Kalahari Duneveld Bioregion.

In theory, biome classification calls for the inclusion of the dominant animal as well as plant growth forms, but this has not proved to be practical or realistic. The first problem is to isolate in an animal a physiological trait that can be identified as an adaptation to certain climatic conditions. Such traits do exist, particularly in arid-adapted animals, but they cannot be easily or readily measured in the field. In this respect, the mobility of animals is an obvious difference between plants and animals. Plants, being sedentary, simply have to endure all climatic extremes, whereas most animals can escape the harshest conditions by burrowing underground, entering insulated nests, or simply leaving the area completely. It is therefore not surprising that plants show clearer growth form patterns in relation to climate. Some biologists argue that it is really not important if animals are excluded from biome classification procedures. They maintain that there should, in any event, be a fairly strong degree of correspondence between plants and animals because the vegetation determines, among other things, the nature of the habitat for animals. Whatever the case, until an appropriate character is identified, zoological-geographical surveys will continue to record simply the presence or absence of animal species.

The mesemb shrub *Drosanthemum striatum* is a member of the Aizoaceae family, the major contributor to the high biodiversity of the Succulent Karoo.

Desert biomes of southern Africa

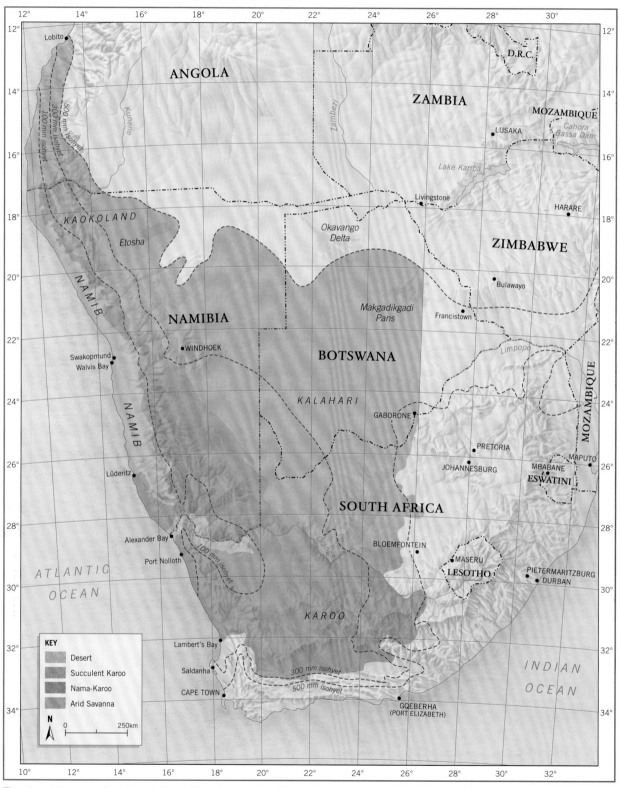

The desert biomes of southern Africa: Desert, Succulent Karoo, Nama-Karoo and Arid Savanna biomes.[16]

The desert biomes of southern Africa

The deserts of southern Africa represent more than half the subcontinent's land mass, covering the western coastal belt between 12°S and 33°S and extending into the Kalahari Basin and the central Karoo plateau as far as about 26°E (see map, opposite page). The following descriptions of the subcontinent's four desert biomes highlight some of their most interesting aspects.

Desert Biome

Southern Africa's Desert Biome coincides with the Namib Desert. It consists of a coastal plain roughly 100 to 150 kilometres wide that extends from 26°S in Namibia to 12°S in Angola. Sloping gently towards the Atlantic Ocean, the coastal plain drops 1,000 metres over its entire breadth. In the south it is patterned by a spectacular sea of linear and crescent-shaped sand dunes that may reach a height of 300 metres above the desert floor. Between the dune sea and the ocean runs a strip of low sand hummocks that are formed when windblown sand is trapped by dwarf shrubs such as the pencil bush (*Arthraerua leubnitziae*) and the dollar bush (*Zygophyllum stapfii*).

The Kuiseb River seldom flows for long but does so often enough to arrest the dunes' northward march, driven by prevailing southerly winds. Originating in the Khomas Hochland, a mountainous area that cradles Windhoek to the east, the Kuiseb once emptied into the Atlantic Ocean. Nowadays, on the rare occasions that it does flow, its passage to the sea is blocked by the sand dunes south of Walvis Bay. The well-known Gobabeb Namib Research Institute is situated on the north bank of the Kuiseb River, about 120 kilometres southeast of Walvis Bay. To the north of the Kuiseb riverbed the dunes give way to gravel plains that are dotted with inselbergs of granite, schist and limestone and a few mountains, the most dramatic of which is the Brandberg (2,573 metres). As the coastal plain tapers northwards into Angola it is traversed by one of the few perennial rivers of the region, the Kunene.

The biome is an extreme desert, having a mean annual rainfall that ranges from 5 millimetres in the west to 85 millimetres along its eastern limits. The persistent lack

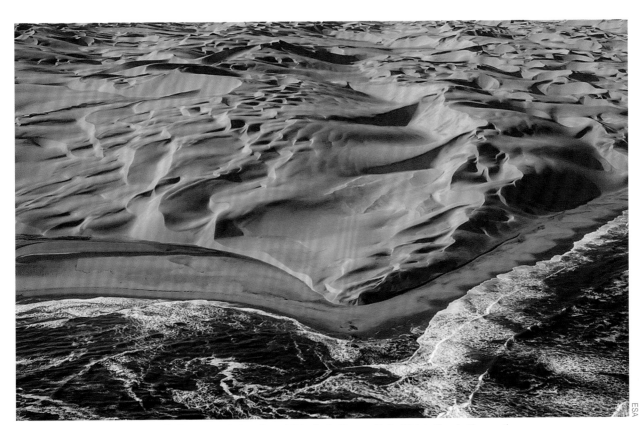

ESA

The vast dune sea of the Namib Desert stretches from Lüderitz in the south to Walvis Bay in the north.

Dominant growth forms of the desert biomes

Desert Biome

Annuals (mostly grasses) that, in the Namib Desert for example, constitute 96 per cent of the canopy cover, excluding drainage lines.

This photograph, taken in the NamibRand Nature Reserve in Namibia, demonstrates the widespread dominance of the short annual Stipagrostis *grasses. Camel thorn trees are confined to the drainage lines and are therefore not considered dominant plant growth forms of the Desert Biome.*

Succulent Karoo Biome

Dwarf shrubs that, in the Robertson Karoo, for example, constitute 85 per cent of the canopy cover.

Taken in the Goegap Nature Reserve near Springbok, this photograph shows vegetation dominated by succulent shrubs. Note the absence of trees and grasses, except for the iconic succulent tree Aloidendron dichotomum.

Nama-Karoo Biome

Dwarf shrubs and grasses that, in the upper Orange River area, for example, make up 63 per cent and 36 per cent of the canopy cover, respectively.

This photograph, taken east of Middelburg in the Eastern Cape, shows typical vegetation of the eastern Nama-Karoo, where grasses dominate and dwarf shrubs are rare. Towards the west in the Nama-Karoo the ratio of grasses to shrubs decreases.

Arid Savanna Biome

Grasses constitute more than 50 per cent of the canopy cover, and woody tree shrubs the balance.

Camel thorn trees – a common tree species of the Arid Savanna – grow on the sands of the Kalahari Desert near Nossob. The photograph also shows various dominant grasses, of which the species Stipagrostis amabilis *occurs on dune crests.*

of rain is caused by high-pressure air masses that are carried south by the high-altitude, anti-cyclonic winds from the equator and descend as dry air (see Chapter Ten). At times, thick fog is generated along the coast as air masses from the mid-Atlantic are cooled over the cold Benguela Current and then blown inland over the desert landscape. This coastal fog is the Namib's crucial life-support system, and is clearly an important factor contributing to the remarkably high diversity of animal life in an extremely arid environment.

Based on the enormous biological importance of the coastal fog, the Namib Desert can be divided into three sectors: coastal, central and inland. The narrow coastal zone has a mean annual rainfall of 5 to 20 millimetres and has thick coastal fog on more than 180 days of the year. In the central Namib, 40 to 80 kilometres inland, the mean annual rainfall increases from 20 to 50 millimetres, temperatures are higher, and fog, although still very important to desert organisms, occurs on only about 40 days of the year. Further inland, fog is rare, temperatures increase sharply, and the mean annual rainfall increases from 50 millimetres to a maximum of 85 millimetres in places.

The vegetation of the Desert Biome is characterised by a dominance of annual grasses that persist through long periods of drought in the form of seeds. An explosion of grasses, mostly species of the genus *Stipagrostis*, can transform the normally barren desert landscape virtually

Life-sustaining fog generated over the chilly upwelled waters of the Atlantic Ocean moves inland at night and retreats again the next morning.

The well-known Gobabeb Namib Research Institute operates from the north bank of the Kuiseb River.

The Kuiseb River is a critically important linear oasis in the Namib Desert, separating the dune sea from the northern gravel plains.

The Namib Desert is not tree country. However, some succulents, such as *Euphorbia avasmontana*, seen here in the NamibRand Nature Reserve, can grow to a considerable size.

overnight after an effective rainfall of about 20 millimetres or more. It is on the basis of these episodic spurts of productivity that annuals qualify as the Desert Biome's dominant growth form. It seems ironic that they should do so, as most travellers, unless they are lucky, are unlikely to witness the full splendour of the grass-covered desert. As quickly as the annuals appear, so they seem to wither away and vanish, but not before setting their precious seeds.

Another easily overlooked form of desert vegetation – indeed one that seems to have been ignored for centuries – is the lichen (see box, opposite page). A multitude of these fascinating organisms abound, and their variety and ecological importance are only now being recognised. Far more visible are the succulent stemmed *Commiphora* and African moringa (*Moringa ovalifolia*) trees and the impressive specimens of *Euphorbia virosa* and *Euphorbia avasmontana* that dot the very rocky parts of the inner and central Namib and the plains with their occasional rocky outcrops.

Strangely enough, botanists do not consider the well-known desert perennials, welwitschia (*Welwitschia mirabilis*) and the camel thorn tree (*Vachellia erioloba*), to be true components of the Desert Biome because they are not directly dependent on rainfall: the former is restricted to run-off areas of broad drainage lines or washes, whereas the latter is found in both run-off drainage lines and dry riverbeds. Such distinctions could be considered academic: not only are both species exceptionally well-adapted to the

Some trees survive in the Namib only on rocky outcrops, above subterranean watercourses and along run-off drainage lines. A good example is the African moringa tree.

desert environment, but both are also crucial members of the biome, providing habitats, refuge, shade, food and water for a multitude of desert creatures. Other trees that, like the camel thorn, occur in dry watercourses are the wild tamarisk (*Tamarix usneoides*) and the enormous ana tree (*Faidherbia albida*), whereas the mustard tree (*Salvadora persica*) favours riverbanks.

Lichens and desert vagrants

The fact that a lichen is formed by a symbiotic association of a fungus and a species of alga has led some authorities to refer to this curious plant as a '1 + 1 = 1 organism'. Lichens occur throughout the fog belt of the Desert Biome, in hot, exposed places where few other plants survive. They are true fog plants, sustaining themselves exclusively on fog and dew, yet they have no roots, stems or leaves that could serve to trap water.

The fungus is the dominant partner and benefits nutritionally from the entrapped algae, which perform the function of photosynthesis. It provides the thallus, the main structure of the lichen that not only houses the algae, but also attaches the lichen to stones, rocks or vegetation structures. The thallus has various designs, depending on the lichen. The orange lichen *Teloschistes capensis*, for example, forms cushion-like clumps on the soil and shrubs. *Santessonia hereroensis* is branch-like, growing on stones east of Walvis Bay. Some lichens, such as *Caloplaca indurata* and *Xanthoparmelia* species, encrust rocks and quartz pebbles, creating delicate, lacy patterns, whereas others, the 'vagrant' lichens, are leaf-like and unattached. German-speaking Namibians refer to this latter type more romantically as *Wanderflechten* ('wandering lichens'), for they are blown back and forth across the desert by the prevailing winds. The best-known *Wanderflechten* are *Xanthomaculina convoluta* and *Parmelia hueana*, which collect, often in dense mats, in washes or roadside ditches.

Orange tufts of *Teloschistes capensis*, seen near Cape Cross, a few kilometres from the Namibian coast.

Xanthoparmelia sp. showing exposed thalli after wetting.

The nomads of the fog belt. Mats of vagrant windblown *Xanthomaculina convoluta* accumulate along drainage lines on the gravel plains of the Namib.

A miniature forest of grey *Santessonia hereroensis* grows above an understorey of orange *Xanthoria* lichens.

Above left: The grass *Stipagrostis sabulicola* commonly grows along the bases of sand dunes in the Namib dune sea.
Above right: The fruit of the spiky nara plant provides food and water for a multitude of animals.

In contrast to the stable and vegetated sand dunes of the Kalahari Desert, the sands of the Namib dunes are continuously shifting, and the dunes themselves are forever changing shape. Nothing grows on the unstable dune crests, but the lower slopes are meagerly dotted with perennial plants that are adapted to life on restless sands. With its higher water content, the sand of the lower slopes supports such perennials as the grass *Stipagrostis sabulicola* and the succulent *Trianthema hereroensis*. The nara plant (*Acanthosicyos horridus*) also occurs among the dunes, most frequently in and around perennial watercourses and vleis where subterranean water exists.

Of the 89 vertebrates that occur in the Desert Biome, no fewer than 29 are endemic. This extraordinarily high figure, representing the most endemics in any of the four desert biomes, is made up largely of reptiles: of the 42 reptiles found in the Desert Biome, 23 (or 55 per cent) are endemic. These include two particularly interesting lizards: the herbivorous desert plated lizard (*Gerrhosaurus skoogi*) and the shovel-snouted lizard (*Meroles anchietae*). Eleven of the endemic reptiles are geckos, two being barking geckos of the genus *Ptenopus*, whereas another four belong to the genus *Rhoptropus* and are unusual for geckos in that they are active during the day. The western keeled snake (*Pythonodipsas carinata*) and Péringuey's adder (*Bitis peringueyi*), well-known for its rapid sidewinding gait over sand, are the biome's two endemic snakes.

The three endemic mammals are a bat, the Namib long-eared bat (*Laephotis namibensis*), and two gerbil species. Although not strictly an endemic – its range extends southwards into the Succulent Karoo – Grant's golden mole (*Eremitalpa granti*) is a remarkable denizen of the Desert Biome, being able to 'swim' through loose, dry dune sands.

Péringuey's adder is one of two snake species endemic to the Namib dune sea.

Of the desert birds, only Rüppell's korhaan (*Eupodotis ruepellii*), Gray's lark (*Ammomanopsis grayi*) and the dune lark (*Calendulauda erythrochlamys*) are found exclusively in the Namib. Vertebrates aside, the Desert Biome is perhaps best known for its very high species richness of beetles, particularly those belonging to the family Tenebrionidae.

Succulent Karoo Biome

Like the Desert Biome, the Succulent Karoo Biome comprises mostly a coastal strip of land about 100 to 150 kilometres wide. It straddles the Namibia/South Africa border, stretching from Lambert's Bay (32°S) in South Africa to just north of Lüderitz (26°S) in Namibia, but in the southern part, to the east of Lambert's Bay, it also extends inland following the valleys of the Tankwa Karoo for about 400 kilometres. Here it is bounded by the Roggeveld Mountains to the north and the Cedarberg, Koue Bokkeveld and Swartruggens mountains to the south. The Succulent Karoo landscape, as typified by the coastal platform, the Knersvlakte north of Vanrhynsdorp, and the Tankwa Karoo drained by the Tankwa River and its tributaries, is generally flat or gently undulating. In stark contrast are the rugged mountains of the Richtersveld in northern Namaqualand, where the biome is dramatically bisected by the Orange River, the only perennial river that traverses the west coast arid zone south of the Kunene River.

The biome's soils, rich in lime but weakly developed, are very shallow and are exceptionally vulnerable to erosion by wind and water. Severe overgrazing of the vegetation that once limited erosion has resulted in extensive gully and sheet erosion, despite the region's low rainfall. This rainfall, between 20 and 290 millimetres a year, is more reliable and predictable than in other arid regions, and its relatively strong winter pattern, especially in the south, accounts for the predominance of succulent plants.[17] In summer, when temperatures can exceed 45°C,

The Orange River separates Namibia on the left and South Africa on the right. This small band of land along the banks of the river, sandwiched between the Nama-Karoo and Succulent Karoo biomes, is best described as Desert Biome. This photograph was taken at Oana Nature Reserve, west of Vioolsdrif.

The mesembs of Namaqualand

Comprising about 1,750 species in 127 genera, the plant family Aizoaceae is the largest in southern Africa and consists of two subfamilies: Mesembryanthemoideae (approximately 100 species in 17 genera) and the Ruschioideae (1,563 species in 101 genera).[18, 19] The name 'Mesembryanthemoideae' is taken from the Greek *mesembria*, meaning 'midday', which aptly describes the plants' noonday flowering habits. The derivative 'mesembs' is familiarly applied to most species, especially to those within the Ruschioideae. They are also known as ice plants in English, owing to the water bladders on the leaves of many species, and vygies in Afrikaans, meaning 'small fig', referring to the seed capsules.

Mesembs are superb examples of succulent plants, and range in size and growth form – from tiny, compact perennials such as *Lithops* species, through small, creeping annuals, for example, the bokbaaivygie (*Cleretum bellidiforme*), to dwarf shrubs such as *Lampranthus* and *Ruschia* species, which represent the common growth form. With the exception of only two genera, all mesembs have brightly coloured flowers.

The Ruschioideae evolved very rapidly with the onset of winter rainfall in an arid environment about 5 million years ago in southwestern Africa, and today the borders of the Succulent Karoo Biome are neatly defined by the distribution of their genera. Their success is owed to wide-band tracheids in the leaf that prevent the collapse of the primary wall during water stress (see Chapter Two); their cylindrical leaf shape, which minimises water loss and heat gain (see Chapter Two); and their highly derived seed capsules. Remarkably, 92 per cent of the genera are endemic to southern Africa, making the Succulent Karoo the most species-rich desert biodiversity hotspot in the world. It is recognised by UNESCO as a world heritage site of international importance.

From left to right: *Conophytum* species, a tiny, flowering stone plant – note the translucent leaves; *Drosanthemum spongiosum*, a glittering shrubby mesemb – note the water bladders on the leaf from which the name 'ice plant' is derived; *Cephalophyllum striata*, a mat-forming mesemb; *Conicosia elongata*, an unusually flat-leafed mesemb.

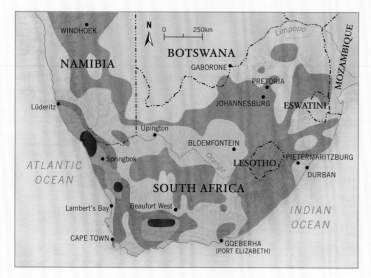

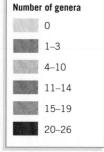

Number of genera

	0
	1–3
	4–10
	11–14
	15–19
	20–26

The density of distribution of the 101 genera of the subfamily Ruschioideae (Aizoaceae) in southern Africa. Note how clearly the highest number of genera neatly define the limits of the Succulent Karoo Biome and the winter-rainfall region.[20]

it is undeniably southern Africa's driest region in terms of rainfall. As in the Namib, the Succulent Karoo's coastal zone enjoys the benefits of moisture-bearing fog, but it is also subject to hot, dry berg winds that occur frequently, causing severe erosion.

The Succulent Karoo is the only desert biodiversity hotspot in the world.[21] The name 'Succulent Karoo' is derived from the biome's astounding richness of plants, mostly low, perennial shrubs that bear succulent leaves, branches and stems.[22–25] It has 63 vegetation units within six bioregions (Richtersveld, Namaqualand Hardeveld, Namaqualand Sandveld, Knersvlakte, Trans-Escarpment Succulent Karoo and Rainshadow Valley Karoo),[26] and encompasses 6,356 species in 1,002 genera and 168 families.[27] Strict endemics comprise 26 per cent of species, and near endemics, which have their centre of distribution within the biome, comprise 17 per cent of species. The succulent growth form is found extensively throughout the families Aizoaceae (1,750 species in 127 genera), Crassulaceae, Liliaceae and Euphorbiaceae. But it was the explosive adaptive radiation of the Ruschioideae 6 to 2 million years ago within Aizoaceae (see box, opposite page) that accounts for most of the species richness (1,563 species).[28, 29] This radiation was triggered by the onset of winter rainfall around 5 million years ago. Well-known plants include the stone plants (for example, *Lithops* species), cryptic mesembs much sought after by the world's succulent collectors and poachers. The dominant shrub throughout the Succulent Karoo is *Galenia africana*, a pioneer species that readily colonises disturbed land and is thus a telltale indicator of severe overgrazing.

The biome is also extremely rich in geophytes, of the Iridaceae and Liliaceae families, and annuals, mostly represented by the family Asteraceae. The spectacular displays of Namaqualand flowers every spring serve as evidence of the localised nature of the annual growth form co-dominance. There are few trees in the biome, apart from some alien species and indigenous acacias, such as the sweet thorn (*Vachellia karroo*), which is confined to dry riverbeds and water run-offs. However, the trees that do occur, such as the quiver tree (*Aloidendron dichotomum*), its close relative the bastard quiver tree (*Aloidendron pillansii*), and the halfmens (*Pachypodium namaquanum*), are some of the largest, rarest and most dramatic succulents in southern Africa. The Succulent Karoo does not seem to have had a significant grassy component, even in historical times, although some biologists debate this.

Annuals are one of the dominant growth forms in the winter-rainfall Succulent Karoo. This photograph, taken at the original Skilpad farm in the Namaqua National Park, shows dense displays of *Dimorphotheca*.

The iconic quiver tree is one of the few trees of the Succulent Karoo that is not restricted to watercourses.

Javier Ábalos Álvarez

One of the rarest trees in the Succulent Karoo, the halfmens ('half person') is restricted to mountainous regions in the Richtersveld and southwestern Namibia.

Eighty-eight desert vertebrates occur in the biome, of which 25 are endemic. Interestingly, three of the species are frogs: two are rain frogs of the genus *Breviceps*, and the third is the Namaqua caco (*Cacosternum namaquense*). As in the Desert Biome, reptiles represent the largest proportion of endemic species: of the 45 species that occur, one tortoise, two snake, seven legless skink, seven lizard, one gecko and one chameleon species are found exclusively in the Succulent Karoo. One of the snakes, the Namaqua dwarf adder (*Bitis schneideri*), is the smallest of the African adders, measuring a mere 18 to 24 centimetres. Although 25 desert birds occur in the Succulent Karoo, the biome has no endemics of its own. Nevertheless, it does share four endemic species with the Nama-Karoo, of which the red lark (*Calendulauda burra*) is probably the rarest and most noteworthy.

Nama-Karoo Biome

Covering about 605,000 square kilometres in part of its distribution south of the Kunene River, the Nama-Karoo is the second-largest desert biome after the Arid Savanna. It straddles the central plateau of the Western and Northern Cape provinces, from which smaller sections radiate into the Eastern Cape. In the northwest the Nama-Karoo covers most of Namibia south of Rehoboth, but also extends northwards as a narrow strip along the edge of the Namib Desert into Angola. The landscape is generally flat or gently undulating, but is dotted with characteristic Karoo koppies topped with erosion-resistant dolerite sills and occasional mountain ranges such as the Nuweveld Mountains near Beaufort West. The Orange River bisects the biome, and one of its tributaries provides the Nama-Karoo with its most breathtaking scenery in the form of the Fish River Canyon.

The canyon of the Fish River, a tributary of the Orange River, lies in southwestern Namibia, one of the driest parts of the Nama-Karoo. The region, including the hot water springs resort, Ai-Ais, is part of the Ai-lAis/Richtersveld Transfrontier Park.

Mean annual rainfall in the Nama-Karoo ranges from 100 to 520 millimetres, most of which occurs in late summer. The low humidity results in temperatures that are extreme: mean minimum monthly temperatures decrease to -9°C in places, and absolute recordings are even lower, whereas the mean maximum monthly air temperature can exceed 40°C. More about the ancient life that once existed in the Karoo Basin is discussed in Chapter Nine.

Fourteen vegetation units occur within three bioregions (Bushmanland, Upper Karoo and Lower Karoo).[30] The co-dominant plant growth forms of the biome are dwarf shrubs and grasses, although the full expression of the grass component as it was before being chronically overgrazed by domestic livestock can be seen in only a few places today. There are many Nama-Karoo shrubs, of which kraalbos (*Galenia africana*), ankerkaroo (*Pentzia incana*) and kapokbossie (*Eriocephalus ericoides*) are just a few that have established local dominance. Important dominant grasses are twabushman grass (*Stipagrostis brevifolia*), blinkhaargras (*Stipagrostis ciliata*) and bushman grass (*Stipagrostis uniplumis*). Once the home of a great diversity of dinosaurs and archaic mammals, today the Nama-Karoo supports 131 desert vertebrates. Of these, 16 species – nine reptiles, five mammals and two birds – are endemic to the biome. The most vulnerable endemic mammal is unquestionably the riverine rabbit (*Bunolagus monticularis*). It is classified as endangered in the South African Red Data Book as its preferred riverine bush habitat is being rapidly destroyed by agriculture. The endemic birds are Sclater's lark (*Spizocorys sclateri*) and cinnamon-breasted warbler (*Euryptila subcinnamomea*).

Arid Savanna Biome

From 12°S in Angola, the Arid Savanna stretches diagonally across northern Namibia, across the southern and central Kalahari Desert in Botswana to about 26°E, and into the Northern Cape in South Africa as far south as 29°S. Most of the biome comprises level plains that form part of the extensive Kalahari Basin, although the Khomas Hochland mountain range and the biologically intriguing Waterberg Plateau break the flatness in central Namibia. In the southern Kalahari Desert, long, parallel ridges of vegetated sand dunes, oriented in a northwestern to southeastern direction, also interrupt the plains. A distinctive feature of the biome is the large number of calcrete pans that occur in it, of which the largest and most famous are the Etosha Pan in Namibia and the Makgadikgadi Pans in northeastern Botswana.

The Karoo koppie known as Teebus ('tea-caddy'). Karoo koppies are capped by hard, erosion-resistant dolerite sills – solidified lava that was forced under very high pressure through the older underlying strata about 180 million years ago.

This Google Earth image shows the linear vegetated sand dunes of the Kalahari duneveld that flank the Nossob River in southern Namibia.

Etosha Pan was formed about 10 million years ago as a deep lake, and was fed by the Kunene River. It became dried out when the river altered course following tectonic activity about 16,000 years ago. Today the pan is 120 kilometres wide and covers an area of 4,800 square kilometres. This photograph was taken from the International Space Station in 2006.

Most of the Arid Savanna Biome receives its rain in the form of convective thunderstorms. Easterly trade winds also bring the remnants of maritime moisture from the Indian Ocean after it has crossed the escarpment.

The average annual rainfall in the Arid Savanna ranges from 235 to 500 millimetres and occurs mainly in summer. Although this amount is relatively high for a desert biome, the region's organisms do not necessarily derive the full benefit from the rain because it characteristically arrives in the form of localised, rather vicious thunderstorms of short duration. The storms are generated when hot convective air currents are set up as the land heats up during the course of the morning; if sufficient moisture is present in the air, cumulus clouds form and amalgamate into storm clouds that may produce a localised shower in the afternoon. Daily fluctuations in temperature are considerable, especially in the southern Kalahari Desert where the temperature may range from -10°C at night to 30°C during the day in winter, and from 5°C on particularly cold nights to 45°C during the day in summer.

The Arid Savanna Biome encompasses 20 vegetation units within two bioregions (Eastern Kalahari Bushveld and Kalahari Duneveld).[31] The co-dominant growth forms are grasses and a variety of trees and shrubs that range in height from 3 to 7 metres. Large camel thorn trees are prominent in the dry beds of the Kuruman, Nossob and Auob rivers, the three largest ephemeral waterways in the biome. Where the riverbeds are composed of fine, alluvial clays, the perennial small buffalo grass (*Panicum coloratum*) prevails. The riverbanks are dominated by driedoring (*Rhigozum trichotomum*) and perdebos (*Monechma australe*) shrubs and by thickets of black thorn (*Senegalia mellifera*).

On the sandy plains and sand dunes, the common shrubs are grey camel thorn (*Vachellia haematoxylon*) and driedoring, whereas the two most abundant trees are the camel thorn and the shepherd's tree (*Boscia albitrunca*). Perennial grasses are represented primarily by blinkhaargras and *Eragrostis lehmanniana*, and the prevalent annuals and geophytes are the tsamma melon (*Citrullus caffer*) and gemsbok cucumber (*Acanthosicyos naudinianus*), respectively, both of which are important sources of water for many animals. The most common summer annual is the Kalahari grass (*Schmidtia kalahariensis*), which transforms the Arid Savanna into a lush, green expanse after good rainfalls. The perennial duinriet (*Stipagrostis amabilis*) is the dominant plant of the dune crests.

This biome supports 72 desert vertebrates, of which 15 species are endemic to the biome. Eleven of these species are reptiles, one is a mammal and three are birds. One of the reptiles is the shy Anchieta's dwarf python (*Python anchietae*). The mammal is the Damara mole-rat (*Fukomys damarensis*), a social species occurring in groups of up to 44 individuals.

A considerable proportion of the biome's endemism can be attributed to the birds and reptiles that occur only in the arid rocky sector of northwestern Namibia – a region that is dominated by broad-leaved mopane (*Colophospermum mopane*) vegetation. In addition to its endemic species, the Arid Savanna supports a large number of other mammals, such as gemsbok (*Oryx gazella*), eland (*Taurotragus oryx*) and blue wildebeest (*Connochaetes taurinus*), which have more widespread distributions in other arid regions in Africa. This lends the biome the highest overall faunal richness of all the desert biomes in southern Africa. The biome also hosts large predators such as lions, cheetahs and hyenas.

Game, such as these blue wildebeest, congregate on the banks of the dry Nossob and Auob rivers, where they feed on the riverine grasses and shrubs such as driedoring and perdebos. Large camel thorn trees are common along these river courses.

Above left: Duinriet grows on the unstable sands of the dune crests in the Kalahari duneveld. **Above right:** Following good rains in summer, the southern Kalahari turns green virtually overnight. Here gemsbok can be seen wading through tall annual Kalahari sourgrass (*Schmidtia kalahariensis*), an unpalatable species that prospers in heavily grazed and disturbed areas, especially along the banks of the Auob and Nossob rivers.

The antiquity of the Namib Desert

How true is the untiring claim that the Namib is the oldest desert in the world? Let's examine the modern evidence.

Early ideas about the age of the Namib focused on the extraordinary adaptations of Namib animals. It was argued that adaptations to hyper-aridity, such as fog-basking behaviour in beetles, must have taken an extraordinarily long time to evolve, perhaps as long as 80 to 66 million years. However, to better understand the origin of the Namib Desert in light of modern data, and to prove or disprove assertions of its antiquity, we need to examine the stages of its development and the drivers of aridity, such as the break-up of Gondwana, the creation of the Atlantic Ocean, the onset of the cold Benguela Current, and the formation of the Namib dune sea.

South America started to move away from Africa about 130 million years ago, starting in the south. By 80 million years ago, the two continents were fully separated, and the Atlantic Ocean was established. Both continents at this time were tropical, which implies that the Namib cannot be older than 80 million years.

The best sources of data that can point to the earliest onset of aridity along the narrow 200-kilometre-wide coastal strip now known as the Namib Desert come from stratigraphic analyses, that is, analyses of sedimentary layering. These analyses provide some evidence of aridity by the Late Cretaceous around 80 to 66 million years ago.[32] The Benguela Current has frequently been linked to both the aridity of the Namib and the formation of its dune sea. However, the onset of aridity had nothing to do with the influence of the cold Benguela Current that developed only 10 to 7 million years ago, during the Late Miocene.[33] Moreover, the dunes are thought to be no older than 2 million years. What can be attributed to the Benguela Current is the onset of regular coastal fog, generated when the warm, dry descending air of the Hadley cell meets the cold surface waters of the Atlantic

A great deal of research on the plants and animals that live in the Namib dune sea, and their adaptation to aridity over time, has given rise to a deeper understanding of the origin and age of the Namib Desert.

Ocean (see Chapter Ten). The icy-cold waters of the Benguela Current are due to easterly trade winds that blow the surface water offshore, causing upwelling of frigid water from about 300 metres deep. These waters bring nutrients to the surface which, when exposed to sunlight, lead to prolific marine life: phytoplankton, fish, seals and seabirds. As a result, like other upwelling systems along the western coasts of other continents, the coastal waters of the Namib are among the most productive in the world.

Another source of information is the fossil record. Animal fossils can be used to reconstruct palaeoenvironments;[34] for example, if a tree-dwelling primate fossil is found, it is highly unlikely that the site was a desert at the time! The Namib Desert does not have a rich fossil record, but nevertheless there are some sites – Silica North and South, and Eocliff in the *Sperrgebiet*, the forbidden diamond zone of the southern Namib – that have proved extremely important in not only establishing the onset of aridity, but also understanding the evolution of mammals and birds in Africa. Palaeontologists such as Martin Pickford and colleagues from the Sorbonne University in Paris have been allowed to excavate these sites for bones. Their studies suggest that semi-arid conditions can be traced back to the onset of the Oligocene, around 34 million years ago, and hyper-arid conditions to the beginning of the Miocene, about 22 million years ago.[35] The Early Oligocene date sounds realistic because it coincides with a major climatic perturbation of the Cenozoic (which spans the last 66 million years): a dramatic cooling and the first formation of the Antarctic Ice Sheet. Cooling brings aridity, because atmospheric moisture gets locked up as ice. It also causes sea levels to drop, which tends to result in coastal water tables dropping as well.

The mammals that the Pickford team uncovered included elephant shrews (Macroscelidea), golden moles (Chrysochloridae), tenrecs (Tenrecidae), hyraxes (Hyracoidea), rodents (Rodentia) and, indeed, primates. Apart from the rodents and primates, which are invaders from Asia, elephant shrews, golden moles, tenrecs and hyraxes belong to the Afrotheria, the clade of mammals thought to have originated in Africa. Tenrecs no longer occur on the African continent, but are endemic to Madagascar. The primate fossil, *Namadapis interdictus* (Adapinae), a primitive primate, is dated to the Lutetian, that is, 47.8 to 41.2 million years ago, when the coastal region that is now the Namib Desert was moist and humid under summer rainfall. In other words, it was a wooded region that could sustain animals that ate fruit. Clearly,

The icy-cold waters of the Benguela Current bring nutrients that sustain large seal colonies along the Namibian coast.

the Namib was not arid during the Middle Eocene, which lasted from about 54 to 48 million years ago. The sub-humid to warm, humid conditions that the Pickford studies proposed for the Middle Eocene environment is also consistent with the reconstructed average temperature of the Earth that shows that the Eocene was the hottest, most tropical period of the last 66 million years.

It would seem that the Namib Desert is at least 34 million years old, although it may be older. It became hyper-arid 22 million years ago with the continued expansion of the Antarctic Ice Sheet. This is more than enough time for unique innovations that would allow organisms to live in a sandy desert and to evolve. However, it was only after the onset of the cold Benguela Current that adaptations to acquiring water in the form of fog evolved in both plants and animals.

How do age estimates of the Namib compare with those of other deserts? Well, there is only one fair contender: the contemporaneous Atacama Desert in South America. This desert has many similarities to the Namib Desert, although it is unquestionably more hyper-arid. Adrian Hartley, University of Aberdeen, and Guillermo Chong, Universidad Católica del Norte, argued that the Atacama is about the same age as the Pickford estimates for the Namib, and that its aridity can be attributed to the same stages of global cooling during the Late Cenozoic.[36] So, I'd argue that the claim that the Namib is the oldest desert in the world is somewhat shaky.

CHAPTER **2** TWO

Water: the currency of life

Above: *Leptostethus marginatus* weevils engage in fog basking in the Namib Desert.

Left: A dust devil passes through a waterhole frequented by ostriches, zebras, elephants, springbok and gemsbok on Etosha Pan in Namibia.

Life on Earth evolved in water, and today no organism can live without it. In deserts, water is the currency of life. It is scarce, difficult to obtain regularly, and disappears rapidly after episodic rainfalls. Successful desert organisms are those that are able to maintain a healthy water balance: the amount of water entering the organism must be more than, or equal to, the amount leaving it. If the amount of water leaving the organism is consistently more than the amount entering it, then the organism will dry out and eventually die. In the course of evolution, the threat of dehydration posed a constant challenge to aquatic creatures as they began to emerge from their ancient watery habitats and colonise the uncrowded expanses of dry land during the Carboniferous Period. The challenge is no different today. For creatures ill-equipped to deal with the problem death by dehydration is stunningly fast in the desert.

Waterproofing

Apart from the considerations of body size, waterproofing is the best way of reducing water loss from the surfaces of desert organisms. Of the total amount of water lost on a daily basis, desert plants lose roughly 10 per cent from the leaf surface, or cuticle, a percentage considerably lower than that of non-desert species. Their waterproofing is made up of thick deposits of lipids (insoluble compounds including fats, waxes and oils) embedded in wax deposits on the leaf surface and in the leaf cuticle. Waxes are continuously deposited on the cuticle surface in several forms, such as plates and rods. These surface waxes can be seen clearly, for example, on the smooth bark of the bastard quiver tree (*Aloidendron pillansii*) in the Richtersveld.

Plants can increase the amount of surface wax on their leaves when the relative humidity is low or temperatures are very high, thus protecting themselves against desiccation. They also lay down thicker wax deposits in response to daylength, or photoperiod. In winter the days are shorter than the nights, but as the days get longer and hotter with the approach of summer, desert plants detect the change in the photoperiod and increase their surface wax deposits.

Evolution has increased the waterproofing of some succulents' leaves in another, rather innovative, way. Plants of the genera *Psammophora* and *Arenifera* (meaning 'sand-bearing' in Greek and Latin, respectively) have very sticky leaves to which windblown sand and dust adhere. The sandy layer not only helps to camouflage the plant, concealing it from herbivores, but also reduces transpiration and water loss through the cuticle.

Other desert plants, such as *Lithops*, *Fenestraria* and *Haworthia* species, minimise water loss from their surfaces by hiding underground. The stone plants of the genus *Lithops* consist of two barrel-shaped leaves which are almost completely buried, with only the camouflaged leaf tips visible at ground level. Thus *Lithops* reduces the surface area over which water can be lost from the plant. Experiments have shown that the rate of water loss from *Lithops lesliei* is 20 per cent lower in buried plants than in exposed ones.[6] Another superb adaptation in *Lithops* for conserving water concerns water recycling: shifting the water stored in the pair of old leaves to the pair of new, developing leaves. By doing this, the plant is not dependent on rainfall to complete a yearly life cycle.[7]

A buried habit may be beneficial in reducing water loss, but it also minimises the amount of solar radiation that can penetrate the plant. Sunlight is essential for photosynthesis. How do these hidden plants obtain the sunlight that they

The wax on the stem of the quiver tree acts as a waterproofing agent and retards water loss from the plant.

The bushman's candle (*Sarcocaulon patersonii*) occurs in very arid regions of Namaqualand. The stems, which bear prolific deposits of waterproofing wax, are used as candles by the local Nama.

The leaves of *Psammophora longifolia* produce a sticky substance that traps sand particles, thus protecting the leaves from heat, damage from sandblasting, and water loss.

need to photosynthesise? This problem has been overcome in another very innovative way: small, translucent 'windows' on their leaf tips allow sunlight to penetrate through to the chloroplasts arranged deep within their underground leaves. In fact, so many succulents sport such windows that German botanists have dubbed them collectively *Fensterpflanzen* ('window plants') (see box below). Not all window plants are buried, but they probably all share the same benefits derived from having the windows.

Insects also need protective waterproofing if they are to avoid dehydration, and the structure of their cuticle is remarkably similar to that of the plant cuticle. Evolutionists would cite this as an example of parallel evolution, whereby a similar structural adaptation fulfils the same function in two genetically distant and essentially unrelated groups: plants and insects. Like those of plants, the cuticles of insects contain several laminated layers of lipid, but underlying these are specialised dermal glands that produce and store wax. Whenever conditions become particularly desiccating, the dermal glands produce long filaments of wax that pass through ducts leading through the various cuticle layers to pores, or tubercles, on the cuticle surface. The wax filaments ooze out of the tubercles and spread, becoming entangled with other filaments and forming interwoven mats that markedly improve the cuticle's waterproofing (see box, page 48). The waxy patterns, or blooms, on the insects are similar to those found on the surfaces of plants. They also impart a range of colours to otherwise black beetles in regions of high temperature

This work by Rudolf Marloth (1855–1931) shows the growth habit of typical window plants. The leaves are underground, with their camouflaged surfaces exposed to the elements.

and low humidity. For example, the tenebrionid beetle *Onymacris plana* is always pitch-black when found along the coastal Namib where the humidity is high, but it is often bluish in the central Namib, which has lower humidity and higher temperatures. In these beetles the diameter of the individual wax filaments falls within the range that causes light to be scattered, thereby producing a bluish colour, the so-called Tyndall blue effect. Typically, however, the waxy blooms of the Namib beetles are white.

Window plants

Jean-Jacques MILAN / CC BY-SA 3.0
Ophthalmophyllum dinteri

C T Johansson / CC BY-SA 3.0
Lithops otzeniana

Dinkum / CC BY-SA 3.0
Fenestraria aurantiaca

Abu Shawka / CC0
Haworthia cooperi

In the leaf tips of many southern African succulents there are small, translucent 'windows' that allow sunlight to penetrate deep into the leaves. Examples of these window plants include various species of *Lithops*, *Fenestraria* (meaning 'window plants'), *Ophthalmophyllum* (meaning 'eye leaf'), *Conophytum* and *Haworthia*. These remarkable plants exemplify the truly unique nature of the Namaqualand mesembs.

Wax bloom on plants and animals

Many desert beetles and plants lay down deposits of wax on their surfaces to improve their waterproofing and thus reduce water loss. The patterns of these wax blooms can only be seen under a scanning electron microscope and, although they are uncannily similar on plant and insect surfaces, there are certain differences. In plants the wax can be plate-like, one per cell (**A**), or it can take the form of a continuous mat of rod-like pieces. In insects the wax is always filamentous in structure, secreted via pores in the cuticle surface. Spilling out from these pores, the wax often forms volcano-like blooms that eventually transform the cuticle surface into a mat of interwoven wax filaments (**B–D**).

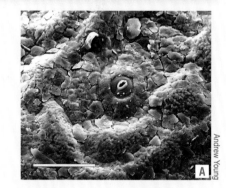

Andrew Young

Thomas Schoch / CC BY-SA 3.0

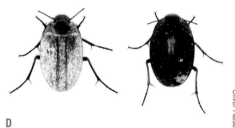

Oliver Halsey

A. The leaf surface of *Conophytum obscurum* subsp. *vitreopapillum* shows granular wax layers.[8] (Scale bar = 100 µm [micrometres or microns]). **B.** The cuticle of *Onymacris rugatipennis*, a Namib Desert beetle, is covered with a heavy wax deposit. **C.** Waxy racing stripes on *Stenocara gracilipes* serve to collect droplets of water that will roll down to the mouthparts. **D.** Differences in the wax deposits on the cuticle of *Zophosis* beetles from the Namib.

Elizabeth McClain from the University of Namibia studied the waxy blooms of the Namib tenebrionid beetles in considerable detail and showed quite convincingly that the incidence of the blooms corresponds with drier, desiccating conditions.[9] As discussed in Chapter One, the temperature increases, relative humidity decreases, and consequently the saturation deficit increases the further inland one travels into the Namib Desert from the sea. McClain showed that this gradient is beautifully matched by an increase in the extent to which the body surface of *Onymacris plana* is covered by the waxy bloom.[10] There is also no doubt that the bloom reduces water loss, for it has been shown that if some of the wax is scratched off, the beetle's rate of water loss increases immediately.

Reptiles have a form of fibrous keratin, beta-keratin, and lipids in the outer skin layers (*stratum corneum*) that make the skin waterproof. Lipids are the primary barriers to desiccation and water loss from the skin in land animals.[11] The more lipids there are in the *stratum corneum*, the more waterproof the skin. The overlapping keratin scales and waterproof skins of some desert reptiles are so successful at providing waterproofing that some species of lizard have the lowest water loss rates ever measured in desert organisms. Indeed, it is not surprising, therefore, that lizards are so common throughout the deserts of the world. Once more there is an astounding overlap of adaptations in very different organisms, for scales like those of reptiles have evolved also in some plants to reduce water loss from their tiny, delicate leaves. The leaves and stem of the worm-shaped, ground-hugging succulent *Anacampseros papyracea* are covered with papery, overlapping scales that presumably protect them from excessive desiccation.

Water loss from the skin of desert mammals and birds is about ten times higher than that from desert reptiles. The comparison is not entirely fair, however, as many mammals have sweat glands that deliberately release water onto the skin surface to facilitate cooling when

Anacampseros papyracea is a succulent plant that has snake-like scales on its leaves that serve to reduce water loss.

With a large surface-area-to-volume ratio, the pygmy hairy-footed gerbil cannot afford to lose much water by sweating.

The southern rock agama obtains its water from insect prey; its waterproof skin prevents water loss.

The Cape flat lizard is a sit-and-wait predator and can tolerate the heat of the day because of its waterproof skin.

Although the skin of the shovel-snouted lizard is waterproof, this reptile can dive into the sand to minimise water loss.

temperatures are high (see Chapter Three). Humans, with their naked skin, have the highest water loss rate ever measured from a mammalian skin in the desert. Even individuals who are well accustomed to desert conditions can lose as much as 4 litres per hour. This high rate would certainly result in death within a few days if the subject did not regularly replace the lost fluid. Even when large amounts of water are lost from the human body, the appropriate drinking response to balance the loss is not always stimulated, so a certain amount of self-discipline is required to maintain a regular water intake and avoid chronic dehydration.

Because gerbils and other desert rodents have large surface-area-to-volume ratios they simply cannot afford to sweat – they would lose too much water daily and would certainly become dehydrated within hours of leaving the sanctuary of their burrows on a hot day. These small desert mammals create their own microclimates in their burrows, where not only is the evaporative power of the air considerably lower than it is above ground (high humidity), but the temperature is lower too. Not surprisingly, most desert rodents are nocturnal, emerging only at night as the relative humidity of the desert air starts to increase in response to decreasing air temperatures after sunset.

Surface architecture

If you measure the temperature of the sand surface of the Kalahari Desert on a hot summer day, it could approach 70°C, whereas the air temperature only a few centimetres above ground level may be as much as 40°C lower. What exists between these extremes is a boundary layer of still, undisturbed air in which a gradient of temperature increases dramatically closer to the ground. Such boundary layers of temperature and water vapour pressure gradients, which exist above all plant and animal surfaces, are strongly affected by wind, and exert an important influence on surface evaporation. Wind erodes and thins the boundary layer, creating steeper gradients of temperature or vapour pressure across the layer. For many organisms it is desirable to maintain broad water vapour pressure boundary layers above their surfaces because these increase the diffusion path over which water vapour must move, thus impeding its movement and reducing water loss. Not surprisingly, the shapes and textures of many desert plant and animal surfaces are such that they maximise the width of boundary layers. Thorns, spines or tubercles, as well as certain arrangements of the branches, stems and leaves of plants, effectively trap air pockets and minimise the disruption of the boundary layers by physical factors such as wind.

In desert succulents, spines and thorns are found in members of the Apocynaceae (for example, *Pachypodium* species), Asclepiadaceae (for example, *Hoodia* species), Euphorbiaceae and Crassulaceae, and in some aloes. *Euphorbia stellispina* is a good example, for its thousands of star-shaped thorns have a dual role: they deter herbivores, and serve to maintain broad boundary layers

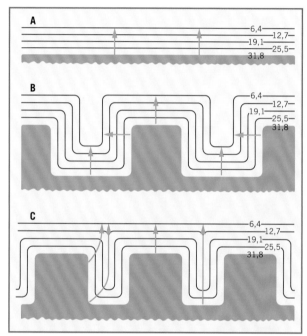

A hypothetical arrangement of boundary layers of water vapour pressure on a plant or insect surface that is flat (**A**), has protuberances (thorns, spines) or depressions (pits, grooves, furrows) that are widely spaced (**B**), or closely spaced (**C**). The numbers refer to water vapour pressure (millimetres of mercury [Hg]) at 30°C, assuming that the air has a relative humidity of 40 per cent and the air immediately above the surface of the plant or insect is fully saturated (100 per cent). Notice that the diffusion paths of water vapour movement down the gradient (blue arrows) remain short for flat surfaces (**A**) and when the protuberances or depressions are widely spaced (**B**), but become considerably longer when protuberances or depressions are closely packed (**C**). The latter arrangement impedes water loss and minimises the disruption of the boundary layers by wind. Plants and insects benefit from the concepts illustrated here with structures such as closely packed thorns, spines, branches, stems, leaves and epidermal cells, as well as sunken stomata and spiracles.

The densely packed spines of *Euphorbia stellispina* help to trap pockets of air against the stem, thus reducing water loss.

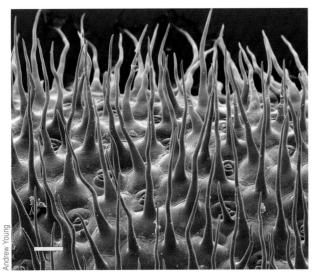

Andrew Young

The microscopic forest of trichomes on the leaf surface of *Conophytum depressum* subsp. *perdurans*.[12] This arrangement possibly plays a role in maintaining water vapour pressure boundary layers over the leaf. (Scale bar = 100 μm [micrometres or microns]).

over the plant's surface. *Euphorbia eustacei*, found in the Nama-Karoo, has such a dense covering of stiff spines that it looks something like a hedgehog when it is not flowering. Many desert plant species possess microscopic 'spines', called trichomes, that are so minute they can be seen only with a microscope.[13]

Many succulents have closely packed branches or leaves that effectively trap air pockets, thus maintaining broad boundary layers. The fur and feathers of mammals and birds also serve this purpose; by restricting the movement of air across the skin surface they minimise evaporation. Unfortunately, this restriction may also work against desert organisms when cooling is required.

The hazards of breathing

The highest percentage of water lost from desert organisms occurs during the exchange of gas between them and the desert air when animals and plants breathe, and also when plants photosynthesise. Animals breathe in oxygen from the atmosphere and give off carbon dioxide, whereas during photosynthesis plants take in carbon dioxide and give off oxygen. The problem for desert organisms is that when they open whatever orifice they use to exchange these gases they bare moist internal surfaces to the dry desert air. Plants open and close their stomata, insects their spiracles and mammals their nostrils. Not surprisingly, though, an appropriate suite of

adaptations has evolved in desert organisms to minimise the amount of water evaporated from these moist surfaces during gas exchange.

Many desert plants solve the problem of losing moisture by opening their stomata only at night, that is, when the vapour pressure of the desert air is highest. This profoundly decreases the daily transpiration – the amount of water lost through the gas exchange necessary for photosynthesis. However, another problem presents itself: how does photosynthesis take place, since it requires the intake of carbon dioxide in the presence of sunlight?

Normally three elements are required for photosynthesis: carbon dioxide, water and sunlight. Carbon dioxide enters the leaf via the stomata, whereas sunlight penetrates to chloroplasts within the leaf where it is absorbed by the pigment chlorophyll. In the course of absorption, chemical energy is generated and used to synthesise three-carbon sugars from the carbon dioxide and water, in a process known as C_3 metabolism (see box, page 52). This sequence of events is simply not possible if the stomata are kept closed during the daylight hours. The secret is that many desert plants circumvent the problem by incorporating an intermediate step: they take in carbon dioxide when the stomata are open at night and convert it into malic acid. The acid is broken down during the daylight hours and the carbon dioxide then released is incorporated into the normal sequence of sugar-producing events. This procedure, known as crassulacean acid metabolism, or CAM, is very common in succulent plants, especially in the family Crassulaceae from which it obtains its name.

It was initially thought that welwitschias *must* be CAM plants, which would explain their persistence in the Namib Desert. But they are not. Instead, they open their stomata fully during the dawn hours, when temperatures are at their lowest. This is also the time of day when the water saturation deficit is at its lowest and evaporation and water loss from the stomata are at their minimum. After a few hours in the morning the stomata close by about 70 per cent, and by dusk they are completely shut. This ability to rapidly switch from active to dormant respiratory states is what Gert Krüger and his colleagues at North-West University think is the most important survival response of welwitschias.[14]

Many desert grasses, including the majority of those in the summer-rainfall deserts, take one step further to minimise water loss during carbon fixation by producing four- instead of three-carbon sugars. Known as C_4 plants, these grasses are very efficient at photosynthesis, for not only do they re-use respiratory carbon dioxide, thus

Distribution of C$_3$, C$_4$ and CAM plants

Plants have three options for capturing atmospheric carbon from carbon dioxide in the course of photosynthesis: they can make three-carbon sugars, they can make four-carbon sugars, or they can temporarily convert carbon dioxide absorbed at night into malic acid before continuing with the sugar-producing procedure by day, in a process known as crassulacean acid metabolism (CAM). The option they use depends mostly on the local desert climate. In general, C$_3$ plants grow well at lower temperatures and predominate along the west coast, although they also do very well on mountain ranges and at high altitudes. CAM plants, which include virtually all the succulents, require little rain, but what there is must be reliable for they cannot tolerate dehydration. Nor can they tolerate very high temperatures or frost, and so are heavily concentrated in the coastal winter-rainfall deserts, mostly in the Succulent Karoo where the climate is moderated by fogs and the oceanic influence. Succulents are not common in the Namib because the rainfall there is too unpredictable. C$_4$ plants, especially grasses, require high temperatures during the growing season and are therefore restricted to the summer-rainfall regions of the Desert, Nama-Karoo and Arid Savanna biomes, except at high altitudes where night temperatures are too low.

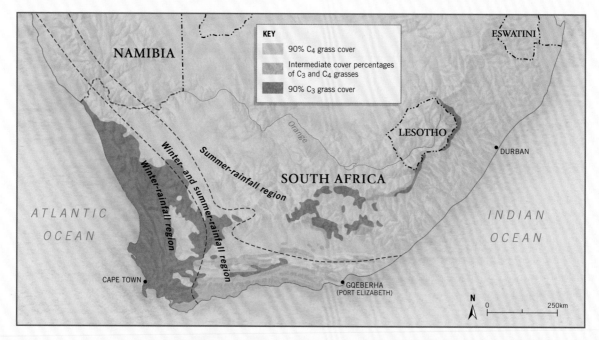

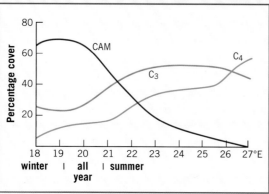

Above: Some grass species have C$_3$ metabolism, whereas others have C$_4$ metabolism, depending on the climate. The distribution of C$_3$ and C$_4$ grasses in southern Africa shows a close relationship to the three rainfall zones.[15]

Left: The percentage cover values of C$_3$, C$_4$ and CAM plants along a west–east transect at about 30°S from the west coast inland to the highveld grasslands. As a general rule, the CAM plants are restricted to the coastal winter-rainfall regions, whereas the C$_3$ and C$_4$ plants assume the dominant plant cover in the summer-rainfall regions.

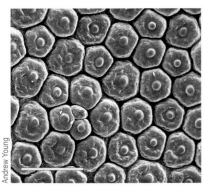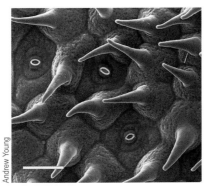

Above left: The leaf surface of *Conophytum jucundum* subsp. *marlothii* lacks surface stomata, which are sunken between the cells. The trichomes are reduced to bumps compared with the longer trichomes of, for example, *Conophytum danielii* (above centre). (Scale bar = 100 µm [micrometres or microns]). **Above centre:** The stomata on the leaf surface of *Conophytum danielii* are not sunken, and are surrounded with epidermal cells that bear long trichomes. (Scale bar = 100 µm). **Above right:** The spiracle on a desert insect is sunk below the cuticle surface, creating a depression that reduces evaporative water loss.

minimising the exchange of this gas through the stomata, but they can also photosynthesise at temperatures higher than 30°C, a capability which is very rare in C_3 and CAM plants. C_4 plants grow particularly well in areas where the rainy season, and therefore the growing season, coincides with the hot season.

Facing a common problem in their attempts to reduce water loss during breathing, plants and insects again show a remarkable similarity in the form of their stomata and spiracles, respectively. Both are valve-like structures that open and shut during gas exchange. The stomata on the leaf surfaces of desert plants open directly into air spaces in the leaves where gas exchange occurs with the cells. Insects normally have ten pairs of spiracles, each connected to a trachea that branches extensively throughout the insect's body, thereby delivering oxygen directly to where it is used.

Spiracles and stomata reduce water losses during gas exchange by broadening the gradient between the external water vapour pressure and that at the openings of these pores. In some desert plants and insects, the stomata and spiracles lie in depressions sunk below the cuticle surface. These sunken respiratory pores have a marked influence on the rate of water loss; it has been estimated that a two-fold increase in the depth of the stomata below the cuticle surface creates a saving in water of approximately 33 per cent during gas exchange. Welwitschias show an extreme form of sunken stomata (see box, page 45). Their stomatal guard cells lie below the plane of the surface epithelial cells of the leaf and are thereby 'doubly sunken'.[16] In some species of the button-like, ground-hugging *Conophytum* mesembs, the stomata lie sunken between the epidermal

leaf cells; in others, the stomata are dispersed between these cells, with their openings at the same surface level as the epidermal cells that are exposed to the air.[17]

In some desert plants the stomata reside within furrows on the stem surface, which further increases the width of the boundary layer over which water loss from the stomata occurs. Good examples are the stems of some euphorbias[18] and the nara plant.[19] Other desert plants, such as the bastard quiver tree and various species of *Haworthia*, also exaggerate this trend by having raised 'chimney' rims around the stomatal opening on the cuticle surface, thus increasing the depth of the stomatal pore.

In insects a pattern of respiration known as discontinuous ventilation cycling has evolved, and also plays a part in reducing water loss.[20] Instead of remaining open for long periods, as stomata do, the spiracles open for a short time when a rapid burst of gas exchange, or 'breathing', takes place, and then close for a much longer period, remaining tightly sealed. The periods when the spiracles are closed may last as long as several hours in some species, if the insect is inactive or cold. Because the burst phase is so rapid (lasting seconds or minutes), the insect loses significantly less water than it would if the spiracles remained open. Although discontinuous ventilation cycling occurs in all insects, it is particularly important for small desert species such as the Namib Desert dune ant (*Camponotus detritus*), saving it quantities of water vital to its survival, especially when it is inactive.[21]

Tenebrionid beetles of the desert have an adaptation that decreases water loss from their spiracles even further. The elytra, two protective chitinous coverings that normally move aside to expose the wings for flight, are fused down

Water gain

So far, the various ways in which desert organisms minimise water loss have been discussed. The other side of the water balance equation – the ways in which the organisms acquire sufficient water for their needs – can now be addressed. In regions where rain seldom falls, organisms must exploit a number of different sources of life-giving moisture, and dew and coastal fog are two of the most important alternatives that are more reliable than rainfall.

Adaptations for capturing water, like those for minimising its loss, involve morphological forms in plants and animals, specialised behaviour as well as physiological responses. Many of the adaptations are obvious and well known, but some of the physical mechanisms involved, particularly those concerning the movement of water vapour into plants and animals, are less well understood and are still being investigated.

Dew and coastal fog

Along the coast bordering the Namib and the Succulent Karoo many desert plants and animals depend heavily on the advective fog carried inland from the chilly Benguela upwelling system to balance their water budgets. They display a variety of methods of trapping this valuable airborne moisture, some of which are quite ingenious. The examples that follow, I believe, represent the tip of the iceberg because there is much more to be discovered about how desert plants capture fog.

Many organisms also depend on dew for their water supply. Because the clear desert air presents an excellent 'window' for the re-radiation of heat from the desert surface at night, temperatures decrease rapidly to below the dew point, and the water vapour carried by the cooling air condenses readily on any chilled surface.

Many lichen species occur throughout the fog belts of the Namib and Succulent Karoo biomes (see box, page 27). Because they are not waterproof, they lose and gain water across their surfaces very easily, and when exposed to moist air they rapidly absorb water and become physiologically active for as long as they remain hydrated. In the Namib and the Succulent Karoo this restricts their physiological activity to the night and early morning, when coastal fogs and dew prevail. At night, as the water vapour content of the air increases, the lichens absorb moisture and respire, then at first light they suddenly start to photosynthesise. Photosynthesis continues until the increasing air temperature dehydrates the lichens again, after which they remain physiologically inactive until favourable conditions

are presented once more. Lichens can survive for years in a desiccated state, withstanding temperatures that range from below freezing point to as high as 85 °C without suffering any apparent harm. Rolled-up *Wanderflechten*, in this condition, look like nothing more than dried-out pieces of dead plant matter. Yet, within 20 minutes or so of the onset of fog, they unfurl, absorb water and expose their green thallus surfaces to the light to maximise photosynthesis before the sun dries them out once more. Some lichens of the genus *Lecidea* actually improve their lot by growing in the finest cracks and fissures in quartz stones on the gravel plains of the Namib. These cracks provide nanoclimates,

Top and above: Within minutes of fog rolling in over the Namib Desert, lichens such as *Xanthoparmelia* (grey-green) and *Xanthoria* (orange) unfold their thalli to maximise absorption of fog water.

Wanderflechten respond to fog by rapidly unfolding their dry thalli to reveal their green photosynthetically active algal hosts.

Lichens adorn a shrub on the Namaqualand coast near the mouth of the Groen River.

protecting the lichens from direct solar radiation. The translucent quartz stones filter out about 90 per cent of the incoming light and therefore most of the heat, but still allow sufficient light to pass through for photosynthesis to take place. They also effectively trap run-off from fog and can maintain increased levels of relative humidity long after the morning fog has lifted, thus extending the period during which the lichens can photosynthesise.

In a similar situation, water frequently collects on the undersides of half-buried quartz pebbles and stones on the gravel plains of the Namib Desert, creating a microclimate that sustains a highly complex and diverse ecosystem of algae, bacteria and viruses which, collectively, are called hypoliths. Hypoliths that live under translucent rocks in extreme deserts, including cold deserts such as in the Antarctic, are protected from the wind, desiccation and harsh ultraviolet radiation. In the Namib, photosynthetic hypoliths require a mere 0.1 per cent of the incident sunlight that falls on the translucent quartz rocks to flourish.[28] Moreover, although rainfall supplies more liquid water per single event than fog does, on an equivalent annual basis, fog provides nearly twice as much liquid water as rainfall to the hypolithic zone.[29]

At least 20 species of hypolithic green algae can survive independently of their protective lichen fungi. Even more remarkable is that some of these algae are diatoms. Typically, diatoms are found only in plankton in the sea or in lakes, and the discovery of at least 52 species in the Namib by a team of botanists from the Goethe University Frankfurt is quite astounding.[30] The most common species that the team identified was *Achnanthes minutissima*, a cosmopolitan species that in Europe is found in inland waters. The algae are known as *Fensteralgen* ('window algae')

because the translucent quartz protects them. They in turn act as an important food source for a variety of desert arthropods that live in the favourable microclimate underneath the quartz stones. The most common microbes are bacteriophages, especially those belonging to the family Siphoviridae, which are viruses that attack bacteria.[31] The hypolith microbial community is thought to play a very important role in nutrient recycling.[32] So the gravel plains of the Namib Desert are not as abandoned and lifeless as they may seem – each quartz pebble supports its own food chain, relying only on the input of small amounts of water, mostly from fog, and is an important yet unappreciated component of desert productivity.

Ironically, the waterproof cuticle of insects and plants that so effectively restricts water loss also prevents the

A host of fog-dependent microorganisms live under quartz pebbles on the gravel plains of the Namib. Turned upside down, this pebble shows a green tinge from algae that receive light transmitted through the quartz in the pebble.

Trianthema hereroensis grows at the base of dunes. These green plants, seen in their habitat in the Namib dune sea, occur about 28 kilometres from the coast, allowing them to take advantage of the fog to absorb water vapour through their leaves.

absorption of moisture. For a long time, botanists have been puzzled as to why appropriate structures have not evolved in desert succulents to enable them to take up water droplets that condense on their leaves at night. This is a pertinent query, especially considering that sources of water in the form of fog and dew occur more reliably in the coastal deserts than rain. Moreover, the amounts of water concerned can be quite substantial: the Richtersveld, for example, has a mean rainfall of 64 millimetres per year, but it has been estimated that an additional 40 millimetres or so occurs as moisture from fog and dew. Why do desert succulents not exploit this atmospheric moisture?

Gideon Louw and Mary Seely, working at the Gobabeb Namib Research Institute, showed that the succulent *Trianthema hereroensis*, which grows at the base of dunes, takes up atmospheric water vapour directly through the leaves.[33] How this actually occurs has never been firmly established. Recently, a group of Swiss, German and Dutch botanists, coordinated by Dieter von Willert, addressed this question in terms of the likely avenues by which water may enter the plant. In their book *Life Strategies of Succulents in Deserts*, they stress that wherever water may find an easy entry point, it will leave just as easily.[34] This may account for the general lack of specialised water-absorbing structures on the leaf.

The small leaves of *Trianthema hereroensis*.

However, some Northern Hemisphere plants, as well as some southern African succulents, do have specialised pore-like structures on their leaves that are implicated in the uptake of water, though as yet there is no definitive scientific understanding of the processes involved.[35] The structures, called hydathodes, are pores found on the leaves of most species of the genus *Crassula*.[36] They often occur in clusters that are sunk into well-like depressions on the leaf surface and consist of valve-like openings similar to stomata, but two to three times larger.

Hydathodes originally evolved in the plant kingdom as pores for getting rid of excess water, but this is unlikely to be their function in the desert-adapted crassulas, as the direction of water flow seems to have been reversed.

The hydathodes of many crassulas are also surrounded by hair-like growths (trichomes) of the leaf epidermis, shown in the SEM photo of *Conophytum depressum* subsp. *perdurans* (see page 51). These growths are thought to play a role in dew condensation and the capture of fog, as discussed later for 'curly-whirly' plants. Rapid radiative heat loss at night causes the tips of trichomes to cool to below the air temperature. Dewdrops condense on the tips and may then roll down into the hydathode wells where they may be absorbed. Rod-like, pointy-tipped structures also seem to capture fog droplets very well.[37] However, the function of trichomes on the surface of plant leaves remains contentious.[38]

Jeroen Schreel and his collaborators at Ghent University have shown that trichomes on the leaves of beech trees are pectin-coated hydroscopic structures that can take up water from a wetted leaf surface and pass it to subepidermal cells closely linked to the vascular bundles that transport water and nutrients in the leaf. Pectins are polysaccharides, or long-chain carbohydrates. However, the water-absorbing function of trichomes has yet to be illustrated for any southern African desert plants. There is an urgent need for research if we wish to understand holistically how desert plants extract atmospheric water.

Even succulents that are not equipped with hydathodes seem able to take up atmospheric moisture at night. In an experiment conducted at the end of the dry season on six different succulents from the Richtersveld, von Willert and his colleagues found that the plants were able to recover between 17 and 49 per cent of the water lost during the day in the course of the following night.[39] Since the measurements were made on leaves of branches that had been cut off the parent plant, this recovery of water could not have occurred via the normal route, from the soil through the roots. One of the six species tested belonged to the genus *Crassula*, so the water could have entered it through the hydathodes or trichomes. As far as the remaining species were concerned, the water could have entered the leaves only via the stomata, by means of so-called reverse transpiration, or across the cuticle. Remember, most succulents are CAM plants, which open their stomata at night. In the past it has often been emphasised that reverse transpiration is not possible in desert plants because no vapour pressure gradient that

Many plants have hydathodes on the surface of their leaves. These are pores that typically exude excess water from the leaf. However, it is possible that the leaves of crassulas (such as the one seen here) and other Succulent Karoo plants within the fog belt may be able to take up water through the hydathodes.

would draw water vapour into the leaf through the stomata could ever exist. The limitation has always been thought to be the fully saturated air of the intercellular spaces within the leaf. Water vapour will only move down a gradient from a high to a low vapour pressure. Since the intercellular air was considered to be always fully saturated and the outside air often not saturated, the options were: there would be no movement of water vapour when the outside air is also fully saturated; or water vapour would move out of the leaf when the outside air is unsaturated, as it most often is. How, then, do succulents take up water from the air at night? Von Willert and his colleagues argued that water uptake occurs because towards the end of the dry season the intercellular spaces in the succulents are not fully saturated with water vapour. So, on cool nights in the Richtersveld, when the air can become fully saturated for a few hours, there can indeed be a reversed vapour pressure gradient, and water vapour will enter the leaves.

There is no doubt that water uptake by the leaves, in what is called foliar water uptake, occurs in many plants, not only in desert plants.[40] It now seems that stomata may well be able to take up water without the requisite favourable water vapour pressure gradient. The process may be mediated by salt ions in water that reduce surface tension.[41] Called the 'hydraulic activation of stomata', the 'salt mediation allows for the creation of a liquid water film that bridges the stomatal pore and enables bidirectional movement of water'.[42] Elucidating the baboons fed on ripe figs from the few large sycamore fig trees (*Ficus sycomorus*) that grow in the riverbed, and on the fruits of the mustard tree (*Salvadora persica*) on the riverbanks. The baboons were unlikely to have been too water-stressed as the figs, for example, have 80 per cent water content.

The vast majority of desert herbivores can maintain their independence of freestanding water by actively seeking out plants with a high water content. Ungulates such as springbok (*Antidorcas marsupialis*), steenbok (*Raphicerus campestris*), gemsbok, red hartebeest

Springbok utilise an artificial water point at Mata Mata in the Kgalagadi Transfrontier Park.

Steenbok (such as this one seen in the Tswalu Kalahari Reserve) are completely independent of standing water.

(*Alcelaphus buselaphus*) and eland (*Taurotragus oryx*) certainly do so and can survive, although most will drink water if it is available.

Many of these species are also quite attuned to the fact that the water content of plants increases at night. Even when the grass of *Stipagrostis uniplumis*, which grows in the dune valleys of the Namib, appears dead and dried out, it increases its moisture content from a minimum of nine per cent in the day to 26 per cent at night in response to fog-induced changes in the relative humidity of the desert air. It therefore makes sense for ungulates to feed at night in order to maximise their water intake when feeding. This is certainly what gemsbok and, to a lesser extent, blue wildebeest, do in the southern Kalahari Desert. Michael Knight, then at the University of Pretoria, conducted research on the feeding patterns of gemsbok and blue wildebeest between 1985 and 1989 while he was resident biologist at the Kgalagadi Transfrontier Park. He observed that 72 per cent of the gemsboks' feeding is done at night.[56] Smaller arid-adapted ungulates that do not need to drink water, such as the steenbok and springbok, probably also feed predominantly at night.

Yet there are some desert herbivores that do not take advantage of the benefits gained by night-time feeding. For some years, biologists have been puzzled by the fact that certain beetles indulge in fog basking and trench building when they need only feed at night in order to balance their water budgets more than adequately. The dead, windblown plant material known as detritus is a principal food source of the tenebrionid beetles and many other dune-dwelling animals. It collects at the bases of sand dune slipfaces and can absorb as much as 60 per cent of its own weight in water on foggy nights. During the day, however, when the beetles actually feed on the detritus, this percentage drops to two to four per cent. Possibly, the evolution of water-capturing behaviour, in addition to the various adaptations that reduce water loss and help the beetles cope with high ambient temperatures (see Chapter Three), is more successful than the evolution of nocturnal foraging with its inevitably higher predation pressures. On the other hand, with the beetles being ectotherms that are reliant on the air temperature to attain their preferred body temperatures, perhaps the lower ambient temperatures and cold, foggy breezes at night retard their capacity to forage.

Many small desert carnivores seem to cope quite well without drinking water, and so must obviously be able to balance their water budgets with the water that they obtain from their prey. Nevertheless, some do resort to alternative sources of water. The brown hyena (*Hyaena brunnea*), for example, feeds on carrion, which is often dried out and dehydrated, and supplements its diet with tsamma melons, gemsbok cucumbers and other fruits that have a very high water content.

Many desert birds can survive without access to water, but some cannot. The most interesting of the latter group are the various species of sandgrouse, although ironically, they can also be regarded as one of the most arid-adapted groups of birds in Africa. Sandgrouse feed exclusively on air-dried seeds that have a very low water content, so they must take in fluid regularly to balance their water budget. Seeds are also poor in salts, with the result that sandgrouse have lost the glands that enable their closest relatives, the marine waders, to rid themselves of the enormous quantities of salt ingested with their water and food. In some respects, this is a disadvantage as the sandgrouse cannot drink salty water, which is often the only freestanding water available in deserts. In the early mornings and evenings, large flocks of these birds, sometimes numbering thousands, fly as far as 60 kilometres to the nearest source of fresh water. Their sweet twittering in flight as they circle a waterhole is one of the truly beautiful melodies of the southern African deserts.

Perhaps the most intriguing aspect of the sandgrouse's adaptations to desert life is how the adults manage to solve the water balance problems of their chicks. The chicks are born highly precocial, meaning that they are able to walk, run and forage for seeds from their very first day, and are not fed by the adults at all. However, they are still too young to fly and cannot get to water. Instead, the adult male carries water to them every day, soaking his ventral feathers in a special way and, on his return to the nest, presenting the fluffed-out feathers of his abdomen to his brood.[57, 58] The chicks take the wet feathers in their beaks and strip the absorbed water from them. Highly specialised to absorb water, the male sandgrouse's belly feathers are unique, and can retain more water per unit weight than a typical kitchen sponge. Apparently, very little water is lost by evaporation during the flight because the water-soaked feathers are held close to the belly, thereby reducing the amount of airflow over the wettest feather surfaces.

Martin Harvey

Brown hyenas in the Kgalagadi Transfrontier Park eat tsamma melons mostly during the dry winter months when the fruit is most abundant.

Peter Chadwick

A male Namaqua sandgrouse (*Pterocles namaqua*) wets its belly feathers as a means of transporting water to its chicks somewhere in the Kalahari duneveld.

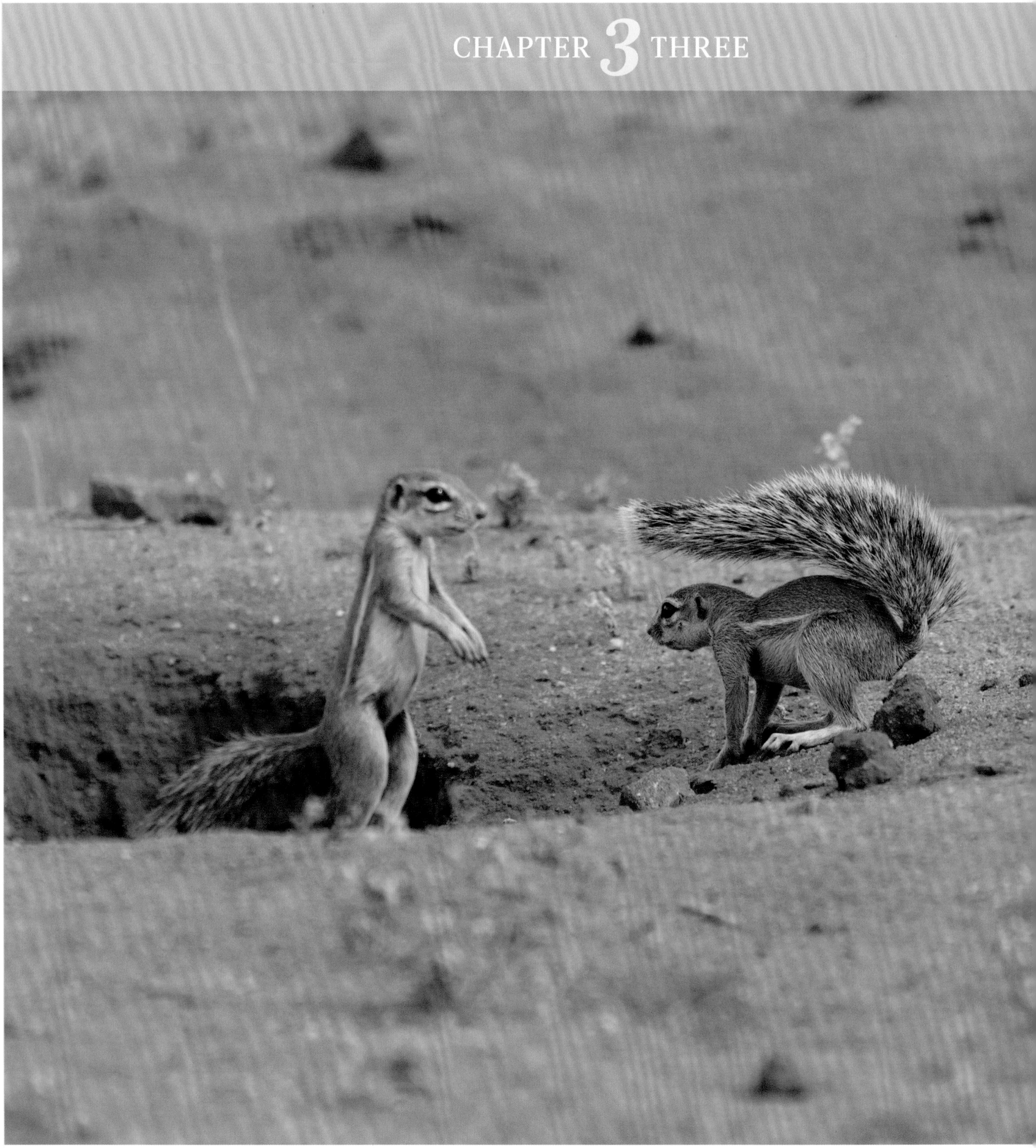

In the heat of the day

Above: Many desert plants have small leaves to reduce heat loading and water loss. Others, such as this *Euphorbia caput-medusae*, mitigate against these factors by having no leaves at all, only flowers on the end of each stem.

Left: Cape ground squirrels forage during the heat of the day – often in very exposed areas but always close to a burrow entrance to allow for a quick escape. They use their tails as parasols to shade their bodies while they feed.

All land deserts have one physical characteristic in common: they experience extreme temperatures. They may be extremely cold, extremely hot, or both. The deserts of southern Africa are both. The heat is derived, in general, from solar radiation, although infrared radiation emitted from the outer atmosphere and from various hot desert surfaces, such as rocks and sand, can also cause the temperatures of desert organisms to rise. In addition to the solar radiation that actually lands on an organism, a certain amount of radiation is reflected off clouds, airborne dust and the desert surface. Although the sun shines everywhere on Earth, deserts receive more radiation than any other part of the planet. In the first place, more solar and infrared radiation

In very hot conditions, desert birds can release heat from their bodies by exposing the sparsely feathered skin under their wings to the desert air, as demonstrated here by a red lark in the Nama-Karoo.

Ryno Kemp

actually reaches the ground because in the desert air there are fewer obstacles such as water vapour and clouds to impede its penetration. Secondly, there are few plants to absorb the sun's energy at ground level and prevent it from penetrating through to the soil and rock below. As a result, the desert surface heats up rapidly, and in the southern Kalahari Desert may approach 70°C by early afternoon.

As readily as the desert surface absorbs heat during the day, so it loses it at night, and for the same reasons. The minimal water vapour in the higher layers of the atmosphere, the rare cloud cover and the sparsely vegetated land provide a meagre barrier to heat flow and, as the clear desert night air literally sucks the day's heat back into the outer atmosphere, the temperature plummets. The tremendous fluctuation in the air temperature over a 24-hour period is one of the hallmarks of the world's deserts that lie close to the tropics of Cancer and Capricorn. Nowhere else on Earth are such rapid changes of temperature experienced on a daily basis, and desert organisms have to be able to cope with them.

The basic law of heat flow is that heat always moves from matter with a high temperature to matter with a low one. If an organism is small and has no adaptations to impede heat flow across its outer surface, then its temperature would follow closely that of the surrounding air or some or other

surface with which it makes contact. Such an organism in the southern African desert regions would thus experience a very wide range of temperatures over a 24-hour period, a situation that is far from ideal. Most desert organisms have a fairly narrow range of temperatures at which they function best, and it is essential that they minimise as far as possible extreme temperature fluctuations within their own bodies.

As far as animals are concerned, the extent to which they tolerate temperature fluctuations in their bodies divides them into two categories: those which tolerate relatively wide temperature fluctuations and therefore sacrifice the ability to function optimally at all times; and those which maintain a fairly constant body temperature at all times, and so can function optimally whenever they choose. Organisms of the first group, which includes insects, reptiles and amphibians, are called ectothermic – the heat of their bodies is derived mainly from outside sources. The second group, represented by mammals and birds, comprises endothermic organisms that generate heat within their bodies. Although endotherms may derive some heat from their surroundings, on the whole they are self-reliant in terms of heat source and temperature control. I have explored how endothermy might have evolved in my book *Fires of Life: Endothermy in Birds and Mammals.*[1]

Plants of desert regions probably experience the greatest temperature stresses simply because they cannot move. In general, they fall into the ectotherm category and are at the mercy of the environment. The different ways in which plants and animal ectotherms and endotherms attempt to solve their temperature problems are the subject of this chapter.

Enzymes and antifreezes

When temperatures fluctuate widely within an organism, deviating too far above or below a specific operational range, they can, and often do, severely restrict that organism's ability to function. Quite simply, its enzymes are unable to do their job properly. Enzymes are proteins that control biochemical reactions in all organisms, and they cannot cope with huge changes in temperature. Witness a lizard on a cold day; its sluggishness is due to the inability of its enzymes to provide its muscles with the appropriate energy that they need to function efficiently.

This does not mean, however, that enzymes cannot function at very low temperatures. Many Antarctic and Arctic fishes have body temperatures barely a few degrees above freezing point, yet they can swim as fast as tropical fishes. However, if their body temperatures were to change by just a few degrees, their enzyme systems would slow down dramatically, and they would become sluggish. In short, enzymes have evolved to work efficiently at many different temperatures, but none can tolerate large deviations from the range of temperatures at which they evolved to function best.

Extreme heat or cold not only incapacitate organisms but can also kill them. Sub-zero temperatures freeze the water in plant and animal cells, turning it into ice that expands and may shatter cells and their membranes. Such total physical destruction is seldom reversible. Even partial freezing of the cell water kills, and all kinds of destruction may occur at localised zones where freezing has started. By removing water from the cellular fluid, freezing generates massive osmotic gradients that force water molecules to move across membranes, upsetting the organism's water balance and causing its entire physiological system to collapse. At the other extreme, temperatures that are too high destroy enzymes permanently. The effect is not unlike the solidification of egg white on boiling. The enzymes' shapes are so radically distorted that they can no longer interact normally with other molecules.

As yet, little is understood about adaptations that may reduce the damage caused by high temperatures. However, the picture is clearer as far as low temperatures are concerned; in many desert organisms a simple but elegant way of preventing their tissues from reaching lethally cold temperatures has evolved. Considering that about 70 per cent of the bodies of most animals consists of water, which freezes at 0°C, how does a lizard, for example, prevent its tissues from freezing solid on a winter's night when the temperature may drop to -15°C?

There are two ways in which insects cope with sub-zero temperatures in winter. Some are freeze tolerant, meaning that they can survive body fluid freezing; others are freeze avoidant and have the ability to prevent freezing. Southern African insects, it seems, are mostly freeze tolerant: 77 per cent were found to be freeze tolerant compared to 29 per cent in the Northern Hemisphere.[2]

The easiest way to prevent body fluids from freezing is to change the colligative properties of the fluid; in this case, to increase the number of non-ionic solutes in solution, which has the effect of lowering the freezing point of water. The tissues of many desert insects and reptiles contain solutes that are particularly efficient at reducing the freezing point of the tissue fluid, and without doubt, the most effective of these is glycerol. As winter approaches, many desert insects increase the content of glycerol in their tissue fluid, sometimes to as much as 50 per cent, in much the same way as one adds antifreeze to the radiator water of a motorcar to prevent it from freezing on a winter's night in the Nama-Karoo. The insects thus decrease the freezing point of their tissues to a few degrees Celsius below the freezing point of water.

However, a more complex freeze-avoidant approach involves supercooling, a mechanism whereby ice crystals are prevented from forming, and body fluids can cool to temperatures much lower than that made possible by freezing-point depression. Insects that utilise supercooling produce special antifreeze proteins that bind to ice crystals, which then inhibits further ice growth.[3] In this way, larvae of tenebrionid beetles, for example, can avoid freezing of their body fluids by as much as 5.5°C below the freezing point of water.[4]

Although antifreeze agents are not effective in allowing animals to be active in the cold, they at least prevent them from freezing solid. Antifreeze agents do not occur only in animals. In many shrubs of the Nama-Karoo high concentrations of salts in the leaves are able to lower the freezing point of the cellular fluid.

Plants and temperature

Plants face one important problem that animals do not: they cannot move and are consequently forced to endure the full ferocity of solar radiation. Unsurprisingly, they can tolerate much wider fluctuations of temperatures than animals can. *Lithops turbiniformis*, for example, can tolerate a minimum temperature of -16.4°C and a maximum of 68.7°C before suffering permanent thermal damage.[5] The latter temperature is staggeringly high if one considers that most small mammals die when their body temperature reaches about 42°C. It is ironical, though, that although succulents are considered to be well adapted to endure long periods of drought that are broken by reliable rainfalls, compared with non-succulents they fare poorly with respect to the absorption of heat in the form of thermal radiation.

Experiments by B.M. Eller, University of Zürich, and colleagues showed this effect very dramatically.[6] Having selected for use five desert plant species with increasing degrees of succulence, they showed that in the near-infrared part of the radiation spectrum, for example at a wavelength of 800 nanometres, the plant with the most succulent leaves, *Othonna opima*, absorbed 50 per cent of incident radiation. The non-succulent *Ozoroa dispar*, on the other hand, absorbed less than five per cent. These succulents evolved during the Ice Ages of the last 3 million years when, during the Glacial Periods, it was about 4 to 5°C cooler than today.[7] This thermal vulnerability has profound implications for the ability of succulents to withstand global heating (see Chapter Ten).

Could this fact explain why some succulents are almost completely submerged in the desert soil? Considering that some species, such as those of *Lithops* and *Haworthia*, reduce their water loss by being partially buried (see Chapter Two), it is tempting to imagine that the thermal buffering effect of soil may minimise wide temperature fluctuations and thus compensate for the plants' relatively high degree of absorption of radiation. In fact, this does not seem to be the case. The temperature of *Lithops lesliei*, for example, follows that of the subsurface soil to within a degree or so.[8] Considering that the daily fluctuation in soil temperature may be 30°C greater than the fluctuation in air temperature, this species has to contend with substantial temperature extremes. The plants are not buried deeply enough to fully benefit from thermal buffering of the soil.

Nevertheless, desert succulents and other plants can reduce the amount of heat that is absorbed by means of some or other structure, shape or texture. In particular, features that increase reflectivity are very important in minimising the amount of radiation that actually enters the plant. The ground-hugging succulent *Anacampseros papyracea* has white, overlapping, reptile-like scales that are thought to reflect a high percentage of incoming thermal radiation (see photograph, page 49). Many *Euphorbia* species sport a dense covering of spines and thorns that not only protect the plant from herbivores and maintain broad water vapour boundary layers to reduce water loss (see Chapter Two), but also effectively scatter and reflect solar rays that strike the plant. The irregular shapes and knobbly surfaces of the stems and branches of *Hoodia*, *Tylecodon*, *Trichocaulon* and *Euphorbia* species have a similar effect.

The 'warts' on the stems of the krimpsiektebos (*Tylecodon wallichii*) are the hardened remnants of old leaf bases. They are effective at scattering incoming radiation.

The snake-like stems of the ground-hugging *Euphorbia caput-medusae* are densely covered in tubercles that scatter and reflect incoming sunlight.

Some of the succulents' structures are microscopic. Minute, hair-like trichomes, similar to miniature spines or thorns, scatter radiation (see SEM photographs of *Conophytum* trichomes, pages 51 and 53), whereas the sloping shapes of individual epidermal cells help to reflect the sun's rays. As a general rule, waxy blooms on the surfaces of succulents also increase the plant's reflectivity and can reduce the absorption of solar radiation by as much as 30 per cent. In some buried plants, the old leaves from the previous growing season provide protection from the elements and help to increase the plants' reflectivity. The new leaves of *Conophytum* species, for example, grow from inside the old ones, which then dry out to form light-coloured 'skins' that cover the plant during the hot, dry season. *Argyroderma delaetii*, a species of the quartz-pebble flats of the Knersvlakte, bears two swollen, light green leaves in the winter growing season; in summer these become shrivelled, light brown and more reflective.

The broad leaves of *Welwitschia* reflect 36 per cent of the radiation that strikes their flat, dull-green surfaces, a level that is made possible by deposits of calcium oxalate in the epidermal cells.[9] Calcium oxalate is an important component of the leaf cuticle in many desert plants. Crystals of calcium oxalate in the outer layer of cells of the plant leaf increase the reflectivity of sunlight and prevent overheating. For example, almost all species of the diverse genus *Conophytum* possess calcium oxalate in the cuticle.[10] *Conophytum* species that do not possess calcium oxalate are those that are buried (geophytic) and rely on transparency ('windows') of the cuticle to allow light to penetrate to the chloroplasts underground (see Chapter Two).

Apart from specific structures, the overall shape of desert plants also plays an important role in reducing heat absorption. In addition to allowing the stems of euphorbias to expand and contract, depending on their hydration status, the characteristically fluted stems also reduce the amount of direct sunlight that lands on the plant surface at any one time. Since the leaves of most euphorbias are too small to provide shade, the deep grooves along the stem ensure that a certain percentage of the plant body is protected from the sun throughout the day.

Whereas large leaves may shade the plant itself, small ones reduce the amount of radiation absorbed by the plant on account of their smaller surface area. The trend towards bearing small leaves in desert regions is illustrated by the clear switch from the fine-leaved acacia-type trees in the Arid Savanna Biome to the broad-leaved mopane-type trees of the Moist Savanna Biome or even the

Most *Conophytum* plants possess calcium oxalate crystals in the epidermal cells of their leaves that help to reduce the plants' exposure to radiation.

This tiny unidentified *Conophytum*, found in the Oana Nature Reserve in Namibia, has translucent leaves that allow sunlight to penetrate the interior of the leaf. Unlike other *Conophytum* plants, it lacks calcium oxalate in the leaf cells.

northern limits of the Arid Savanna Biome. In addition to absorbing less radiation, small leaves help to keep the plant's temperature low because their large surface-area-to-volume ratio promotes effective evaporative cooling (see box, page 42). The drawback, though, is that the plant loses moisture in the process. For all desert plants and animals, staying cool becomes a compromise between how much water the organism can afford to lose and how high it can permit its internal temperature to rise.

Frequently, the scarcity of water precludes any choice at all. In desert plants that use C_3 and C_4 metabolism, gas exchange – and therefore evaporative cooling – occurs during the heat of day when the water vapour pressure of the desert air is lowest (see box, page 52). The rate of

Displaying a phototactic response, the growing tip of the halfmens is pointed towards the sun, and tracks its movement across the sky each day. The 'hat' of leaves protects the heat-sensitive growing tip from direct exposure to the sun's rays.

Cheiridopsis denticulata illustrates one of the secrets of success of many dwarf succulents in the Succulent Karoo: the vertical orientation of the swollen leaves. This arrangement minimises the exposure of the surface area of the leaf to the sun, as the leaf can be struck by the sun's radiation from above and by radiation reflected from the desert floor below.

evaporation is thus high, and the leaf temperatures remain comfortably within the range over which chloroplasts can easily convert the sun's energy into the chemical energy that is subsequently stored in the sugars produced.

Many of the C_3 plants in the deserts are large, deep-rooted trees, so water losses in aid of leaf cooling are relatively affordable since the trees have access to deep groundwater. For this reason, they can be found in the washes and run-off lines of even the driest of deserts. C_4 plants, on the other hand, are mostly grasses with shallow roots and have no access to deep groundwater. Perennial C_4 species are therefore uncommon in the drier deserts, where rainfall patterns are unpredictable. Where they do occur in abundance, in the summer-rainfall deserts, they can tolerate high growth temperatures and so do not need to use up as much water on cooling as C_3 plants do (see map, page 52).

Different desert plants depend on this evaporative cooling during stomatal gas exchange to differing extents, but all achieve at least some cooling from it. For instance, at midday, 14 per cent of the total heat absorbed by the broad leaves of *Welwitschia* is discarded from the leaves through evaporative cooling.[11] This may seem relatively little, but at the hottest time of the day it is enough to prevent the leaf temperature from reaching a damaging level. In order to minimise the amount of heat absorbed by their leaves and stems, many succulents, especially the mesembs, hold them upwards, thus reducing the surface area that receives direct solar radiation. One drawback of this leaf orientation is that the sensitive growing tips of the leaves or stems are exposed to the most intense radiation. In the halfmens (*Pachypodium namaquanum*), which bends the tip of its stem towards the sun, this problem is solved by a rosette 'hat' of leaves that provides shade at certain times of the year. Notice the 'curly-whirly' leaves of the leaf rosettes (see page 60); could this be an adaptation to capture fog that occurs frequently where they grow?

Guy Midgley, from Stellenbosch University, showed that the life expectancy of succulent mesembs during a prolonged experimental drought was about 250 days, half that of typical deep-rooted Karoo shrubs.[12] One reason he suggests for the difference in longevity is the vertical orientation of the leaves and stems. Although this sounds contradictory, and although succulents can withstand fairly long dry spells, it is crucial that the droughts be interrupted on a reliable and regular basis. If they are not, the succulents start to wilt, their leaves can no longer be maintained in the upright position, and the added heat-loading of their wilted horizontal leaves rapidly exacerbates their dehydration and demise. This is one of the important factors that accounts for the predominant restriction of the succulents to the predictable winter-rainfall regions of the Succulent Karoo. It is also, sadly, likely to be the cause of mass extinctions in the Richtersveld and Namaqualand as the winter-rainfall zone contracts southwards with climate change (see Chapter Ten).

Ectotherms: insects and reptiles

Most desert ectotherms, such as insects and reptiles, rely heavily on the heat of the sun to reach their preferred operational temperatures. This they do by behavioural means, by shuttling between the shade and the sun. Consequently, the majority are active when temperatures in the deserts are tolerable, from soon after sunrise until sometime before noon, and again from late afternoon until sunset. During the hottest hours they retire beneath the sand or into other refuges where the temperatures are lower. In winter, when the days may be cooler, they may be active throughout the day.

On the one hand, an ectotherm's reliance on external heat sources is a disadvantage in that it cannot be active all the time; on the other, it saves a lot of energy on a daily basis. This is because temperature has a direct influence on the rate of energy expenditure. As the body temperature of insects and lizards decreases at night, so too does their energy expenditure, usually a two- to three-fold reduction for every 10°C decrease – known as the Arrhenius Effect.[13] These daily energy savings are crucial in ecosystems where food and water are scarce, and can be considered to be one of the principal factors accounting for such a high species richness of reptiles and insects in deserts. Most endotherms do not benefit from this energy saving because they keep their body temperatures constant.

Given that temperature restricts a desert ectotherm's potential to be active, it would be to the ectotherm's advantage if it could extend its activity time into the hottest hours of the day. Some unique adaptations that serve just this purpose have evolved in some ectotherm species. The tenebrionid beetle *Onymacris plana* traverses scorching hot desert sand in true athletic fashion: it runs faster than any other insect on Earth! Most can cover 1 metre in less than a second, but a maximum of 1,15 metres per second (4,14 kilometres per hour) has been recorded.[14] When the sand temperature exceeds 40°C, these speedy beetles dash from the shade of one nara bush to another, and are thus able to extend their daily activity time.

Another desert beetle, *Stenocara phalangium*, extends its activity time in a similar record-breaking manner – it has the longest legs of any beetle in the world. It literally walks on stilts and is thus able to lift itself above the temperature boundary layers that exist above the desert surface. These beetles inhabit the gravelly inter-dune 'streets', so they cannot dive below the desert surface as dune-dwellers do when temperatures become extreme. Instead, they perch themselves on top of the largest pebble within their territory. In fact, the highest pebbles become so sought-after that individuals vigorously defend them against other beetles.

For small desert-dwelling insects, with their large surface-area-to-volume ratios, high temperatures always pose a major problem. It is not surprising that many are remarkably tolerant of body temperatures that would kill most animals.

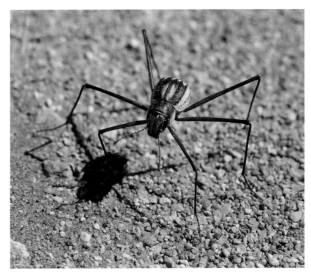

The beetle with the longest legs in the world, *Stenocara phalangium* is a denizen of the gravel plains of the Namib Desert. Its long legs raise its body above the hot boundary layer overlying the surface of the sand.

Oliver Halsey

Perhaps the fastest beetle in the world, *Onymacris plana*, a Namib dune sea endemic, dashes from one shrub to another at great speed to minimise exposure to both the sun and the hot desert sand.

For example, the Namib Desert dune ant prefers its body temperature to be around 31 °C, but it is routinely active on the sand at any surface temperature between 10°C and 55°C without suffering any lasting thermal damage.[15] These ants also have long legs, which lift them that critical 5 millimetres or so above the temperature boundary layer overlying the sand surface. At the highest temperatures, this is enough to keep their body temperature 10°C to 15°C below that of the sand surface. Like many diurnal dune-dwellers, they are active in the mornings and afternoons, but differ from other diurnal species in that they don't always retire to their nests during the hottest part of the day.

One ant in the Namib and Kalahari deserts, *Ocymyrmex*, is a true heat specialist, foraging during the hottest part of the day when its insect prey has become heat-stressed and is therefore easy to capture. The worker ants have been recorded on sand surfaces with temperatures ranging from 27°C to 67°C, and are able to endure such heat by means of thermal respiting.[16] While foraging, they periodically climb 10 to 20 millimetres up objects such as grass stems, faecal pellets or pebbles to get above the thermal boundary layers overlying the desert floor. *Ocymyrmex* ants have considerably longer legs than other ants, which elevates them even further above the boundary layer.[17] Even at this elevation the air temperature may be as much as 15°C lower than that of the sand. The ants spend only about six seconds above ground level before continuing their hunt for prey. Depending on the sand temperature, they may repeat the exercise as frequently as seven times per minute. Although six seconds does not sound like a long-enough time period in which to cool down to any meaningful extent, calculations show that the ants can lower their body temperature by as much as 6°C in this time. It has also been suggested that *Ocymyrmex* workers can tolerate such high temperatures because they are sterile and do not run the risk of overheating eggs or sperm, which are sensitive to heat stress.

At a mere 3 millimetres long, tiny spider beetles (Ptinidae) spend quite some time thermal respiting in the Namib Desert during the heat of the day. They climb on top of the faecal pellets of hares and ungulates, on which they also feed. A tiny wolf spider has also been reported to scurry periodically onto pebbles to dissipate heat while foraging during the heat of the day.

Reptiles face similar temperature problems, and their methods for coping depend to a certain degree on the nature of the surface on which they live. Those that inhabit hard or stony areas emerge sluggishly from their nocturnal shelters before the sun has had a chance to heat up the desert surfaces. They manoeuvre themselves into positions on rocks and in sunny spots where they can warm up quickly. As they are vulnerable to attack by predators at this time, it is essential that they become fully active as quickly as possible. They expose their largest surface areas to the sun by positioning themselves side-on to its rays, and by spreading their legs and flattening their bodies. They also increase the amount of blood flowing to the skin so that the blood heats up more quickly, allowing the heat to be circulated to the deeper parts of their bodies via the bloodstream. Only when the lizards reach their preferred temperature do they begin to move freely and are then best able to escape the attacks of predators, find food, defend their territories and engage in breeding matters.

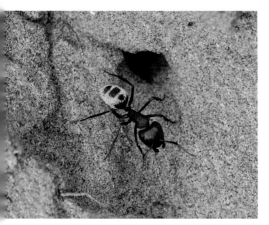

Chantelle Bosch

Above left: The boss ants of the Namib dune sea, Namib dune ants can tolerate very high sand temperatures – helped by their long legs. **Above centre:** After having captured a heat-stressed insect, a heat-tolerant *Ocymyrmex* ant dissipates heat by climbing on a plant for a few seconds to get above the thermal boundary layer. **Above right:** A heat-tolerant wolf spider interrupts its rapid hunting on the hot desert sand by lingering temporarily on a quartz pebble to cool down.

This beautiful male Cape flat lizard (*Platysaurus capensis*) warms itself in the morning sun.

As the day gets progressively hotter, the lizards continue to heat up and their body temperature starts to approach what is known as the critical temperature maximum, at which they can no longer move. To avoid this, they rapidly seek shade or the shelter of their burrows to cool down again, and then for the rest of the day shuttle between the sun and the shade, thus fairly accurately controlling their body temperature between the upper and lower limits at which they operate best.

The Namaqua sand lizard (*Pedioplanis namaquensis*) is a typical example of a lizard that is able to remain active throughout the day, even in summer, without having to retire underground. Even during the hottest hours in the Kalahari Desert and the Nama-Karoo, the lizard can be seen in the shade of a grass clump or small shrub, waiting patiently for a suitable prey insect to pass by. It then dashes out from cover at unbelievable speed, captures its quarry and returns to its shady refuge. The species' preferred body temperature ranges from 36°C to 42°C, so it can cope with even the hottest of days in its habitat. Another species of lizard, the ground agama (*Agama aculeata*), regularly climbs vegetation in the morning to bask or to avoid the hot desert surface and offload heat during the day. It is widespread throughout the Arid Savanna and Nama-Karoo biomes.

In habitats where the ground is soft, such as the Namib dune sea, there is very little shade, and the various lizards that live there behave quite differently. The sand-diving lizards, the wedge-snouted sand lizard (*Meroles cuneirostris*) and the shovel-snouted sand lizard, for example, do not cool down at night to the same extent as a lizard in a non-sandy habitat because the temperature of the sand

The Namaqua sand lizard, a sit-and-wait predator, keeps watch for prey items during the heat of the day.

The ground agama will climb up shrubs and bushes when its body temperature gets too high. This also affords it a lofty spot from which to spot prey.

Above and top right: When running over the hot sand of the Namib dunes, the shovel-snouted sand lizard periodically comes to a halt and performs a thermal 'dance' by lifting its feet and tail off the surface to cool them down. Another move in its repertoire involves alternately lifting opposing front and hind feet off the sand for a few seconds to offload heat (top right). **Centre right:** The thermal dance has evolved in another closely related sand-diving lizard, the wedge-snouted sand lizard, from the same habitat. **Bottom right:** The Namib sand snake moves very rapidly over hot sand by restricting bodily contact to short sections that propel the snake forward. Note the contact marks in the sand behind the snake.

into which they burrow remains higher than that of the air. Nevertheless, they are in no hurry to emerge in the mornings and do so only when the temperature of the sand surface has reached the same level at which they can operate most efficiently. In order to minimise the risk of predation while warming up, the lizards stick only their heads out of the sand. The heat is absorbed through the head and transported to the submerged body via the blood.

As the day progresses, the wedge- and shovel-snouted sand lizards remain active – even though the sand surface temperature may exceed 40°C. When the sand becomes too hot for comfort their first response is to stiffen their legs, thus elevating their bodies as high above the sand as possible. Although this behaviour reduces the amount of heat absorbed by these lizards from the surface, their feet can still become intolerably hot. To give each foot a few

minutes respite, both species perform a somewhat amusing thermal 'dance'. Using their hardened tails for support, they lift alternate front and back feet off the scorching sand, lowering them after a few moments before lifting the opposite pair. These sand-diving lizards evolved very rapidly from other southern African *Meroles* sand lizards in response to the fairly recent emergence of the extreme environments of the Namib dune sea (see Chapter Ten).[18]

Sluggish until the sun has heated them up, lizards often adopt postures that will speed up the process. Here the common Namib day gecko suns itself on granite close to a rocky crevice to which it can retreat if threatened.

When body temperatures continue to rise, all dune-dwelling lizards seek shelter below the dune surface, and are amazingly adept at diving into the soft, bone-dry sand. Since the lizard's entire body surface is in full contact with the cooler subsurface sand, heat flows rapidly out of the body by conduction. The shovel-snouted sand lizard or the desert plated lizard can be visible on the surface one moment and be gone in another, leaving hardly a ripple in the sand to show its point of entry. The snouts of both species are spade-shaped to decrease resistance as they 'swim' through the sand using lateral, undulating motion. Depending on the cause, the lizards may remain buried for longer than 24 hours without suffering any apparent breathing problems – oxygen and carbon dioxide pass through the dune sand with ease. The desert plated lizard is routinely found at depths of up to half a metre below the sand surface, apparently descending in a slow corkscrew fashion accompanied by small wriggling movements.

The Namib sand snake (*Psammophis namibensis*) minimises contact with the hot sand when hunting at speed for lizards. It does this by elevating its body and thrusting it forwards, employing only short sections of the body when making lateral contact with the sand surface.

Many rock-dwelling reptiles can also use rock crevices to escape the heat of the day by shuttling in and out of the sun. A good example is the several species of gecko in the Namib Desert that are active during the day. The Namib day gecko (*Rhoptropus afer*), for example, lives on granite sheet rock and shuttles between the areas of exposed gravel and the shelter of overlapping exfoliating granite flakes. It can hide there during the heat of the day and dash out to grab a passing insect on the exposed gravel sheets.

Another equally curious desert reptile is the Namaqua chameleon (*Chamaeleo namaquensis*), which hunts and stalks its prey throughout some of the most arid zones of southern Africa. Active throughout the heat of the day, this large, ground-dwelling reptile uses shade if it is available but does not seem to be reliant on it. Instead, it is armed with a formidable array of adaptations to conquer temperature problems, foremost of which is its remarkable ability to change its skin colour in relation to its temperature control needs. For instance, after emerging from its burrow or a rocky retreat after sunrise, the chameleon is almost black in colour and is thus able to absorb the sun's radiation very rapidly. To further speed up this heating process, it takes up a position side-on to the sun, deflates its lungs and dramatically stretches its skin, thus flattening its sides considerably. It thus enlarges the surface area onto which the sun's rays fall, more than doubling its surface-area-to-volume ratio. This flattening posture is highly adaptive, since it can also be adopted at high temperatures to minimise heat gain. In this case, the chameleon orientates the long axis of its body to the sun, thus reducing the surface area directly exposed to the sun. When its body temperature starts to approach the upper limit of its preferred range, about 39°C, it gradually changes colour, taking on a very pale white or grey hue, which increases the amount of solar radiation reflected off the skin. At the highest end of the range it also pants, keeping its body temperature well below that of the desert air by means of evaporative cooling. It is presumably able to replace the moisture lost during this process from the prey that it catches, for its appetite is ferocious and it may easily catch and consume a hundred beetles in one day.

Olga Ernst / CC BY-SA 4.0, Wikimedia Commons

The Namaqua chameleon can change its colour according to its thermal status. Here, close to the mild climate of the coast, it is in its dark phase, which promotes heat absorption so that the reptile can reach its optimum body temperature.

Chantelle Bosch

This Namaqua chameleon is in its light phase, which promotes the reflection of heat.

Like many small antelope, springbok orientate the long axis of their bodies in line with the sun's rays to minimise the full impact of the sun.

Most antelope, such as this herd of springbok, feed predominantly at night in the Kalahari Desert and spend much time in the shade during the day.

Because of their relatively thin fur, springbok suffer severe heat loss on cold nights or during rainstorms, which can lead to mass mortalities in winter.

stance when foraging at air temperatures above 30°C: they orientate the longest axis of their bodies to the sun, thus minimising the amount of solar radiation striking them. The springbok's pelage is exquisitely adapted to facilitate the task, for although the fur is generally thin, the springbok carries on its lower back a furry surprise. It has very long, pure white hairs, tucked into a skin pocket, or marsupium, hence the species name. These hairs can be erected by special pilo-erection muscles to produce the characteristic and very beautiful 'pronk' hairs on the lower back. Together with the white belly fur, the white hairs reflect about 75 per cent of all direct and reflected radiation that strikes these parts of the pelage.[33] When the springbok is orientated in line with the sun's rays, the pronk hairs can reflect as much as 95 per cent of the radiation.

At night the springbok and steenbok pay a price for their thin fur, for they have to shiver to produce enough heat to keep warm. As Gideon Louw and Mary Seely argued in their book *Ecology of Desert Organisms*, 'this situation, together with low primary production of herbage in deserts which does not usually allow the deposition of large fat reserves, means that these animals are frequently walking an energetic tight-rope. Severe cold after prolonged drought can therefore lead to extensive mortality in desert antelope, particularly when they are prevented from migrating to more favourable areas.'[34] And indeed, quite the most pathetic sight I have witnessed in a desert is a herd of shivering springbok enduring a rain shower on a windy day!

Large desert ungulates

When large desert ungulates such as eland, gemsbok, red hartebeest and blue wildebeest become water-stressed and can no longer spare water for evaporative cooling by skin sweating or panting, their body temperature increases but the brain temperature remains fairly constant. This is called selective brain cooling.[35] The mechanism relies on a 'blood-flow radiator' known as the carotid rete system, discovered more than 2,000 years ago by the Greek physician Herophilus. The system's form is simple, elegant and effective: it cools the blood going to the brain.

If an animal is water-stressed and can no longer afford the loss of body water, it stops sweating and its body temperature rises, sometimes to as much as 43°C. In effect, it is storing heat, which is an advantage in that it increases the temperature difference between the body and the air and heat can thus flow out of the animal down this temperature

gradient. But the gemsbok does not carry an elevated body temperature for the whole day. Being a large animal, it has a small surface-area-to-volume ratio compared with springbok or steenbok, and it heats up slowly. Its maximum body temperature is reached in the afternoon.[36] The stored heat can then easily be offloaded passively to the cooler evening air and the 'normal' body temperature restored.

The carotid artery feeds the brain with blood freshly renewed with oxygen in the lungs. This blood, which is at the same temperature as that of the body, would damage the brain if it were to enter the brain case at a temperature of anything approaching 41°C to 43°C. Fortunately it doesn't: immediately before entering the brain case, the carotid artery splits into a maze of smaller arteries which intertwine closely with a similar maze of veins that carry cooler venous blood back to the heart from the nasal sinuses in the gemsbok's nostrils. This network of interwoven blood vessels constitutes the carotid rete. When the gemsbok's blood temperature rises, it starts to pant, thus reducing the temperature of the venous blood in the nasal sinuses through evaporative cooling. As this cooler blood flows in the opposite direction to the warm carotid blood in the carotid rete system, heat flows from the warmer to the cooler blood by a process known as 'countercurrent heat exchange'. Maartin Strauss and collaborators from the Brain Function Research Group at the University of the Witwatersrand have shown that the carotid rete can cool the blood entering the brain by about 1°C in the Arabian oryx.[37] This may seem a small difference, but in terms of survival it is all the difference.

The function of monitoring the temperature of the blood belongs to the hypothalamus, a region of the forebrain that coordinates and regulates a range of systems in the body. It is able to monitor the temperature of the blood very precisely and accurately; moreover, it is also sensitive to and monitors increases in the blood concentration as a consequence of the loss of body water, and responds by shutting off the normal thermoregulatory responses such as sweating and panting. Thus, selective brain cooling can save large mammals considerable amounts of water daily that they would have used to maintain a constant body temperature, for example, in conditions of water stress.

But selective brain cooling can also be shut off in seconds when the antelope faces a threat. As the Strauss team argue, 'should an artiodactyl [even-toed ungulate] in a hot environment and implementing selective brain cooling be confronted by a flight-or-fight situation, its selective brain cooling would be abolished immediately by increased sympathetic tone. Consequently, hypothalamic temperature would increase, and the hypothalamic drive on evaporative cooling would be restored immediately, with the full power of evaporative cooling invoked to dissipate the extra metabolic heat. Immediate survival outweighs the longer-term benefits of body water conservation, and the artiodactyl makes temporary use of full evaporative cooling to avoid a potentially lethal hyperthermia. When the threat has receded, selective brain cooling can again be initiated, and evaporative water loss suppressed.'[38]

The carotid rete system may be the most important adaptation that allows antelope – and not only the larger ones – to inhabit the hot and dry deserts of southern and northern Africa. If desert ungulates were to attempt to maintain their normal body temperature by skin sweating alone, they would lose more water than they could ever hope to replace on a daily basis without drinking.

Robyn Hetem, also from the Brain Function Research Group, has analysed data for 17 species of large, desert-dwelling ungulates. Her analyses show that, when desert ungulates are short of food and water – and thus the energy needed to maintain a constant body temperature and the water needed to offload heat through evaporative

cooling – they can also relax control of the daily rhythm of body temperature.[39] In essence, what they are doing, like selective brain cooling, is prioritising the control of the body fluid concentration over body temperature control. Remember, if water is lost from the body fluids, the concentration of solutes in the blood increases and so, too, does the blood osmolarity, which can cause severe osmotic tissue damage. The body temperature in the carotid artery does display heterothermy, meaning that there are exaggerated body temperature fluctuations – both increases and decreases – around the normal body temperature. But this is considered to be more of a pathological than an adaptive response. Large ungulates under severe energy and water stress will survive for longer with elevated or reduced body temperatures that teeter towards lethal levels, than they will if their body fluid homeostasis is compromised. So, in short, large desert ungulates will progressively store heat in the body over the course of a hot day and dissipate the heat at night, thereby minimising the commitment of water for evaporative cooling. The critical response to potential hyperthermia in large ungulates is simply behavioural regulation, resting in shade during the hottest times of the day, and foraging at night.

Members of a gemsbok herd seek the shade of a camel thorn tree in the Pro-Namib.

Birds and temperature control

In their physiological responses to high air temperature birds are no different from mammals. For example, birds employ gular flutter, similar to panting in mammals, whereby the upper throat muscle flutters and acts as a 'pump', moving air rapidly in and out of the buccal cavity to promote evaporative cooling.

The only real differences between birds and mammals concern some of the behavioural methods they employ to thermoregulate, and the fact that their body temperatures are, on average, about 3°C higher than those of mammals. This latter difference means that birds face fewer thermal stresses when it is very hot than mammals do, for their relatively high body temperatures ensure a ready flow of heat out of the body as long as the air temperature remains below about 40°C.

Some birds, such as the sociable weaver (*Philetairus socius*), minimise their costs of thermoregulation by building their own thermal shelters (see Chapter Six). Most other species, however, do not rely on their nests for shelter and so have to face the heat of the desert.

Two types of desert birds, sandgrouse and larks, illustrate nicely how exposed birds cope with heat stress. As soon as the air temperature exceeds 31°C, sandgrouse put their impressive thermoregulatory repertoire into operation. It commences with wing-drooping behaviour, a common response employed by all birds when the temperature becomes too high for comfort. By exposing the sparsely feathered underwing skin to the desert air, the birds open 'thermal windows' through which heat can be discarded. Then, when the air temperature starts to approach or exceed their body temperature, sandgrouse do something quite unexpected – they fluff out their feathers and huddle together! Ironically, although these responses are effective at reducing heat loss in very cold temperatures, they are also effective at reducing heat gain. If the air temperature exceeds the birds' body temperature of 41°C, heat attempts to flow into the body. Huddling limits this inward heat flow but is effective only up to a certain point. As a last line of defence against very high temperatures, gular fluttering takes over its extremely effective role. This response, again common to all desert birds, is so effective that the Namaqua sandgrouse and double-banded sandgrouse (*Pterocles bicinctus*) are able to keep their body temperature below 42°C even when the air temperature reaches 50°C. Again, this illustrates the tremendous power of evaporative cooling.

Much of the success of ostriches in the deserts of southern Africa can be attributed to the behavioural actions they employ to maintain their body temperature. When the air temperature is high they use their generously feathered wings as sun umbrellas to shade their bodies and their huge, naked thighs. They also orientate their long axis with that of the sun, droop their wings laterally to provide maximum shading, and raise the feathers on their backs to allow even the slightest breeze to remove heat trapped over their skin surfaces. Again, when the air temperature exceeds their body temperature (about 40°C) they, like the sandgrouse and all other desert birds, rely almost exclusively upon the

Above: The enormous, communal nests of the sociable weaver adorn a camel thorn tree. The nests act as thermal shelters from the heat and cold. **Above right:** Sociable weaver.

Ostriches and other ratites have not flown for many millions of years, yet their generously feathered wings have been retained. This is because the wings perform crucial thermoregulatory functions, such as shading the naked thighs and, perhaps more importantly, their chicks. The wings also play a role in mating displays.

evaporative cooling provided by gular fluttering. At the other extreme, ostriches use their wings as blankets on very cold winter nights: they sit on the ground with their legs folded beneath them to reduce the exposure of bare skin, and trap warm air between their wings and the ground.

When birds fly, their massive pectoral flight muscles produce a lot of heat within their bodies. At moderate air temperatures, a flying bird has little difficulty in getting rid of this unwanted heat because the fast air movement over it rapidly removes the heat by forced convection. However, when the air temperature in the desert is very high, offloading this flight heat can become a real problem. The birds' solution is elementary: they trail their legs below their bodies during flight. Presumably, by not

being tucked away to reduce drag in the normal fashion, trailing legs offer additional bare surfaces from which heat can be lost through forced convection.

The chicks of desert birds are particularly vulnerable to overheating, and they rely heavily on their parents for protection. Sclater's lark, an endemic of the Nama-Karoo, breeds on rocky plains where vegetation cover is very sparse. Its nest, a cup-shaped depression among stones and pebbles, is completely exposed to the elements, and after the single egg has hatched the parents take great care to ensure that the helpless chick does not fry to death on the scorching hot, stony ground. They take turns to stand over the nest and shade the chick, one shading while the other hunts for harvester termites to feed it. The chick itself, however, also has a safety procedure if it is left unshaded for too long: it raises its head and points its gaping mouth in the direction of the prevailing wind or breeze. Behavioural patterns that exploit the massive benefits of evaporative cooling are evident in birds such as Sclater's lark, even at a very early age. The chicks of this and other larks also sport a bizarre headgear of hairy feathers which, when exposed to the sun, is probably useful in scattering solar radiation as it strikes the young bird's head.

Like the smallest mammals, the smallest birds would suffer the most when exposed to very high and very low

Sclater's lark parents take turns to shade their chick and go out to forage in the Nama-Karoo Biome.

The scaly-feathered weaver is the smallest bird in the deserts of southern Africa.

temperatures if they did not have some physiological or behavioural adaptation that cushioned the effect of the extremes. Scaly-feathered weavers (*Sporopipes squamifrons*), the smallest desert birds in southern Africa, keep warm on cold winter nights by huddling together in small flocks. They follow the example of the sociable weavers and, on a smaller scale, build roosting nests into which up to 12 birds cram to keep warm. Laboratory measurements showed that a group of 12 huddling birds in one nest halved their nightly energy expenditure.[40] On hot days, they presumably roost in deep shade and limit their activity as much as possible to save water. Another small Kalahari bird, the white-browed sparrow-weaver (*Plocepasser mahali*), builds a number of roosting and breeding nests in single or neighbouring trees that can be as much as 10°C warmer than the air temperature. These social birds also huddle for warmth in the roosting nests.[41] There is a nasty consequence of physiological and behavioural responses to high air temperatures – the time that the birds have for foraging during the day is reduced. All small birds lose body weight overnight when they are unable to forage. Typically, they recoup this weight loss the following day with their foraging activities. However,

on very hot days, the birds spend so much time panting, wing drooping and retiring to shade that they do not have sufficient time during the day to make up the previous night's body-weight shortfalls. So, during heat waves lasting a series of consecutive days, small birds rapidly lose condition and may ultimately die. Measurements of the deterioration of body condition caused by hot temperatures is the basis of predictions for how Kalahari birds will respond to global heating in the near future[42] (see Chapter Ten).

A white-browed sparrow-weaver perches at the entrance to its roost nest.

A camel thorn tree is host to several white-browed sparrow-weaver nests. Some nests are used for roosting during the day and night, whereas others serve as breeding sites.

CHAPTER 4 FOUR

The struggle for food

Maxime Briola

Hennie de Klerk

Above: Harvester ants (*Messor capensis*) carry grass leaves, stems and seeds into their underground nest.

Left: A desert-dwelling elephant reaches for acacia leaves in the dry bed of the Hoanib River.

Desert organisms not only need to conquer the challenges of scarce water and extreme temperatures in their environment, but also need to find and process enough food to balance their energy budgets. A healthy energy budget is one in which the amount of energy, acquired from the sun by plants and from their food by animals, is more than sufficient to meet the organism's everyday energy costs.

Scientifically speaking, we expect animals to adopt the most efficient and least energy-expensive method of finding food on a yearly basis so that in the long term they can optimise their breeding successes and produce as many offspring as possible. By so doing, the plant or animal is maximising its inclusive fitness. In this context 'fitness' refers to a measure of how many genes an

A gabar goshawk snatches a Namaqua sandgrouse over the waterhole at Cubitje Kwap in the Kgalagadi Transfrontier Park.

organism passes on via its offspring to future generations. This is what the continuity of life is all about and, in our case, it is driven by the energy acquired from the desert.

But finding food in deserts is not always simple. Rainfall is not only very meagre but also unpredictable, and since it influences the food sources of every desert animal in some or other way, the availability of food tends to follow the pattern of rainfall. Nor is it only a question of quantity: herbivores experience an additional problem in that although there may be enough food to eat, what is available is often of very poor quality. So, in the quest for food, desert animals face two major problems: firstly, they must find a reliable source of food in a fickle and unpredictable desert environment; and secondly, many of those that eat plant material must be able to process and digest poor-quality food.

In order to decrease the amount of food they have to seek, most desert animals are able to minimise their energy requirements by maintaining very low metabolic rates.[1] Many plants and animals also bring into play a suite of fascinating traits to simply 'opt out' when conditions are unfavourable (see Chapter Seven), while at the same time opting out of the need to find food. Some animals also increase their chances of finding food by foraging as members of cooperative social groups, sharing the food that any one individual finds (see Chapter Six). Solutions such as these partially solve the problem of finding sufficient sustenance, but there are other strategies that many desert animals employ to ensure for themselves an adequate food supply. The alternative solutions are the subject of this chapter. First to be discussed is the likely role of competition between plants and between animals as a means of securing available food. Then organisms that are equipped to store food during times of plenty are introduced, and finally, we take a look at some of the intriguing ways in which desert animals turn poor-quality food into a viable energy source.

Securing a reliable food supply

The problem of finding a reliable, year-round food supply is not confined to desert organisms, although the harsh and unpredictable habitat in which they exist no doubt makes the task more difficult. All organisms in all ecosystems of the world face the same problem to some extent, and some of the solutions observed in desert regions can also be seen on a global scale.

One way in which a certain species may secure a food supply is to compete for it against other species that have similar ecological requirements and lifestyles. Competing for food – or any other resource, such as a crucial nesting site – is a fact of life in the deserts as elsewhere in the world. Biologists recognise two distinct types of competition: interference and exploitation. Classically, interference competition, also known as 'contest' competition, involves the use of threats, fighting or poison by one species to exclude another. Exploitation or 'scramble' competition, on the other hand, occurs when a resource is rapidly exploited by one species at the expense of competitors without the use of direct aggression. In their book, *The Ants*, sociobiologists Edward O. Wilson and Bert Hölldobler delightfully sketched the difference between these two forms of competition as being analogous to 'the difference between small boys running a race to see who wins a pile of coins (contest competition) and the same small boys racing to pick up as many coins as possible thrown in front of them (scramble competition)'.[2]

Competition between different species of plants and animals – interspecific competition – is a decidedly thorny subject among biologists. Although most will concede that competition between similar species does occur, only about half believe that it plays an important role in structuring plant and animal populations in nature. For example, we know that beetles compete for food and habitat space in the Namib, but the question remains: are the numbers of beetles there controlled by interspecific competition or by other factors, such as predators? Such questions are fascinating and will be encountered again and again as we explore the ways in which desert organisms secure their food. By presenting both sides of the story I give the reader the opportunity to decide how important interspecific competition is in moulding desert communities into the complex and ever-changing patterns that we observe in the field from one year to the next.

Competition in plants

In many wetter ecosystems of the world, especially in biomes that are heavily forested, competition among plants is, most importantly, for light. In deserts, where there is ample light, plants compete instead for water and nutrients, the most significant of which are nitrogen and phosphorus. Because plants can take up nutrients only when they are dissolved in the soil water, there is a strict association between water scarcity and nutrient scarcity. So, when suitable rains fall in the desert, there is a mad scramble by plants for the few nutrients available.

In the Nama-Karoo, the kapokbossie and the ankerkaroo are two common perennial shrubs that tend to dominate the landscape. They owe their success to a rather spiteful trick – they are gluttonous wasters. When the soil in which they grow receives a good wetting, these two species capture the water at an astoundingly rapid rate. The plants make no attempt to use it efficiently, however, and open their stomata as wide as possible, losing much of the moisture that has been taken up back to the desert air by transpiration. Why, one may ask, should a desert plant respond so illogically to rainfall? Would it not be wiser for the plant to use the soil water sparingly and thus be able to extend its growth period for as long as possible?

Guy Midgley, formerly attached to the Stress Ecology Research Unit at the South African National Biodiversity Institute in Cape Town, believes that this seemingly

The kapokbossie rapidly absorbs water from the soil, thereby denying its competitors – seedlings and other shrubs – access to moisture and nutrients.

Mounds and circles of mystery

Three of southern Africa's four desert biomes feature a curious landscape phenomenon that is particularly noticeable from the air: evenly spaced circles, each about 30 metres in diameter. The circles are visually accentuated by abrupt changes in the vegetation pattern on and between them. They can be seen over vast parts of the Namib Desert, Nama-Karoo and Succulent Karoo biomes, as well as parts of the Fynbos Biome.[11] In the winter-rainfall areas of their range, south of the Orange River, the circles, consisting of mounds of soil up to 1 metre high, are known as *heuweltjies* ('small mounds').[12] In the more arid summer-rainfall regions, north of the Orange River, such as in the NamibRand Nature Reserve in the southern Pro-Namib and on the Giribes Plain in Kaokoland, the circles are flat or slightly concave and here they are known as fairy rings.[13] From time to time these circles seem to disappear for a number of consecutive years, but make their appearance again after good rains.

The origins of the circles have generated interest and speculation for centuries. The oldest published theory dates back to 1726 when Francois Valentyn, an employee of the Dutch East India Company, arrived at the Cape of Good Hope. In describing a company cattle post which he could clearly see some distance from the Castle in Cape Town, Valentyn provided this description of the surrounding hills: 'They are called the Tygerbergen, not because these wild beasts dwell there, but from certain darker or browner patches which clearly distinguish them from all the other hills, and these are caused by the dung of the deer thereon, which also enriches the soil.' Deer do not occur naturally south of the Sahara, so clearly he meant the dung of African ungulates. The hills he could see are still called the Tygerberg Hills, and the patches are still there today. It has been established that plants growing on them are markedly different from the surrounding vegetation, which creates the differences in the colour of the patches. Valentyn probably heard the explanation he gave from one of the permanent residents at the Cape, and it was followed by many even more wild and wonderful theories: some claim that the circles are UFO landing sites; others that they are sacred San marriage sites; and others still that they are, quite literally, fairy rings, where the fairies sing and dance. Sadly for some, and fortunately for others, most of the theories are just delightful nonsense.

Most serious *heuweltjie* and fairy ring pundits have implicated termites in their hypotheses.[14–17] The southern harvester termite (*Microhodotermes viator*) is unquestionably

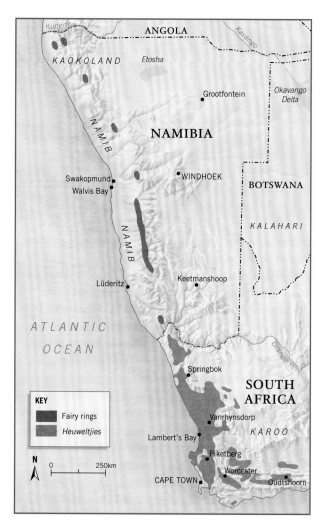

The distribution of *heuweltjies* and fairy rings in southern Africa.[18]

Northern harvester termites carry grass underground on the rim of a fairy circle.

Above left: Found only north of the Orange River, fairy rings display a remarkably uniform spacing pattern that suggests that their creators compete for space. **Above right:** A close-up view of a fairy ring in the Pro-Namib. This photograph was taken in the NamibRand Nature Reserve at the time of a nine-year drought.

Above left: The crest of this *heuweltjie* in the Strandveld of the Namaqua National Park shows the intense disturbance created on these mounds by digging mammals, such as aardvark, in search of termites. From the air the mounds consequently appear to lack vegetation. **Above right:** *Heuweltjies* – fairly evenly spaced vegetated mounds of soil up to 1 metre high – occur predominantly in arid areas south of the Orange River. Seemingly barren when seen from afar, they in fact harbour diverse plant communities.

associated with all the mounds south of the Orange River, whereas the desert termite (*Psammotermes allocerus*) and the northern harvester termite are often associated with the fairy circles in Namibia. These different patterned-earth phenomena are separated by a mere political boundary.

One feature of *heuweltjies* and fairy circles is the remarkable uniform spacing pattern between them,[19] believed to result from the competition for resources between whatever biological agents are responsible for their formation. Termites can account for the spacing pattern of the mounds and circles on the basis of competition between colonies for food, but they may not be the only animals responsible for building the *heuweltjie* mounds in the south. Bearing in mind that mounds characteristically occur on shallow soil, which readily becomes waterlogged in winter, the mound elevates matter, thus releasing their nutrients back into the soil. Such decomposers occur in very much smaller numbers in deserts than they do elsewhere because conditions are simply too dry for them to survive in the soil. However, the microorganisms are safe from desiccation in the guts of termites, and there they carry out their decomposer tasks to the benefit of themselves, their hosts the termites and, in the long run, the entire ecosystem.

The scarcity of microorganisms in desert soils results in very slow decomposition rates, and dead plant matter can lie around for years without being broken down. Valuable nutrients are therefore kept 'locked up' and prevented from re-entering the soil where they could again be taken up by plants. Only with the aid of insects – beetles, silverfish and termites – can the nutrients be 'unlocked' and returned to the soil via the insects' faeces.

The extent of soil enrichment by termites can be seen very clearly and dramatically if one examines the nutrient

The flightless dung beetle *Pachysoma rotundigenum* feeds on detritus, which it also buries for food for its larvae.

One of the Namib's most important decomposers, silverfish are among the few insects that can produce cellulases.

composition of the soil of *heuweltjies*. These earth domes have exceptionally high nutrient levels compared with the soils between the mounds. For example, nitrogen levels are double those found in the soils between the *heuweltjies*, and calcium levels are about 14 times higher.[53] These higher soil nutrient levels have a profound influence on plant growth on the *heuweltjies*, and are undoubtedly responsible for the dense bush clumps and better crop growths that they support in some areas. The mounds act as carbon dioxide traps and oxygen generators.

The next most important group of desert caeco-colonic fermenters are the rodents. To understand and appreciate their adaptations, we need to go back a few million years. All modern rodents evolved from an ancestral insect-eating animal that existed about 66 million years ago. Insectivorous animals do not need complex guts to digest their high-quality protein food; all that is required is a fairly large sac-like stomach to temporarily store the food after meals, a relatively short intestine, and an efficient enzyme system to break down and absorb important foodstuffs into the circulatory system. The very earliest rodents either remained insectivorous, like their ancestors, or became omnivorous, like humans, and could thus consume any high-quality plant or animal food. Omnivores also do not require very complex guts to ferment their food.

Then, starting in the Miocene and accelerating during the Pliocene some 7 million years ago, huge changes unfolded on the African landscape that were to change the animals of Africa forever – the forests started to retract and were replaced by grasslands and open wooded savanna. As these changes took place, the rodents carved out their niches in the new habitats. One family of rodents, the Cricetidae, which originally evolved in North America,

Termites rely on protozoans and bacteria in their gut to ferment cellulose.

Dead trees such as this one in the NamibRand Nature Reserve can persist for decades without decaying, spared by the dearth of decomposers.

had in fact already crossed into Africa via the Palearctic landmass during the Miocene, about 20 million years ago. Another family, the Muridae, poured into Africa out of the Asian forests. We still do not really understand where the family of subterranean rodents known as the Bathyergidae came from, but certainly by the early Miocene they were making their presence known. And so, the battle for a niche in the 'new Africa' by these rodent families commenced, and today we can still witness the action.

Although many of these rodents remain omnivorous today, some adapted to the open African habitats by becoming true herbivores, switching from high-quality diets to poor-quality plant material. And, as one might expect, ingenious modifications to the simple, ancestral digestive system to accommodate cellulose fermentation evolved in them. Instead of fermenting plant roughage in the rumen stomach as ungulates do, the rodents ferment their roughage in large outgrowths of the lower intestine, the caecum, or appendix as we call it. Here, they too maintain enormous numbers of microorganisms that break

down plant cellulose into fatty acids. Some desert-dwellers have taken this modification to extremes. The Damara mole-rat of the Arid Savanna Biome feeds extensively on the tubers of the gemsbok cucumber, of which about 60 per cent of the edible part consists of tough, stringy cellulose fibres – appallingly poor-quality food. These mole-rats have the largest and most complex folded caecum of all rodents in southern Africa; it comprises no less than 10 per cent of the mole-rats' body weight![54]

However, the truly interesting battles for an ecological niche raged above ground, between the Muridae and the Cricetidae. The murid rodents brought with them from Asia the ability to breed rapidly and have large litters, and so it would appear that they outbred the cricetid rodents in the choicest of the new African habitats. To avoid this competition, the cricetids had little option but to retire to the less desirable, harsher habitats – the swamps and the deserts. These remarkable adaptations evolved in them to cope with these environments, and consequently they still reign supreme there.

One of two subspecies of mountain zebra in the deserts of southern Africa, the Cape mountain zebra is a resident of the Nama-Karoo Biome. Like the Hartmann's mountain zebra, it makes use of caeco-colonic fermentation, a digestive process that helps to break down cellulose only after it has passed through the stomach.

The Hartmann's mountain zebra's remarkable capacity to endure in some of the driest and hottest parts of the southern African deserts is largely due to its ability to digest grasses of very poor quality.

Most genera of the Cricetidae in southern Africa, including the genera *Gerbilliscus*, *Gerbillurus* and *Desmodillus*, which represent the diverse desert gerbil fauna in the Namib Desert, have become the true desert specialists. In their case, it is their remarkable water conservation adaptations that account for their numerical dominance and success in the extreme deserts of southern Africa (see Chapter Two).

However, another subfamily of the Cricetidae, the Otomyinae, became swamp and marsh specialists, and today they are surprisingly well represented in deserts by the genera *Parotomys* and *Myotomys*. All the Otomyinae have very large caecal fermentation chambers that have evolved to cope with a diet of poor-quality marsh grasses and reeds. What really is of interest to us, though, is that these large caecal fermentation chambers armed some species with the perfect adaptation to move out of the swamps and invade those deserts that could provide food in the form of grasses and dwarf shrubs. Today two species, Brants's whistling rat and the bush Karoo rat, considered to be the smallest mammalian herbivores in southern Africa, feed exclusively on the stems and leaves of perennial desert shrubs – relatively poor-quality food for rodents.

Irrespective of how efficient caecal fermentation may be, one thing is certain: it is not nearly as efficient as rumen fermentation. Urea recycling does not occur, and the volume of the caecum is considerably smaller than that of the rumen. But the biggest problem for small caeco-colonic fermenters is that the food moves through the caecum too fast for effective and complete fermentation to occur. To compensate for this, a bizarre way of improving the rats' cellulose fermentation has evolved in them – they eat their own faeces, passing the undigested cellulose through their entire digestive system two or three times before it is finally discarded. Two types of faeces are produced: the normal firm, dark rodent faecal pellet which is the final discard stage; and a soft, lighter-coloured faeces which is not discarded by the animal but is instead eaten directly as it emerges from the anus. This process, called coprophagy, is a highly adaptive means of increasing the efficiency of cellulose digestion in the absence of an ungulate-type rumen. As we discussed for ungulates, efficient fermentation requires a long time and a large vat. Now, even though rodents have attempted to maximise their caecal volume for this, not enough fermentation can take place on the first pass. Multiple passes have therefore proved to be the successful way of increasing fermentation time.

The other advantage of coprophagy is that dead microorganisms passed out with the faeces are re-ingested, thus forming a valuable protein source for animals that do not recycle urea. Coprophagy is practised by many desert rodents as well as rabbits and hares, and starts at a very early age. As soon as rodent pups are able to eat, they beg the faeces from their parents, thereby allowing them to start their own microorganism populations in their caeca, which they will sustain there for the rest of their lives.

Caeco-colonic fermentation also occurs in large mammals and, in the deserts of southern Africa, the champions are Hartmann's mountain zebras (*Equus zebra hartmannae*). It has always amazed me how these large herbivores manage to eke out an existence in the Namib Desert. There have been many arguments, some ongoing, about the relative evolutionary success through time of rumen fermentation in even-toed artiodactyls, such as antelope, versus caecum fermentation in odd-toed perissodactyls, such as horses. Clearly, rumen fermentation is more efficient than caeco-colonic fermentation, but what seems clear is that caeco-colonic fermenters can survive on grasses with very high cellulose contents, that is, very poor-quality roughage, provided that this food source is available in abundance. So, to me, here's the puzzle: where do Hartmann's mountain zebras obtain large quantities of grass on a daily basis? Whenever I have seen them on the gravel plains of the Namib, there is not a blade of grass in sight. This animal is in urgent need of more research.

Animals with cellulases

Unlike many microorganisms, vertebrates and most insects do not produce their own cellulases that would allow them to digest cellulose. Interesting exceptions, however, are a few specialist insects that feed on detritus in the Namib dune sea. Various beetles belonging to the genus *Onymacris*, for example, appear to be able to digest cellulose. This ability is so advanced in *Onymacris laeviceps* that this beetle can, apparently, digest cotton wool! Even more remarkable is the fact that other desert beetles that belong to the same family – the Tenebrionidae – but occur in Israel and Arizona do not produce cellulases. The special adaptation that evolved in the Namib tenebrionids presumably did so in response to the vast amounts of available food in the form of detritus in the dune sea.

Silverfish, known as fishmoths, can also digest cellulose, as proved by the long-tailed silvermoth (*Ctenolepisma longicaudata*), a common household insect that eats cellulose-rich books, clothes, photographs and other items. How this habit evolved is not really known, for households and their contents are newcomers to the landscapes of the world. One thing is certain, however: silverfish are one of the most abundant groups of insects in the deserts of southern Africa, especially in the Namib.

Working from the Desert Ecological Research Unit of Namibia at the Gobabeb Namib Research Institute, John Irish and Rick Watson spent two years undertaking valuable pioneering research on these interesting insects.[55] Their research painted the first clear picture of the importance of silverfish as decomposers in southern African desert ecosystems (see box, page 115). To date, about 40 silverfish species of the family Lepismatidae have been identified in the Namib Desert, and of these, nine live in the dune sea, where their ecology has been studied to some extent.

In principle, one could argue that the evolution of cellulases in silverfish and tenebrionid beetles may be the single most important factor accounting for the remarkably high diversity of life in the Namib dune sea. Remember, only a handful of plant species occur there, certainly not enough to act as the primary food source of the many animals that inhabit the region. The insects' ability to tap the energy contained in poor-quality detritus has added a multitude of additional food chains to the ecosystem. Without this activity, the Namib dune sea could not have boasted the large number of animal species that it does.

Tenebrionid beetles are extremely successful in the Namib Desert as they can produce their own cellulases and are thus able to eat dry detritus and other plant material. Here *Onymacris plana* is snacking on the flower of a nara plant.

Above: Toad grasshoppers quite easily sport the most impressive camouflage of all desert-dwelling insects in southern Africa.

Left: The formidable scales of the slow, lumbering ground pangolin (*Smutsia temminckii*) illustrate the concept that flat-footed (plantigrade) mammals are armoured because they cannot run fast enough to escape predators.

Numerous adaptations have evolved in desert animals and plants that solve problems of water scarcity, temperature extremes and energy budgets, yet all would be quite superfluous if the animals and plants could not avoid being eaten by whatever may prey upon them.

The driving force in the life of all creatures, whether desert-dwellers or not, is to produce many offspring which in turn may equally successfully produce vast numbers of descendants. In this way, combinations of genes of a particular species are passed on from one body to its progeny, as they have been for millions of years. The genes are the most ancient survivors on Earth. In their quest for immortality they programme each body that carries

Wendy Panaino

them through time to ensure that they are passed on again, mostly through sex but also asexually, before their host dies naturally or is killed and eaten by another creature.

It is not surprising, therefore, that through the process of natural selection subsets of genes carry the programmes that arm their hosts with an endless variety of weaponry. Such adaptations to avoid, deter, minimise, or in some cases, even exploit attacks on them by their enemies have been channelled into most species as part of their survival blueprint. Many of these adaptations have yet to be identified, and no doubt they will continue to function effectively without our ever knowing about them. This is particularly true at the microscopic level, where all organisms wage an incessant war against an invasion of their bodies by harmful bacteria, viruses and fungi. Other structures or behaviour patterns are more familiar to us, although it may not always be obvious that they serve as defensive adaptations.

This chapter, however, examines some of the defences that we do know about and think we understand to some extent. It describes the armoury used in battles that rage in the southern African deserts, commencing with the most widespread conflict: that between plants and the herbivores that eat them. As long as plants continue to capture the sun's energy and convert it into the sugars and other foods that serve as the principal energy source of all animals, this conflict will persist. Yet plants did not evolve to serve as food for animals; each remains its own discrete entity, with a survival drive as strong as any animal's.

Chris & Mathilde Stuart

The southern African hedgehog curls up into a tight ball when threatened, with its short but sharp spines protecting its head and underparts.

For immobile plants, nutrients and water are scarce and difficult to find, and once acquired are worth protecting from other organisms.

In both plants and animals, the widespread use of camouflage, deception, bluff and mimicry provides some truly intriguing examples of the versatility of life's colour codes. Another commonplace form of defence – the use of thorns, spikes and horns – can be seen in virtually every form of desert life. In building an organism's armoury, genes programme their host to produce not only proteins and enzymes that are involved in the manufacture of appropriate defensive poisons or in the evolution of growth patterns and shapes, but also proteins that are responsible for behaviour. In closing the chapter, some examples of bizarre but highly adaptive behaviour that helps certain creatures escape from predators are presented.

Biochemical warfare

Plants face attack from herbivores and, not being in a position to run away, employ methods of defence aimed at discouraging them. Unquestionably, the most widespread of these is their use of chemicals that upset herbivores in some or other way. Known as secondary compounds, the plants themselves produce these substances but they have no day-to-day physiological function in the plant itself, having evolved purely in response to herbivore pressures. In other words, the plants would survive quite well without them – and save themselves valuable resources – if they did not need to protect themselves.

The range of defensive chemicals produced by plants is staggering and reflects the outcome of countless evolutionary wars that have raged between plants and their enemies over millions of years. Some of the more common groups are alkaloids, rotenoids, cyanogenic and cardiac glycosides, oxalates, fluoro fatty acids, tannins and phenols, and each acts in a different way. Most are very toxic: the alkaloids, for example, include highly poisonous substances such as strychnine. Others are not directly toxic but they reduce the quality of plant material ingested by herbivores. Tannins, the most common secondary compounds, occur in varying quantities in all vascular plants. They act by interfering with the digestive processes of herbivores, forming relatively indigestible complexes with leaf proteins and thereby reducing the amount of protein that the herbivore can digest and absorb in the gut.

The properties of tannins and their usefulness in processing leather have been known to human beings for centuries. Applied to untreated hides, tannins bond with the proteins in the leather to form insoluble compounds that render the leather impervious to attack by microorganisms. One group of tannins, called condensed tannins, work in exactly the same manner in the rumens of ruminants, rendering proteins indigestible to gut microorganisms and thus blocking the fermentation process (see Chapter Four).

One of the most fascinating interactions between plants and their herbivore foes is illustrated by the geophytic growth form (plants with bulbs, corms and tubers). Certain geophyte species are extremely toxic to humans and animals. *Moraea pallida*, *M. miniata* and *M. polystachya*, all members of the family Iridaceae, are well known for causing 'tulp' poisoning, which is responsible for extensive stock losses in the Nama-Karoo and Succulent Karoo each year. The compound responsible is a cardiac glycoside that causes heart failure. Various bulbous geophytes of the family Liliaceae are also highly toxic and include desert species such as *Urginea physodes* and *Ornithoglossum viride*. Again, the poisonous compound is a cardiac glycoside. Most species of the genus *Ornithogalum*, which are commonly known as chincherinchees and belong to the Liliaceae family, are remarkably toxic, causing severe diarrhoea that may lead to death after a few days. Horses have been fatally poisoned after eating no more than eight dried flower heads, and in cattle chincherinchee poisoning, if it is not fatal, may cause temporary or permanent blindness. (See table on page 124 for a list of common chemical compounds in toxic plants and their effects.)

The evolution of poisonous compounds specifically in geophytes can be readily understood when one considers these plants' extreme vulnerability to attack by herbivores both above and below ground. Geophytes remain dormant during either the dry or the wet season, depending on the species, and whether they grow in a winter- or a summer-rainfall desert. Many, in fact, sprout even before the first rains fall, taking their cue from their internal circannual clocks and using up the food reserves in their corms or bulbs to do so. Thus, they are already photosynthesising when the first rains occur, at a time when the condition of the veld is at its poorest and herbivores are hard-pressed to find good-quality food. Not surprisingly, the emerging tender, green shoots of geophytes become the immediate focus of the animals' attention.

For the long-term survival of perennial geophytes, it is obviously important for them to protect their reserves and thus their best chances of flowering and setting seed. Unlike trees and shrubs, which can survive repeated visits by herbivores and sustained consumption of their many leaves, most geophytes bear only a single stem and a few leaves. In one or two bites the plant can lose its entire photosynthetic above-ground parts. This is a loss it definitely cannot afford, for if the reserves remaining in the underground storage organ are too depleted to sustain sprouting once more, the whole plant will die. This is where the poisons enter the conflict, for secondary compounds have evolved to prevent such disasters.

The war against herbivores during the growing season above ground is not the only conflict geophytes have to face; they also wage an ongoing underground war against subterranean herbivores such as mole-rats of the genera *Cryptomys*, *Fukomys* and *Bathyergus*. These underground burrowers go straight for the 'vault', feeding on the plants' own precious food store in the form of their corms, bulbs and tubers. In the long term, they have probably put greater pressures on geophyte populations than above-ground herbivores, especially in southern Africa where the diversity and abundance of subterranean mammals are unsurpassed anywhere in the world. This underground war is intense, for most of the mole-rat aggressors eat storage organs and little else.

Considering the pressures that geophytes are subjected to, it is no wonder that so many species are highly toxic. But matters are not that simple. Why should it be within any plant's 'interest' to kill a herbivore by poisoning it? If an ungulate drops dead from cardiac arrest after eating one or two flower heads, neither party benefits. The animal loses its life but learns nothing, and the plant in the long term derives no nutritional benefit from the animal's faeces, which would have been deposited on the soil and returned to the nutrient cycle. It is much more important that the herbivore should merely suffer a very bad experience so that in future it learns not to touch that species of plant again. And this, in fact, is what generally happens. Mild poisons, which induce vomiting or some other disagreeable experience, have evolved in many plants, and the plants themselves have an unpleasant taste so that the herbivore learns from the very first bite that the plant is toxic. In large doses, however, these mild poisons can become lethal. Towards the end of the dry season, or during extended droughts when vegetation quality is at its poorest, herbivores are forced to switch to the bad-tasting plants which they fastidiously avoided during more productive times. As the condition of the grazing deteriorates further, they consume these plants in ever-increasing quantities.

Whereas tannins are not directly toxic, they too can be fatal in times of extreme hardship. Animals are able to detect high tannin content in a plant and are usually careful to avoid any plant that has a tannin content of about three per cent or more. If a herbivore persists in feeding on tannin-rich plants, as it may sometimes be forced to do if there is nothing else to eat, it rapidly loses condition and eventually dies.

If many plants survive by being only mildly toxic and by warning herbivores off with their unpleasant taste, why should the geophytes have become extremely toxic? Although part of the answer lies in their extreme vulnerability, another important consideration is the possible response from the original aggressor, the herbivore itself. It takes two to fight an armed conflict and, as in any arms race, the herbivores have their own biochemical defences that nullify the potentially harmful effects of plant poisons. The plant in turn must always strive to be one step ahead of the herbivore, so

Toxic plant	Secondary compound	Effect and cause of death	Comments
Milkweed (*Gomphocarpus fruticosa*)	Cardiac glycosides	Heart failure	Produces white latex that contains cardenolides. Poisoning is acute.
Red tulp (*Moraea miniata*) **Blue tulp** (*Moraea polystachya*)	Cardiac glycosides	Heart failure	All *Moraea* corms are potentially toxic and contain bufadienolides. They cause tulp poisoning. Poisoning is acute.
Pig's ears (*Cotyledon orbiculata*) **Krimpsiektebos** (*Tylecodon wallichii*)	Cardiac glycosides	Heart failure	Several Crassulaceae cause krimpsiekte ('cramp illness') in ungulates. They contain cotyledoside, tyledoside and orbicuside. Poisoning is acute or cumulative.
Large bietou (*Dimorphotheca cuneata*)	Cardiac glycosides	Respiration blockage; tissue hypoxia	Prussic acid poisoning follows the release of hydrogen cyanide.
Vermeerbos (*Geigeria ornativa*)	Sesquiterpene lactones	Vomiting, paralysis, asphyxiation and heart failure	Causes vermeersiekte ('vermeer illness') in ungulates. They contain the lactone vermeerin which deters herbivory.
Spiny ruschia (*Ruschia spinosa*)	Tannins	Binds to protein, enzymes and sugars, which prevents digestion or function	High concentrations of tannins reduce food quality and deter herbivory. Death occurs by starvation.
Chincherinchee (*Ornithogalum thyrsoides*)	Cholestane glycosides	Diarrhoea and blindness	Can be fatal to horses.

Some relatively well-known secondary compounds produced by southern African desert plants (also see opposite page) and their effects.[1] Most observations were obtained from livestock, but it is likely that other animals that consume these plants would also be detrimentally affected in some or other way.

Milkweed

Red tulp

Blue tulp

Pig's ears

Krimpsiektebos

Large bietou

Vermeerbos

Spiny ruschia

Chincherinchee

the herbivore's defensive response merely stimulates the evolution of more potent toxins in the plant. This is followed by a more powerful defence from the herbivore – and so the arms race rages on and on through evolutionary time.

The herbivore's defence against the secondary compounds of the geophytes takes the form of various mechanisms for rendering it safe. Once a toxic compound has been ingested by the herbivore, it must pass a number of obstacles before it can find its way to the target organ, where it can do its damage. The compound may be attacked and degraded by enzymes, barriers may stop it, it may be rapidly excreted, or it may find that it cannot properly interact with its target tissue because of some or other structural alteration there. By far the most significant defence is that provided by the enzymes – most importantly, by mixed-function oxidase enzymes, or MFOs. Unlike other enzymes, MFOs are remarkably non-specific and will act on a wide variety of chemical substances.

The mole-rats have a defence against toxic compounds that is not understood but is particularly remarkable in that it reflects a very advanced stage in the stepwise race for biochemical domination. As mole-rats expend large amounts of energy in burrowing, and therefore cannot afford to be choosy about the bulbs they locate underground, one would expect them to eat every bulb, corm or tuber they encounter. And this is what they do; they delight in eating all kinds of bulbs and corms, including those of chincherinchees and tulips that would induce immediate heart attacks in other herbivores.

Of all the herbivores, insects seem to achieve the greatest immunity to highly toxic plants and, in most cases, this is due to the efficiency of their MFO enzyme systems. Many take advantage of this immunity and become specialist feeders of poisonous plants. In some cases, however, they 'steal' or sequester the poisons from their food plant to make themselves poisonous and thus avoid attack by vertebrate predators. A classic example concerns the wide-ranging African monarch butterfly (*Danaus chrysippus*), also known as the African plain tiger, whose larvae feed on highly toxic milkweeds of the family Asclepiadaceae. The butterfly lays its eggs exclusively on milkweeds, which contain high levels of cardiac glycosides. When the caterpillars hatch, they feed on the plant, but instead of succumbing to the toxin, they accumulate it in their bodies. The toxin is not degraded by MFO enzymes but is passed on through the pupal

stage to the butterfly. Both caterpillars and butterflies are thus afforded a certain degree of impunity from attack because their common predators, birds, learn to avoid them fastidiously. A bird that consumes an African monarch, like a herbivore that eats a mildly toxic plant, usually becomes violently ill but survives, and will not attack a similarly coloured caterpillar or butterfly again.

The toxins of some plants have been well utilised by desert-dwelling humans. *Commiphora africana*, a common arid-adapted plant in South Africa, Namibia and Botswana, is the host plant of the beetle *Diamphidia*. The larvae of the beetle feed on the plant and accumulate diamphotoxins in their bodies that get passed on to the pupae in their cocoons. The San dig out these cocoons, extract the pupae, and squeeze the body juices onto their arrow shafts or tips. This poison is lethal to mammals. It causes muscle paralysis and haemolysis, that is, the destruction of red blood corpuscles. When the adult beetles emerge from the cocoons, they sport bright red and yellow colours, called aposematic coloration, which advertises their toxicity to predators.

Unlike insect larvae, mammals seldom feed specifically on certain poisonous plant species. Whereas the larvae cannot move from their food plant, mammals are mobile

Dr. Raju Kasambe / CC BY-SA 4.0, Wikimedia Commons

The larvae of the African monarch butterfly feed on poisonous milkweeds with impunity, accumulating the toxin in their bodies. It is passed on to the adult butterflies, which are then fastidiously avoided by predators.

Top left and middle: San hunters lace their arrows with a toxin produced by beetles such as *Diamphidia nigroornata*; the poison is passed on to their larvae and pupae. **Top right and above:** The larva pupates in a cocoon in the ground. It is then dug up and the contents extracted and dried before it is mixed into a paste that is applied to the arrow shaft.

and can more easily avoid bad-tasting plants by moving on and selecting something else to eat. They can also dilute the effects of mild poisons by diversifying their diet. Nevertheless, they still rely on their MFO complexes, which have evolved to cope with the plants they have most frequently encountered through evolutionary time. In this respect, it is not surprising that domestic livestock fares so badly against poisonous plants in the southern African veld, especially in the drier regions. Cattle, goats and sheep have not evolved alongside the various geophyte species and so do not possess an adequate measure of biochemical defence. Thus, although substantial proportions of domestic herds are known to have died from chincherinchee poisoning, there have been no reports, to my knowledge, of significant numbers of wild ungulates having suffered the same fate in desert habitats.

The economics of biochemical warfare

How plants and animals achieve a balance in the biochemical arms race depends, as in all wars, on the economics involved. For some decades now biologists have been intrigued about how the costs and benefits of these conflicts may determine the balance that is finally reached. What, they ask, are the costs to the plant of producing secondary compounds versus the benefits they enjoy? Costs and benefits are not arbitrary quantities – they can be quantified in terms of the growth rate and reproductive output of the plant. The latter – measured, for example, as the number of seeds that a plant produces each year – represents one criterion of the plant's 'fitness', or its ability to preserve the continuity of life.

The general consensus is that secondary compounds do indeed cost the plant important resources to produce and store – resources that could have been used elsewhere to enhance growth or reproductive output. The amount that a plant invests in secondary compounds clearly must bear some relation to the risks or the severity of the herbivore attacks to which it is subjected. If the risks are so high that the plant may not be able to produce any seeds at all, then it must benefit that plant to invest heavily in secondary compounds so that its reproductive output, and therefore its fitness, can be improved. The direct costs involved concern not only those of actual metabolic manufacture, such as the amount of adenosine triphosphate molecule (ATP), nitrogen, phosphorus and enzymes which may be required to produce secondary compounds, but also the formidable expense of storing the compounds once they are produced. It should be borne in mind that, with very few exceptions, plants are just as susceptible to being poisoned by the compounds that they themselves produce, as are the herbivores for which the compounds are actually intended. For instance, cyanogenic glycosides release free cyanide (HCN), a potent inhibitor of respiration in both plants and animals. Also, many phenolic compounds are broad-spectrum toxins to plants and animals. They damage cell membranes and interrupt ATP production and several other biochemical processes. These secondary compounds must therefore be stored in a safe place and in a safe way within the plant, where they can do no damage.

Most compounds are stored in special vacuoles and vesicles within the plant cell where they cannot interact with its vital organelles. Tannins, on the other hand, are stored in specialised tannin cells. Other substances, such as the toxic latexes in euphorbias, are stored in specialised tissues separated from the other water-bearing tissues of the plant. All of these storage facilities are structural in nature, and all are therefore expensive to produce.

The most important factor that influences the balance between cost and benefit is the nature of the habitat itself. In the southern African deserts, one might expect that perennial plants, whose growth is limited by a scarcity of water and nutrients, simply could not afford to 'waste' these precious resources on the production of secondary compounds. In fact, virtually the opposite is true: most desert plants invest quite heavily in secondary compounds (or some other form of defence) at the expense of growth rate and seed production. In regions where vegetation is relatively scarce, herbivore pressures can be extremely high and undefended plants would rapidly become locally extinct.

On the other hand, annual grasses and herbs tend not to invest too heavily in secondary compounds. The resources they save in this respect, as well as those they save by not having to maintain extensive root systems (see Chapter Four), contribute substantially to their very fast growth rates and prolific seed production. After rain they 'flood' the food market to such an extent that the herbivores are unable to make a severe impact on them before they have had a chance to set their seeds.

To swing the balance in their favour, plants economise wherever possible. One way that they do this is by producing and maintaining secondary compounds only in the parts of the plant that are most vulnerable to attack. For example, it would be wasteful for Karoo shrubs to maintain tannins throughout their extensive root systems in response to springbok browsing their leaves and stems. In Karoo plants that are known to possess significant amounts of tannin – such as the succulents *Ruschia spinosa* – the highest tannin concentrations are frequently in the leaves, since they are the part of the plant that offers the lowest cellulose and highest protein content, and therefore the highest nutritional value to herbivores. Roots also come under attack, and not only from burrowing creatures such as mole-rats, but also from microorganisms and insect larvae. Some plants that are subject to attack underground economise by maintaining tannins only in the outermost tissue layers of their roots – the first line of defence.

Some plants also save vast amounts of resources by producing secondary compounds only when they are needed. This they can do because many herbivores, especially insects, often become a problem only at certain times of the year, such as during their breeding season. Some plants even display a remarkable, yet poorly understood adaptation to cope with transient as well as seasonal pressures: they produce secondary compounds only when they perceive an attack. These so-called 'induced plant defences' are best developed in plants in which the costs of producing and storing secondary compounds are particularly high, for example, ones that produce large quantities of tannins. When an animal begins to browse, the plant immediately becomes 'aware' of structural damage to its leaves and stems. In order to deter further damage, it responds by increasing the concentration of tannins in the immediately afflicted tissues, as well as in all similar tissues.

Willy Stock, University of Cape Town, and some of his colleagues investigated induced defences in three shrub species commonly found in the Karoo: *Osteospermum sinuatum*, *Pteronia pallens* and *Ruschia spinosa*.[2] They established that of the three, only *Ruschia spinosa* contains quantities of tannins which would be effective in deterring herbivores. They also found clear evidence of an increase in the tannin concentrations in the plant's old leaves – by as much as 350 per cent – in response to simulated browsing.

However, the fact that two of the three Karoo shrubs that Stock investigated have low tannin concentrations and no measurable ability to induce tannins when attacked suggests that these plants may be investing their nutrients in other survival mechanisms. *Pteronia pallens* is certainly toxic to ruminants, and it is suspected that this species may contain alkaloids. Stock suggests that the bietou species does not invest in secondary compounds at all. Instead, it has extremely deep roots and can afford to be deciduous, losing its leaves during a period of drought and then regrowing them when conditions are good. It therefore pours its resources into the rapid regrowth of the missing parts.

Camouflage: the cryptic way out

The easiest way to avoid predators is to hide from them, either by taking refuge in burrows or other shelters or by being difficult to see. An organism that uses the latter method, demonstrating crypsis or camouflage, is one that sports a colour pattern or surface texture which effectively breaks up its distinctive outline and shape, allowing it to blend in with its background surroundings.

In the plant kingdom the desert mesembs of the subfamily Ruschioideae provide superb examples of crypsis. For instance, it is well known that many species of the genus *Lithops* ('stone-like') and *Argyroderma* display an astounding resemblance to the stony ground of their habitats. Growing at ground level, these plants are almost indistinguishable from the surrounding stones and pebbles, and it is very difficult for grazing herbivores to locate them. Only when they flower in spring do these 'flowering stones' betray their presence.

There are, however, other cryptic genera besides *Lithops* and *Argyroderma*. The genus *Pleiospilos* ('full of dots'), which is restricted to the Nama-Karoo and Succulent Karoo, also bears two succulent, stone-like leaves above ground. *Lapidaria* ('a group of stones') *margaretae* adds to the cryptic simplicity of the paired leaves of *Lithops* by having a further four or five camouflaged leaves. The species *Didymaotus lapidiformis* ('shaped like a stone') has only two leaves, but instead of the single flower that characterises all *Lithops* species, it pushes out two flowers, one on each side of the paired leaves.

Some species of the genus *Gibbaeum* form mats or clumps of velvety, light-coloured leaves at ground level. The pebbly shapes and colours of these leaves blend well with the white quartz pebbles in their habitats. This ground-hugging, clumping pattern is also evident in the genus *Conophytum*, but here the leaves are round or button-shaped, and are covered by a dried skin during the dry season. In some species, such as *Conophytum pellucidum*, these dried leaves blend in very well with their surroundings and look more like small pebbles than anything else.

The genus *Avonia*, a member of the family Portulacaceae, includes many species that also merge into their surroundings. One of these, *Avonia papyracea*, is endemic to the southern African desert regions, where it is an excellent mimic of the quartz pebbles among which it grows.

When not in flower, the succulent *Argyroderma delaetii* can be hard to spot among the quartz pebbles of the Knersvlakte.

Argyroderma delaetii in flower.

The speckled brown surface of *Pleiospilos compactus* – seen in its habitat in the Karoo National Park – bears an uncanny resemblance to the stones on the right.

Freeze behaviour, the requirement to remain still to avoid detection, is practised by all cryptic animals. On the sandy substrates of the inter-dune valleys in the Namib, the colour of the solpugid *Metasolpuga picta* closely matches the sand grains of its habitat. This spider-like creature can run very rapidly across flat, sandy ground, but when it detects danger it freezes immediately and can then be difficult to find. Wolf spiders in the Namib Desert are particularly well camouflaged when practising freeze behaviour. Freeze behaviour is also extremely well developed in many adults and chicks of cryptic ground-dwelling desert birds. Again, the sandgrouse is a good example, for it freezes when approached and flies away only at the very last moment. If chicks accompany it, the young birds remain still until their parent calls them after the danger has passed. The chicks are highly cryptic and extremely difficult to see on the ground, so if you disturb a parent bird, great care should be taken that you don't tread on a chick.

As well as reducing detection by predators, freeze behaviour serves a very useful associated purpose: it reduces the number of escape flights that an animal would be required to make each time that a predator should pass nearby. A decrease in escape flights not only saves energy, but also – and more importantly – it reduces the high respiratory water losses that accompany them.

Nocturnal birds are generally very cryptic because they need to hide during the day. Owls sport particularly good camouflage. The tiny African scops owl (*Otus senegalensis*) favours the drier savanna areas where it roosts with its back against a tree trunk, its feather patterns blending in remarkably well with the background patterns of the bark. Then, to further break up its distinctive owl outline, it has a habit of markedly

Above left: Being nocturnal, owls need to rest during the day, and their cryptic plumage helps avoid detection and disturbance. This African scops owl has chosen an alien pepper tree at Nossob in the Kgalagadi Transfrontier Park as a daytime roost. **Above right:** It is not usual to see spotted eagle-owls roosting close to the ground, but if the habitat sports no trees, they have no choice. **Right:** Nightjars, like owls, are strictly nocturnal, and need to hide during the day. In the deserts of southern Africa, they roost on the ground, as this freckled nightjar is doing.

Chantelle Bosch

Above left: The head of a Péringuey's adder. **Above right:** When this adder shuffles itself into the loose sand of the Namib Desert, only its eyes and nostrils are visible.

elongating its body and extending its ear tufts, and at the same time closing its eyes to mere slits. Even large owls, such as the spotted eagle-owl (*Bubo africanus*), rely on crypsis for concealment during the day. But it is the nightjars that are the cryptic champions. Freckled nightjars (*Caprimulgus tristigma*) roost in recesses in granite outcrops and are almost impossible to spot during the day.

Although many animals use crypsis to hide from predators, it is equally useful to predators lying in wait for their prey. The sidewinding Péringuey's adder shuffles its coiled body into the sand until it is completely buried. Only its eyes are visible, and even they are camouflaged to match the sand grain patterns. These snakes lie still for hours on end, waiting for an unwary prey item, such as a lizard, to pass within striking distance. It is fortunate that their venom is very mild to humans because they are easily trodden upon when they lie submerged in the sand.

Even very large carnivores rely on crypsis to increase their hunting success. In the Kgalagadi Transfrontier Park, where dwarf driedoring shrubs dominate the vegetation on the banks of the Nossob River, the black and straw-coloured mane of the lion blends in superbly with the shrubs and golden grasses. When these large cats adopt their stalking posture, with belly and head held close to the ground, they are extremely difficult to distinguish, and it is not surprising that solitary males can successfully ambush even the most cautious adult gemsbok.

Kalahari lions are well camouflaged in riverine vegetation along the Nossob and Auob rivers, and are able to prey on game that comes to feed on the grasses.

Leopards are cryptic whatever their environment.

The spotted pattern of the leopard (*Panthera pardus*) is an obvious aid to the animal's concealment in trees, its preferred daytime resting place, but it also has a cryptic effect even in exposed shrublands of the Kalahari Desert. The fact that leopards rely heavily on crypsis is clearly illustrated by the number of differently coloured fur markings they display throughout their extensive distribution in Africa and Asia. The ground colour of the fur can vary from white through off-white, buff and golden to pitch black, and is presumed to match the prevailing colour and tones of the relevant habitat.

By far the most unusual form of crypsis is chemical crypsis, which has been observed in the puff adder (*Bitis arietans*) – a common ambush snake in the deserts of southern Africa. This snake has very camouflaged scales but, in addition and unlike all other actively foraging snakes, it has no scent and cannot be detected by predators. Trained dogs and meerkats were unable to sniff out puff adders but could easily detect other snakes.[4] It most likely pays not to stink when trying to be unobtrusive.

Deceit and bluff

Like animals of all southern African biomes, a number of desert species employ cunning tricks to deceive their predators or their prey. For example, Péringuey's adder, lying buried in the sand, attracts inquisitive lizards to within striking distance of its position by wriggling the exposed tip of its tail. This action simulates an active insect on the dune surface, and invariably lures the lizard to investigate a possible meal.

Some animals bluff their enemies into believing that they are considerably larger than they really are. The masters at this deception of size are undoubtedly the aardwolf, a harmless, dainty termite-eater that belongs to the same family as the hyenas, and the brown hyena. The relationship of the aardwolf to hyenas is obvious, for its dog-like face and darkened muzzle are like those of the brown hyena. But the similarity ends there; the aardwolf weighs a mere 8 kilograms, the brown hyena about 40 kilograms, but their killer cousin, the spotted hyena, has a mass of about 60 kilograms. Moreover, the aardwolf

Derek Keats / CC BY 2.0, Wikimedia Commons

Derek Keats / CC BY 2.0, Wikimedia Commons

Above: A brown hyena raises its hair to convince its attackers that it is much larger than it really is. **Left:** This hyena's bluff was good enough to steal a springbok kill from five cheetahs. The force of a brown hyena bite is considerably stronger than that of a cheetah. The cats cannot risk bites and subsequent infections from carrion eaters.

cannot bite, for its teeth are reduced to a few rounded pegs suitable for eating termites, and it certainly does not hunt in packs and kill large game such as gemsbok. When threatened, the aardwolf immediately erects its extraordinarily long mane hairs, the effect of which gives it a most formidable appearance and seems to double its size. Sometimes it adds deep-throated growling to this bluff, presenting itself as an adversary with which to be reckoned.

Some owls also exaggerate their size when confronted by danger. The southern white-faced owl (*Ptilopsis granti*), like the African scops owl, normally elongates its body and closes its eyes to slits to blend in with the branches of its daytime roost. When a potential predator approaches too closely, however, it holds out its wings, dramatically fluffs out its feathers and keeps its eyes wide open, hissing all the while. The whole performance gives the impression that the owl is considerably larger and more fearsome than it really is.

The pearl-spotted owlet (*Glaucidium perlatum*) has a rather bizarre feather pattern that affords its 'blind side' some protection. Two black spots surrounded by white rings look like eyes in the back of the owl's head, giving it a false face. This presumably bluffs potential predators into believing that the bird is fully aware of their presence, and that a surprise attack is therefore out of the question.

Butterflies use false eyes quite extensively to deceive their predators, but in some cases they seem to invite attack rather than avoid it. Many butterflies in the subfamily Theclinae have eyespots and tails that create the impression of a false head. A resident of the Succulent Karoo and Arid Savanna, the dusky marbled sapphire (*Stugeta subinfuscata reynoldsi*) has at the tail end of its hind wings a pair of dark eyespots that are very conspicuous when the butterfly is at rest with its wings folded. Even more remarkable are two black hair tails adjacent to each false eye, which look like antennae and forelegs. In fact, the whole butterfly looks like a double-headed freak. The false head fools predators into attacking the butterfly's tail end – the harmless tips of the wings – rather than the real head. When it is attacked the butterfly can escape with its vital organs intact, suffering at worst only a nick out of its hind wing.

Anyone who might eat a handful of African monarch butterflies (*Danaus chrysippus*) stands a very good chance of suffering massive cardiac arrest, for they are crammed with cardiac glycosides. Even the ingestion of a single butterfly would induce violent vomiting and illness. The predators of these bad-tasting toxic butterflies know this only too well, having learned it from their own past bad experiences. They have also learned to recognise the coloration of the African monarch: the black, white and orange colours that typically advertise its toxicity. The display of such bright warning colours (aposematic coloration) occurs in many bad-tasting or toxic insects to alert predators to the hazards of attack.

But that is not the end of the story. Other butterflies have jumped onto the African monarch's bandwagon, displaying aposematic coloration almost identical to that of the toxic butterfly, despite the fact that they are quite

Above: Southern white-faced owls fluff themselves out to look more formidable. **Right:** The pearl-spotted owlet's feathers are patterned to form a pair of false eyes on the back of the head, useful in deterring predators.

Peter Steyn

CHAPTER SIX

Social contracts

Above: Southern pied babblers live in groups of up to 16 birds. Mutual preening (known as allopreening) is an important bonding behaviour within the group.

Left: A trio of meerkats clusters near a burrow. Meerkat sociality has been studied extensively over the past four decades to understand the extent to which group living ensures a successful existence in the Kalahari Desert.

Why do so many animals form colonies, herds, flocks, prides, clans, troops, and so on? The answer to this is of great interest to biologists, since it throws light on the problems that animals face in their respective habitats. The study of animal sociality is an integral component of evolutionary theory and, as we shall see, certain of its implications continue to provide some interesting challenges to the modern biologist. Sociality in animals is, of course, not restricted to deserts, but as a generalisation I am happy to argue that it is very well developed in deserts, particularly in those of southern Africa. As Tim Clutton-Brock, University of Cambridge, argues, 'fitness of all group members commonly increases with the size of their group, because group size increases the capacity of group members to catch, produce, or defend food, to detect or repel predators, to disperse in large subgroups, or to raise young successfully'.[1] These essential activities of life are challenging to undertake successfully in deserts at all times of the year because food is scarce and widely distributed in space and time, and habitats are open, offering little cover against predators.

The theory of evolution by natural selection has been touched on in preceding chapters, mainly in connection with adaptations in plants and animals that help them to overcome some or other desert-related problem. In order to understand animal sociality in an evolutionary context, it is now necessary to examine the theory more closely.

Accepting that the one 'rationale of life' of all plants and animals is to produce as many successful offspring as possible, it is logical to deduce that all adaptations we can identify in them help them to do so. By producing offspring that will survive to breed successfully in turn – in other words, by optimising their reproductive output – they pass on as many of their genes to future populations as they can. How, then, in desert animals, does sociality and the apparent altruism towards others in the clan – kindness, if you wish – help to optimise their reproductive output?

In deserts, eking out a living is a risky business: food and water are scarce, scattered, sporadic and difficult to find; temperatures range from extremes of hot and cold within very short periods of time; and, with little

refuge among the sparse vegetation, predators and prey animals can see each other over great distances. In the face of such formidable difficulties a solitary individual may find it well-nigh impossible to fulfil any rationale of life successfully.

In evolutionary time, many animals have struck 'I'll scratch your back if you scratch mine' deals with other members of their own species, and even with other species, in order to overcome problems through group cooperation and cooperative breeding. But there is a condition: each individual cooperates only if by doing so, it is able to pass on more of its genes to subsequent generations than it would if it were not social. If this condition were not fulfilled, an individual would be seen as being merely helpful or altruistic towards the group at the expense of its own reproductive objectives.

The really interesting aspect of sociality in animals lies in trying to identify the frequently not-so-obvious reasons why members of some species cooperate within a group and how they benefit from doing so. This chapter will examine some of the factors that drive some desert animals together, the benefits that accrue from sociality, and how individuals optimise their reproductive output by cooperating.

A subadult Cape ground squirrel interacts with a parent in the Kgalagadi Transfrontier Park. Like meerkats, Cape ground squirrels rely on the social group for early predator detection.

The extreme deal: eusociality

Most species of insects of the Hymenoptera – ants, bees and wasps – display the most extreme levels of sociality in the animal kingdom: eusociality. In eusocial societies, only one female breeds in the colony and all workers are sterile. Trying to understand how eusocial insects fit into Charles Darwin's vision of evolution has always been difficult. Darwin saw social insects as the major threat to his theory of evolution. Why would social nonbreeders assist a single queen to breed when they could go off and breed on their own? To explain this, it is necessary to delve a little into the mysteries of genetics, one of the most interesting subjects of modern biology and to which Darwin had no access.

All mammals are diploid, meaning that one half of their chromosomes come from the sperm of the father and the other half from the egg of the mother. At the most, you would be related to your mother by 50 per cent, to your father by 50 per cent, but also to your brothers and sisters by about 50 per cent. By the same token, if you had children, they would be related to you by 50 per cent. So, in terms of passing on your genes, each child that you raised would carry a maximum of 50 per cent of either you or your partner's genes. If you had many children and they in turn also had many children, then your genes would spread far and wide in the gene pool of humans. You would score highly on the fitness scoreboard.

For many years, evolutionists have been concerned that, because the workers in social insect colonies are sterile, they do not have the opportunity to pass on their genes. Why do they labour away for the colony if they derive no benefit? Why does one bee waste its time and energy helping another bee – the queen – to pass on her genes when it could be doing the same thing itself? Moreover, how do non-productives evolve if they don't breed?

Insight into this problem was gained in 1964 when William Hamilton, then at the University College London, realised that it is not necessary for individual workers to breed; even though they are sterile, they can pass on the same number of genes as they would have if they had bred by helping the queen to breed.[2] All workers in the Hymenoptera – the sterile females – are related to each other by 75 per cent and not by 50 per cent, a result of the fact that their fathers are haploid, that is, they have only one set of chromosomes that they inherit from their

Hamilton's Rule

'W D Hamilton is a good candidate for the title of most distinguished Darwinian since Darwin,' wrote Richard Dawkins in his obituary of Hamilton. Hamilton died tragically of complications from malaria in 2000, after returning from the Democratic Republic of the Congo, where he was trying to understand the relationship between polio vaccinations and the transmission of the AIDS virus.

William 'Bill' Donald Hamilton (1936–2000)

George Robert Price (1922–1975)

the altruist and the beneficiary. The value of r ranges from 0–1.

George Price developed Hamilton's Rule further, by showing mathematically that natural selection can select for altruism not only in family groups of related members, but also at higher levels of groups in which the assemblages need not necessarily consist of related individuals, provided that there is a threat from an opposing group. Price's equation formed the foundation of Group Selection Theory.

Hamilton's Rule is the basis of the theory of inclusive fitness and Kin Selection Theory, and is described by the simple equation $C < r$B; where C is the fitness cost to the altruist in performing the altruistic task, B is the fitness benefit to the recipient, and r is the relatedness between

The history of the development of these mathematical formulations of how altruism can evolve is brilliantly told in the book *The Price of Altruism* by Oren Harman.[3]

Damara mole-rats are the most social of all mammals in the deserts of southern Africa.

Damara mole-rats use their teeth to dig burrows in search of tubers and bulbs. It is a risky way of foraging, but the risks are overcome through cooperation within the colony.

mothers. This means that all the grubs in the colony have the same mother and father. The potential queens, which will one day disperse as fertile alates, are therefore actually sisters of the sterile female workers. By helping to raise these potential new queens, the workers are helping to pass on thousands of fertile 75-per cent copies of themselves, which is better than the 50-per cent copies they would have achieved if they themselves had bred. Thus, even nonbreeders are gaining 'part scores', what are called indirect fitness benefits.

Although this hallmark explanation, now known as Hamilton's Rule (see box, page 147), and which forms the basis of Kin Selection Theory, seems to solve the problem

of the Hymenoptera, it does not clarify the situation of sterile workers in termite colonies, where all individuals in the colony are diploid. Sterile termites may never get a chance to breed, and the benefits of sociality certainly cannot be explained by a haploid chromosome argument. Yet termites are probably the most successful of all desert animals, having evolved about 175 million years ago, during the Middle Jurassic.[4] The answers may be found by looking not for indirect fitness benefits but for direct fitness benefits, which are less obvious and often very subtle.

The same scenario can be explained in some eusocial mammals. Two species of arid-adapted, subterranean rodents (Bathyergidae) are eusocial: the Damara mole-rat[5] from the Arid Savanna, and undoubtedly other lesser-known *Fukomys* species to the north and east of the Kalahari Desert,[6] and the naked mole-rat (*Heterocephalus glaber*) from East Africa.[7] A naked mole-rat colony has one queen, different grades of workers and a few heftier soldiers – just like the social insects. The Damara mole-rat also has one queen, but there is much debate about whether there is a division of labour among the rest of the colony.

The naked mole-rat, which weighs between 25 and 70 grams, occurs in the arid regions of East Africa, in colonies that number as many as 300. With a mass of between 100 and 250 grams, the Damara mole-rat is larger, and lives in colonies of up to 40 animals throughout southern Africa's Arid Savanna Bbiome.[8, 9] Both species live permanently underground in sealed burrow systems and seldom, if ever, venture onto the surface. The fact that these mammals are eusocial has been puzzling biologists since the discovery by Jennifer Jarvis, University of Cape Town, was announced in 1981.[10]

I continue to argue that common to the sociality of these mole-rat species is past and present aridity, and its influence on the spatial distribution of their food – tubers and bulbs.[11] Aridity in Africa has waxed and waned over millions of years. The current deserts in Namibia, Botswana and South Africa were linked by a desert corridor that passed through the currently more mesic countries of Zambia, Zimbabwe, Tanzania and Kenya to the arid horn of Africa (Ethiopia and Somalia). All of the eusocial mole-rats today, especially the many species of *Fukomys*, inhabit the current or former arid regions of Africa. That the arid corridor has opened and closed over time is reflected in the current distribution of mammals, such as the Damaraland dik-dik, gemsbok and bat-eared fox (*Otocyon megalotis*), that display geographically isolated populations in southwestern and central-eastern Africa.[12]

If the most recent phylogeny (family tree) of the mole-rats is correct, it suggests that eusociality evolved twice, independently, within the two eusocial genera.[13] The ancestor of the Damara mole-rat, *Heliophobius*, is a solitary species, so this mole-rat did not inherit eusociality from its ancestor. Thus, eusociality may have evolved separately in the two arid hotspots of sub-Saharan Africa.

In a Damara mole-rat or naked mole-rat colony only the queen breeds, and in order to ensure this she completely suppresses the reproductive ability of the female workers: eggs do not develop in their ovaries and they do not come into oestrus (the physiological state of readiness when mating can take place). In naked mole-rats this suppression occurs through aggression from the queen and a few 'hench moles' that she allows to mate with her. The naked mole-rat queen is considerably larger than the other females and she suppresses them for as long as she rules. When she dies a few of the larger females suddenly start growing again and may double their body size within a few weeks, a remarkable capacity for a mammal. These potential new queens then physically battle it out in bloody conflicts until there is eventually only one winner – and she then becomes the queen. Much the same happens in Damara mole-rat colonies, except that there is less difference in body size between the queen and the other females. Inevitably, some females never get a chance to become the queen.

In terms of earlier arguments, the all-important question may already be crossing your mind: why do these females stay in the colonies, allowing themselves to be reproductively suppressed when they could set off with a male and form a new colony? This is the crux of the matter.

Veiled benefits

Hamilton's explanation clearly cannot show why individuals in the majority of diploid-diploid bird and mammal species display cooperative behaviour. Indeed, it is often the case that completely unrelated individuals are accepted as helpers into groups. There must be direct fitness benefits that individuals accrue when no obvious indirect fitness scores can be identified. There must also be selection for altruism in groups of unrelated individuals.

It is now thought that altruism can evolve in groups of individuals not related to one another, provided that the group itself faces a persistent threat to its existence.

Formerly of the University College London, George Price argued that selection for altruism can occur at multiple levels of groups.[14, 15] In essence, by joining a group of unrelated conspecifics, such as a herd of zebra, and helping to defend the herd against threats, the individual and the group as a whole enjoy fitness benefits. But what are these veiled benefits and why should altruism evolve in groups?

Consider again the naked and Damara mole-rats. A pair of mole-rats that decided to elope from the colony would not survive to breed as they would not be able to find sufficient food.[16] This is where the desert plays its vicious role, for these mole-rats feed exclusively on underground bulbs, corms and tubers located by random burrowing.[17] In Africa, the more arid a habitat becomes, the larger the underground storage organs seem to be. The tubers' large size is advantageous to the mole-rats because a single tuber can provide enough food to sustain a colony for days, but the drawback is that they occur further away from one another than tubers in a wetter habitat. In the absence of giveaway clues, they are therefore hard to find and are only encountered by chance burrowing. And herein lies the risk to solitary individuals – the probability of finding food is strongly dependent on the number of animals searching.[18]

Under typical dry conditions in the southern Kalahari Desert, a solitary Damara mole-rat would have no more than a two to ten per cent chance of finding a tuber before dying of starvation.[19] On the other hand, any one of a group of 25 cooperative mole-rats sharing their finds would have a virtually hundred per cent chance of finding food. Another way of looking at it is that only two to ten out of every hundred solitary mole-rats that attempted to disperse on their own would survive – a very low percentage indeed. But by staying in the colony they still do not pass on their genes. Or do they?

In the case of the naked mole-rats, individuals gain indirect fitness scores, which means that their genes are passed on without the animals themselves actually breeding. So far, we have considered this only from the point of view of the suppressed daughters, but the queen herself is also faced with a serious problem. Because solitary dispersal is so risky, there are no available unrelated males out there with whom she could mate if she did disperse. Whereas the nuptial flights of potential termite queens are synchronised to take place one or two days after rain, and therefore coincide with the flights of unrelated males and other potential queens from neighbouring colonies, potential mole-rat queens cannot do this. And so, the inevitable must happen – the queen mole-rat has no choice but to mate with her sons!

Inbreeding – horror of horrors? Not necessarily. Traditionally, inbreeding is considered to be a bad thing because recessive genes combine with each other to produce offspring with abnormal structures and behaviour. However, if animals breed fast and have large litters, abnormal animals die without substantially affecting the population size. At the same time, the recessive characteristics tend to die out with these fatalities, thus removing the bad genes from the population.

Another result of perpetual inbreeding is that all mole-rats in the population steadily become genetically more and more similar to each other. Studies detailing the results of DNA-fingerprinting have found that individuals within and between naked mole-rat colonies are related to each other by about 81 per cent rather than 50 per cent.[20] Such close genetic similarity means that daughters are more than 80 per cent related not only to their mothers, but also to their fathers, brothers and sisters. For the genes of any member of the colony to be passed on, it therefore does not matter who breeds, just as long as one mole-rat in the colony does. As long as the contribution of each individual ensures that the queen breeds, which it does because it increases the chances of finding tubers, then individuals still pass on more than 50 per cent of their genes each time that the colony successfully raises a mole-rat pup. This is the essence of Hamilton's Rule. It clearly pays individuals to stay in the colony and help to find food, defend the burrow system against intruders and assist in raising the pups, all of which are tasks whose success depends on the so-called differentiation of labour seen in eusocial societies.

However, Damara mole-rats do not inbreed and the relatedness among colony members is about 50 per cent.[21] Importantly, the breeding female and her mate are completely unrelated to each other, which means that foreign males have entered established colonies. I suspect that this arrangement occurs because dispersing males do not need to face the high risks of establishing new burrow systems to find their own food. All they need to do is disperse after rain when the soil is damp and the cost of burrowing is cheaper,[22] find a neighbouring colony, and burrow down to its tunnel system. But this argument does not apply to nonbreeding females born into a group of Damara mole-rats because they would need to establish their own new colony. We need to identify the veiled fitness costs and benefits of forming groups.

Taming the climate

Before animals can produce offspring, they have to reach reproductive age and be in good condition for breeding. This, of course, means that they first have to cope with the extremes of the desert climate. As we have seen in earlier chapters, animals possess many physiological and behavioural adaptations that help them to deal with climatic extremes. The most common is the tendency to seek refuge underground when conditions on the surface are particularly harsh. But what happens to those animals that do not, or cannot, go underground?

One species simply builds its own thermal shelter. The nests of the sociable weaver (*Philetairus socius*) are characteristic features of the southern Arid Savanna and northern Nama-Karoo biomes, and they can attain impressive proportions. Sociable weavers are desert endemics, and, without any doubt, they provide the best example of how group cooperation can overcome harsh physical factors – temperature and water shortage – in desert habitats. Colonies of up to 300 birds build the communal nests. The sites vary: some nests are built in the higher branches of camel thorn trees, some in kokerboom trees (*Aloidendron dichotoma*), some on windmill platforms, and some even on the crosspieces of telephone poles. A single nest may be 6 metres long and 2 metres high, and it may weigh more than 1,000 kilograms. The structure as a whole may comprise as many as 50 individual compartments, each with its own tube-shaped entrance on the underside of the nest. These haystack-like apartment blocks are occupied throughout the year, so nest building is a never-ending task,

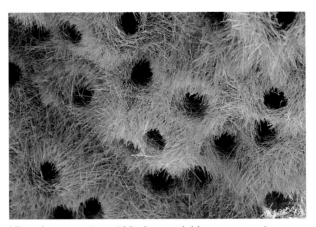

Like a huge apartment block, a sociable weaver nest comprises many separate chambers that are built into the underside of the structure. The chambers are insulated from the sun's rays by a thick thatched roof.

Trees such as this quiver tree in the Namib Desert are not the only sites for sociable weaver nests; the birds also build on windmills and telephone poles, making it difficult for snakes to reach the nests.

with all birds adding grass stalks and straw to the thatch dome every day. In view of this continual building activity it is not surprising that the weight of some nests sometimes brings even the thickest camel thorn branch crashing down.

The thermal characteristics of sociable weaver nests in midwinter and midsummer were investigated by George Bartholomew, University of California in Los Angeles, and his colleagues.[23–25] Their results paint a clear picture of the benefits of building such large nests, the most important of which is that the nests buffer the desert's minimum and maximum temperature extremes. As we have seen, small animals are very susceptible to heat loss and gain, and sociable weavers, which have a mass of about 27 grams, would have to spend vast amounts of energy and water to maintain a constant body temperature.

In winter, the insulation provided by the air pockets trapped within the thatch structure prevents the temperature inside the nest from decreasing to the same level as the outside air temperature. The difference may be 20°C or more, the temperature inside an occupied

nest remaining at a comfortable 23°C while the outside air temperature hovers at or below freezing point. Much of the heat trapped within the nest is generated by the birds themselves – with as many as five huddling together in a compartment – and their huge grass and straw 'blanket' prevents this heat from being lost to the cold environment. Within the shelter of the nest the birds can save more than 50 per cent of the energy that they would have had to expend on staying warm if they had roosted alone outside. Translated into the currency of insects, the birds' chief food item, this amounts to a saving of some 5,000 insects that would have had to be found each day for a colony of 150 sociable weavers! The reduced requirement for food means that this species can occur at much higher densities than other insect-eating desert birds in which sociality has not evolved.

In summer, the nest serves exactly the opposite purpose in that it stops the internal temperature from rising to the extreme levels of the outside air. For instance, when Bartholomew and his team measured the outside air

This camel thorn tree in Tswalu Kalahari Reserve supports a large sociable weaver nest.

temperature in the shade of the nest tree, they recorded fluctuations of between 16°C and 33.5°C, while the internal nest temperature varied between 23°C and 29°C. The much smaller range inside the nest minimises the cost to the birds of keeping a constant body temperature. The scientists did not record air temperatures higher than 33.5°C, although in February the maximum air temperature at about midday frequently exceeds 42°C. In these extreme conditions the nest provides a thermal shelter for the weavers during the hottest daytime hours, when the temperatures may be lethal to them or are so high that the birds use up vast amounts of water for evaporative cooling. So, at about midday, the sociable weavers retire to every available empty chamber for a 'siesta'. Usually only one bird occupies a compartment, but if there are not enough chambers to go around, they are forced to double-up. This dispersed roosting arrangement, also adopted at night, is in contrast to the one practised in winter and minimises the heating effects of huddling together.

An important consequence of the benign year-round temperatures within the nest is that the birds can breed throughout the year whenever sufficient food is available. Not surprisingly, sociable weavers are well equipped with the physiological adaptations to deal with the unpredictability of rainfall. Their reproductive preparedness, such as the development of the male testes, does not appear to be as strongly influenced by photoperiod (daylength) as

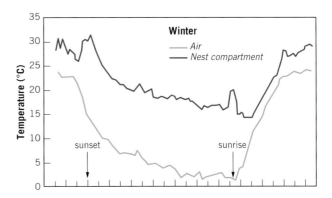

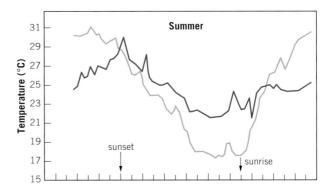

Top and above: The temperatures inside a sociable weaver nest remain relatively constant in winter and in summer, compared with the extremes of heat and cold of the outside air temperature.[26, 27]

it is in the majority of animals (see Chapter Eight). Instead, they are one of the few bird species in which the ability to reproduce is triggered by significant rainfall events, and so they can capitalise on unpredictable rainfall by breeding as soon as the rains occur. Up to four broods may be raised in a year of good rains.

These birds are also cooperative breeders, with birds from previous clutches helping to feed the current chicks. Helpers are particularly important in increasing breeding successes in years of poor rainfall.[28]

Together, these factors not only provide sociable weavers with distinct breeding advantages over other ecologically similar desert birds, but also optimise the reproductive output of breeding pairs in a harsh ecosystem. The success of sociable weavers is attributed to the concept of group augmentation, whereby individuals benefit directly from a large group size that, in this case, enables the construction of a massive nest that tempers the desert climate and affords the opportunity for year-round breeding, whenever favourable conditions are present. Group augmentation, we shall see, confers other critical direct fitness benefits in the deserts of southern Africa.

Finding food

Mole-rats provide the best vertebrate example of how group augmentation can overcome the problem of finding food, but they are by no means the only example. Another desert endemic whose sociality has evolved as a means of finding widely dispersed food items is the brown hyena. Its social structure has been studied extensively in the southern Kalahari Desert by Gus Mills, who published some fascinating papers and a book, *Kalahari Hyenas*.[29] Up to ten brown hyenas live in a clan, which is dominated by one or two adult females and for the rest consists of up to three adult males and a number of subadults and cubs. Instead of being hunters, like the spotted hyenas, brown hyenas are highly efficient scavengers. Mills recorded that less than six per cent of their food was obtained by hunting, although along the Skeleton Coast, where thousands of seal pups are born every November, they are routinely observed killing the helpless pups.

To drastically reduce water loss, hyenas forage mostly at night. Every evening in the southern Kalahari Desert individual animals leave their den or daytime resting place, usually under the heavy shade of a shepherd's tree, and set off on their own. In their search for carrion they cover an average distance of about 30 kilometres each night, although the maximum distance often exceeds 50 kilometres. An invaluable aid in these scavengers' wide-ranging hunt for food is their superb sense of smell – they can detect a carcass from a distance of more than 3 kilometres!

Although brown hyenas feed on anything edible, between 40 and 50 per cent of their food is obtained from the leftover carcasses of prey killed by lions, and another 30 per cent from animals that have died from natural causes. Any carrion they find which is small enough to carry and has some meat left on it is taken back to the den for the cubs. In this respect brown hyenas differ from spotted hyenas that do not, as a rule, carry food back to their young. Of particular interest in terms of the brown hyenas' sociality is the fact that foraging males in the clan are just as inclined to take food back to the den as are the females, even though the cubs which benefit from the food are not necessarily their own. Because the cubs' fathers are invariably nomadic and roam other territories in search of receptive females with which to mate, most cubs are half-brothers, half-sisters and half-cousins to the males in the clan and are related through mutual mothers or aunts by between 12 and 25 per cent. Sometimes, if the mother was mutual and the mutual father was an immigrant male that joined the clan, the relatedness may be as much as 50 per cent.

Gus Mills

Unlike spotted hyenas, all members of a brown hyena clan help to feed the cubs. This brown hyena is carrying the remains of a springbok carcass back to a den in the Kgalagadi Transfrontier Park.

Brown hyenas allow a sister's cubs to suckle, something not seen in spotted hyenas.

The spotted hyena's reputation as a scavenger is undeserved, for a pack can kill large antelope such as gemsbok. These carnivores are unlikely to carry food back to the den for their pups.

Many biologists, including Gus Mills, argue that by helping to raise the cubs within a clan, a large number of natal males (that is, those born into the clan) are gaining 'part scores' and thus optimising their own reproductive output. It works like this: they carry food back to the cubs and thus lighten the feeding load that the females would otherwise have had to carry on their own. Saved much of the burden of foraging, the females can breed more often and thereby optimise the reproductive output of all hyenas in the clan, irrespective of how closely related they are. These 'part scores' enhance indirect fitness and are better than scoring nothing at all. The other direct benefit of staying in the natal clan's territory is that the males can keep a close watch on events in adjoining territories. When females there are receptive, they can mate with them, thus gaining a 'full score'. This example

illustrates how individuals within a group can enjoy direct and indirect fitness benefits by means of cooperation.

As in the case of the mole-rats, one may ask why males born into the clan do not leave and become nomadic, since they can then at least pass on 50 per cent of their genes each time that they mate successfully. The answer is that many do, and in the southern Kalahari this seems to be the most common option. Whether or not they are better off being nomadic is still not certain, but the advantages are that they do not have to share their food with their cubs since the clan-living males take care of that. The disadvantage is that they do not get to know a territory well, and so may not be maximising their foraging potential.

In brown hyena societies it is usually only the matriarch female who breeds, but Mills did observe that 25 per cent of the dens that he investigated were shared by cubs belonging to the matriarch's daughter or sister. On average, brown hyenas have three cubs, and all males and females in the clan take part in raising them. Although females preferentially suckle and bring food to their own cubs, they also tolerate the cubs of daughters and sisters drinking their milk, magnanimity seldom observed in spotted hyenas. Like females in spotted hyena clans, female brown hyenas rarely leave their natal clans to join neighbouring clans. Although additional females may not be able to breed as frequently as the dominant female in the clan, they may one day get the chance to become the matriarch when the dominant female dies.

In certain respects, analogies can be drawn between brown hyenas and mole-rats in terms of cooperative foraging. Having a number of animals simultaneously searching in different places within the territory for widely scattered food items must improve the chances of any one of the foragers finding something worth carrying back to the young. Cooperative foraging also reduces the risks of a mother on her own not being able to find enough food for her offspring. Like hyenas, mole-rats take food back to their pantries if the item is small enough to be carried. However, for all the well-known reasons, brown hyenas avoid inbreeding, so the average relatedness in the clan is lower than that in naked mole-rat colonies, being somewhere around 26 per cent in the clan studied by Mills.

Because of their differing diets and drinking requirements, brown hyenas inhabit much drier regions than can be tolerated by their spotted cousins. They can survive without water by eating fruits and birds' eggs, whereas spotted hyenas apparently require a local source of drinking water in their territory. Brown hyenas also feed

Waterholes are extremely dangerous places for water-dependent birds such as sandgrouse and this Cape turtle dove (*Streptopelia capicola*).

on a very wide variety of different-sized food items, ranging from bits and pieces scavenged from large carcasses to small prey animals such as polecats and mice. This is clearly a benefit in very arid regions that do not support dependable herds of medium- to large-sized herbivores, the prey of the spotted hyena. Although herds of large ungulates may be found there, they occur infrequently, in response to sporadic and localised rainfalls (see Chapter Seven). Spotted hyenas depend on prey animals that are large enough to feed the whole clan of up to 20 members and, hunting in coordinated packs, they regularly kill adult gemsbok, eland and, in the Namib Desert, Hartmann's mountain zebra. They also steal large kills from lions. Their reliance on large prey items, as well as on drinking water, restricts their penetration into very arid zones, limiting them, for instance, to small clans in the Kuiseb River of the Namib Desert where they hunt the sparse populations of gemsbok and mountain zebra.

The sociable weaver apart, there are other cooperative breeding desert birds in which offspring from previous clutches cooperate in raising their mother's young. In these cases, it would seem that the offspring cannot disperse to breed on their own because of the lack of unoccupied and suitable territories or a lack of suitable nest sites. Instead, they gain indirect fitness part scores by helping to raise their siblings while waiting for an opportunity to breed one day and gain full scores. They also gain direct fitness benefits through group augmentation – for example, from grooming by other members of the group – and more effective territory defence and vigilance. Such species include the white-browed sparrow-weaver (*Plocepasser mahali*)[30] and the southern pied babbler (*Turdoides bicolor*),[31] but additional ones are likely to be identified as more data are collected.

Safe haven

The four-striped grass mouse is an excellent model animal for investigating the influence of aridity on social structures in small mammals because it ranges throughout all four desert biomes. It is also diurnal (crepuscular), thus allowing comparisons with other diurnal mammals that endure the heat of the day. In particular, long-term studies, which were led by Carsten Schradin, University of Zurich, and conducted continuously over more than ten years in the winter-rainfall Succulent Karoo Biome at Goegap Nature Reserve, offer superb insights into how the four-striped grass mouse responds to seasonality, low winter rainfall and population fluctuations (density dependence).[32–39]

During the long, dry summer, when population sizes are at their highest following the winter breeding season, these mice live in groups of up 30 animals made up of several breeding females, one breeding male and nonbreeding adults from previous litters.[40] And all of this in one nest! In essence, surrounding territories are fully saturated with mice and there is little opportunity for dispersal, so individuals from previous litters remain within the safe haven of the natal nest. There are costs to remaining in the natal nest, mostly in the form of reproductive competition between females. Nevertheless, the benefits outweigh the costs.

However, as population sizes decrease, for example as a consequence of the intense predation from animals such as jackal buzzards (*Buteo rufofuscus*), horned adders (*Bitis caudalis*), Cape foxes (*Vulpes chama*), caracals (*Caracal caracal*) and black-backed jackals, some mice become solitary breeders after winter rains, when high-protein annuals and insects appear in numbers.

So, four-striped grass mice maintain an interesting social system whereby the communal nest acts as a safe refuge when population sizes are high, and in which nonbreeders delay dispersal to remain in the natal nest and help to raise pups, defend the territory and maintain the nest during inopportune times. In simple terms, this is good training for nonbreeders; with their skills as solitary breeders, they can rapidly disperse as soon as the veld responds to winter rain and neighbouring territories become available. There is clear evidence that this social system is an adaptation to aridity because, on the eastern fringes of the Nama-Karoo, at the interface with the Grassland Biome, these mice never form colonies – they remain solitary, opportunistic breeders.[41] Their reproduction is discussed further in Chapter Eight.

Many eyes see more

If one were to generalise about sociality among the desert-dwelling vertebrates, then it may be fair to argue that, more than any other factor, the threat of attack by predators drives animals into groups. Depending on the species, the resultant degree of sociality can range from short-term aggregations of unrelated animals to levels of sociality that border on eusociality.

The simplest form of sociality is the habit of ring-necked doves (*Streptopelia capicola*) and sandgrouse to form large flocks when they go to drink at desert waterholes.[42] These birds forage on their own during the day, but congregate in large flocks around waterholes in the mornings and evenings. Ring-necked doves normally approach the waterhole singly or in groups of two or three and then settle in a nearby tree to wait. When 100 to 200 doves have arrived, they fly down to the water's edge in groups of six to eight birds, drink very rapidly (for no more than a few seconds) and then return to the surrounding trees. A sucking mechanism has evolved in these birds that allows them to take in fairly large amounts of water at speed, compared to the slower 'dip-raise' action employed by most birds when drinking.

Sandgrouse always arrive at the waterhole in large flocks, which presumably steadily increase in size as more and more birds join those flying in from the furthest point from the waterhole. The characteristic flight calls of the Namaqua sandgrouse may serve to advertise to other grounded sandgrouse that they are welcome to join a flock on its way to drink water. Having arrived at the waterhole, the flock circles it a few times before landing a few metres from the water. They survey their surroundings well before moving closer to drink, and then spend a remarkably short space of time drinking before they take off again.

Flocking behaviour at waterholes has evolved in response to the fast and efficient attacks launched by falcons, hawks, goshawks and jackals at waterholes. In the case of the southern African deserts, one could easily generalise and argue that the chief culprits are lanner falcons (*Falco biarmicus*) and gabar goshawks (*Micronisus gabar*), which seem to specialise in attacking birds at waterholes.

Roy Siegfried, former director of the Percy FitzPatrick Institute of African Ornithology at the University of Cape Town, made various studies of anti-predatory behaviour in animals and he showed experimentally that a large flock of laughing doves (*Streptopelia senegalensis*), which also congregate in flocks at waterholes, has a higher

Namaqua sandgrouse circle a waterhole several times to scan the terrain for predators in the NamibRand Nature Reserve.

One of the major predators of birds at a waterhole is the black-backed jackal, which here sneaked up under cover of a low wall to launch its attack.

Peter Chadwick

chance of detecting a swooping predator than a small flock – conclusive proof that many eyes see more.[43] By joining a large flock, individual doves can increase the time they spend drinking at a waterhole because they can reduce the time that they would have had to spend watching out for predators.

An early warning gives the flock more time to react and take off. Even if the birds react too slowly, the chances of any one individual in the flock being attacked are lower than if that dove were on its own; this is because lanner falcons prefer to hunt by directing their aerial attacks at single, isolated individuals. There are two likely reasons for this strategy: firstly, falcons avoid the high probability of injury through accidental collision, which would occur if they routinely dived into flocks of a few hundred panicky doves; and secondly, falcons, and for that matter all predators that attack large aggregations of moving prey, get confused during the attack and in the heat of the moment they simply can't decide which individual to strike. So, there seems little doubt that a solitary dove or sandgrouse at a waterhole stands a much greater chance of being attacked than it would if it formed part of a drinking flock. This is known as the dilution effect – safety in numbers.

Apart from dove and sandgrouse species, the majority of desert-dwelling, seed-eating birds, such as finches, canaries and waxbills, also form large flocks – both at waterholes and more permanently while foraging and roosting. However, it is not easy to generalise about the benefits that these smaller-sized birds accrue from flocking. Ornithologists continue to argue the issue fiercely, which suggests that no single reason will ever be agreed upon. However, it remains reasonable to assume that these birds also gain a certain measure of protection from predation by the dilution effect and undoubtedly derive huge thermoregulatory benefits from communal roosting and huddling at night. For instance, consider the smallest of the desert birds, the scaly-feathered weaver.

Scaly-feathered weavers build roosting nests in which they huddle to save energy.

This diminutive bird weighs a mere 10 grams, so it is likely that if it did not practise the observed habit of roosting in tightly packed groups of six to 20 birds at night, it would suffer severe hypothermia in winter.[44]

It is well known that large desert ungulates, such as eland, gemsbok and blue wildebeest, are better able to defend themselves and their calves from packs of lions and hyenas when they form large herds. It can also be argued that the dilution effect accounts for the herding behaviour of desert-dwelling ungulates. Another theory that supports the formation of herds is that there is an optimal group size that maximises the chance of early predator detection, so that individuals can spend more time on grazing and less on vigilance. For instance, Siegfried's research shows that individual springbok in groups comprising fewer than 20 animals have to spend more time surveying their surroundings for predators than do those in larger groups, which can rely to a certain extent on the eyes of their neighbours.[45] A similar saving in vigilance time has been found in flocks of desert ostriches.[46]

There may be more to it than just time spent on grazing, for the quality of grazing to be had in very large herds may be better than it is in smaller herds. If springbok form one large, continuously moving, grazing herd, they are less likely to encounter areas that other groups have already grazed, whereas many smaller herds feeding independently would often expend energy and time covering ground denuded by previous foragers. Siegfried suggests that this might be the basis for the historical accounts of the spectacular and sporadic appearances of trekbokken – herds of springbok numbering countless hundreds of thousands reported in evocative detail by early travellers in the Karoo.

Meerkats exhibit the most advanced level of sociality that has evolved in response to predation pressures in the southern African deserts. These endearing little carnivores are true desert endemics and live in groups that include the breeding pair and subordinates. Their highly organised system of predator detection, probably equalled only by that of the common dwarf mongoose (*Helogale parvula*), involves the use of sentries and babysitters. Jackals, snakes and large raptors, especially martial eagles (*Polemaetus bellicosus*), are the meerkats' main predators.

Once their bellies are full, sentries choose to take 'raised guard' duty by climbing up tree trunks or small trees.[47] The benefit of having sentries is that the rest of the group can forage without having to waste valuable time scanning the skies and horizon for predators. Indeed, in summer in the southern Kalahari Desert and the Nama-Karoo, time

is valuable because the heat of the day limits their foraging to a few hours in the mornings and late afternoons, when the sand and air temperatures are tolerable. Meerkats forage by digging numerous shallow holes searching for insects, larvae and scorpions, so they are invariably looking down and cannot easily spot potential predators. This job is left to the sentries, whose remarkable repertoire of calls is uttered continuously to keep all members of the group informed about what is going on around them. Different calls elicit different responses.[48, 49] The most dramatic is a shrill, sharp bark that carries the message 'worst-case scenario – bolt!' and has all members diving for the nearest burrow. This call is used when a well-known predator, such as a martial eagle, has been spotted close by or is actually attacking. The sentries have other, less dramatic calls. For instance, one may carry the message 'aerial predator spotted – probably not a problem – decide for yourself what to do'; it may cause only one or two less experienced meerkats to edge closer to a burrow while the rest of the animals sit on their haunches and observe the threat themselves. This call would be uttered in response to raptor species that, from experience, they know do not attack. There is also an alarm call that is reserved specifically for the presence of a jackal nearby.

The sentries are invariably subadult males which take turns at standing guard so that each one gets a chance to forage. The safety of the group is highly dependent on its size, and therefore the number of sentries available for duty. If the groups become too small in the southern Kalahari Desert, they do not survive for long. Less time is spent on vigilance, the rate of predation increases, and slowly the troop is whittled away. This may happen in drought years, when sentries are forced to abandon their duties because they have to spend more time foraging for scarcer food. At such times the meerkats become desperate and frequently join up with troops of Cape ground squirrels and yellow mongooses (*Cynictis penicillata*), a sort of interspecific group augmentation. Both these warren-dwelling species are also desert endemics and face similar pressures in tough times.[50] The squirrels do not clash with the meerkats over food because they are herbivorous, and they also benefit from the meerkats' repertoire of alarm calls. Consequently, they can spend less of their own time on vigilance and more on foraging.[51] The mongooses, it seems, are merely commensal, benefiting from the burrows made by the squirrels and the meerkats.

The co-existence of these three species is quite extensive throughout the southern African deserts and can be observed even in good years. By combining, they

Top left: Ever vigilant, a group of meerkats bask in the morning sun. **Top centre:** Meerkats are extremely vulnerable to aerial attacks by raptors because they spend much of their time with their heads down a hole digging for food. **Top right:** Scorpions are one of the favourite food items of meerkats. **Above:** A lone sentinel atop a small camel thorn tree keeps watch while the rest of the troop forages.

An erect stance demonstrates vigilance, a primary aspect of the social system of Cape ground squirrels.

Yellow mongooses often share burrow systems with meerkats and ground squirrels.

For some carnivores, group cooperation is not essential for hunting large antelope. Here a male lion rests near its kill.

Gus Mills

Size and distribution of prey herds is thought to determine the size of carnivore groups, but other factors, such as rabies, common among spotted hyenas, can also play a role. Here, a young, rabid spotted hyena attacks two adults in its clan.

It is interesting that the resource dispersion hypothesis still applies in deserts despite profound differences in territory and group sizes between moist and arid habitats. For instance, the territory sizes of spotted hyenas in the southern African deserts vary between 383 and 1,776 square kilometres compared with between 30 and 60 square kilometres in East Africa. Clan sizes range from four to 14 in the desert compared with 35 to 80 on the East African plains. Whereas differences such as these clearly highlight the smaller herds and scarcity of ungulates in southern Africa's desert expanses, they also illustrate the wonderful adaptability shown by the social system of large carnivores when it comes to exploiting prey to the best advantage.

Amid all this theory about group sizes and hunting efficiency, one wonders how nomadic male lions and spotted hyenas manage to procure food on their own without the cooperation of others. Do they attempt to kill large ungulates independently, or are they forced to tackle smaller prey? Lions seem to do both. In the southern Kalahari nomadic lions frequently throw caution to the wind and pounce on slow-moving porcupines. Although porcupines may provide a sufficient meal, the lions take great risks in attacking them because infections caused by porcupine quills can ultimately prove fatal (see page 139). On the other hand, nomadic males are frequently successful in ambushing large ungulates at watering points. Again, this lends support to the resource dispersion hypothesis, which claims that factors such as hunting efficiency and group size are secondary to the issues of prey patchiness and quality.

Social insects

In a chapter on sociality among desert-dwellers it may seem surprising that, as yet, no mention has been made of insects – after all, no other group of animals on Earth can be considered to be more social than the ants, bees and termites. There are a number of reasons for a discussion of insect sociality having been delayed. In the first place, it is not necessarily any better developed in the deserts of southern Africa than it is elsewhere. Secondly, apart from some excellent pioneering work on the ecology and biology of ants in the Namib Desert conducted by Alan Marsh and Barbara Curtis, there still remains a paucity of published data concerning the ecology of southern African desert-dwelling termites and ants. Scott Turner, though, from his research in Namibia, has elegantly described the physiology of termite mounds, that is, how they 'breathe'.[59] Thirdly, there are so many diverse advantages to insect sociality that one cannot generalise and isolate any single advantage that may promote the gene output of individuals. In fact, individual colonies of ants and termites may enjoy many of the benefits of sociality already discussed, plus many more.

The remarkable impact that the harvester termites can have on the desert landscape and vegetation structure has been discussed earlier (see Chapter Four) and it is clear that they, as well as ants, play a dominant ecological role as ecosystem engineers. It is therefore worthwhile exploring some of the adaptations that we suspect have enabled these eusocial insects to do so well in the subcontinent's deserts.

Alan Marsh identified three or four ant species in the Namib Desert that, by their numbers, are dominant in their habitats.[60–62] Both he and Barbara Curtis studied one in particular, the Namib dune ant, which is endemic to the Namib dune sea where it reigns supreme.[63] By ant standards it is large (7 to 16 millimetres), thus benefiting from lower water loss and heat loading. These diurnal ants live in colonies numbering several thousand and are extremely aggressive towards ants from neighbouring colonies. They feed primarily on the honeydew exuded by aphids, mealy bugs and scale insects that infest certain plants in their territories, and the workers constantly guard these helpless sap-sucking insects from predators. They also fiercely protect their food plants against foreign ants by rapidly summoning aid and attacking and killing unwanted invaders of their territory. A Namib dune ant colony does not include distinct soldiers, but there are major, media and minor workers; of these the large majors are the most aggressive. They are especially aggressive when their nest has been disturbed, and they will attack anything nearby. Trip Lamb, East Carolina University, was collecting *Onymacris bicolor* beetles in the dune fields of the northern Namib and noticed that one of his specimens had the head of a *Camponotus* ant firmly attached to its right antennae.[64] The beetle was obviously attacked as an innocent dune pedestrian, and responded by biting off the ant's body with its own impressive mandibles.

The defence of *Camponotus* territories and their main food resources by the thousands of workers ensures that each colony has at least one reliable food source throughout the year – crucial to their dominance and success in the unpredictable Namib dune sea.

Aware of the potential hazards of 'keeping all their eggs in one basket', Namib dune ants split the colony and the brood, which consists of eggs, larvae and pupae, into three or four sister nests spaced within their territory.[65] This is a highly effective adaptation not only against catastrophic events in the form of raids on the nests by predators such as bat-eared foxes, aardvarks (*Orycteropus afer*) or chacma baboons, but also against natural disasters. For instance, in the ants' unstable sandy habitat strong winds frequently blow nests apart or cover them up with sand. Surviving workers from destroyed nests can take any brood members that remain to the refuge of one of the colony's sister nests. In this way some members of the colony have a chance of surviving a local catastrophe. The advantage of being social and the important role played by the workers in preserving their gene 'outputs' is quite obvious.

On the Namib's gravel plains the harvester ant *Messor denticornis* takes over the dominant role. Unlike Namib dune ants, these ants are nocturnal and feed predominantly on seeds produced during the episodic flushes of annual grasses that follow rain. They are far less aggressive than the dune-dwelling ants. Similarities are that the workers are fairly large (5 to 11 millimetres), and that the colony maintains a few sister nests within its territory to reduce the risk of being destroyed by a catastrophic event.

Left: Namib dune ants cooperate to defend their honeydew-producing scale insects from rival colonies in the Namib dune sea. **Above left and right:** This is what happens when a transgressor gets too close to its enemy. Once bitten, the *Onymacris bicolor* beetle severed the head of an attacking ant from its body. Notice the ant's head attached to the beetle's antenna, seen from above (left) and below (right).

A single ant colony is spread out over three or four nests. If one is destroyed, surviving workers can transfer eggs, larvae and pupae from one nest to another.

There are clear analogies between the harvester ants and the mole-rats with regard to the benefits of cooperative foraging. The ants' food items are also patchy and difficult to find, and their chances of finding good-quality patches before other seed-eating animals do so are profoundly increased by having a large number of foragers searching simultaneously. In deserts where food is scarce, it is important to be able to locate and harvest new food patches as quickly as possible. Again, the role of large group sizes is crucial, for when individual foragers have found a good patch of seeds, they lay a chemical trail back to the nest which other excited workers then follow to retrieve the seeds. The adaptive advantage of having different sized workers also plays a major role, because whereas the smallest ants concentrate on carrying seeds, the largest major workers build trails to the seed patches by moving large sand particles and small pebbles to one side. These foraging trails greatly increase the speed with which the carriers can run and retrieve seeds. Vast quantities of the seeds are stored in underground pantries and are eaten during the lean, dry spells when no food is available – the perfect 'insurance' against bad times.

It would obviously be very difficult for individual Namib dune ants or harvester ants – or even pairs – to attempt to compete with these formidable foraging armies and their defences. Of course, winged alates of these and many other desert-dwelling ants do disperse in nuptial swarms that are carefully timed to coincide with the nuptial swarming of other alates from non-related colonies in the area. This pattern maximises the chances of dispersing females to find non-related males so that they can pair, start new colonies, and thus minimise inbreeding. Nuptial swarming occurs very infrequently in deserts, taking place only after rain, and few of the newly paired alates are successful in establishing a new colony. Consequently, even though this form of dispersal is widespread among the social insects, in desert habitats, where food is limited, it is considered a very expensive way of passing on genes. When it does succeed, it does so only by virtue of the vast numbers of alates involved and the resources provided by the large and efficient foraging worker forces, which acquire sufficient food to 'finance' the production of the reproductive alates. Leaving the issue of expense aside for the moment, as a general rule it seems clear that insect eusociality – having thousands of sterile sister workers helping each other to indirectly pass on fertile 75-per cent copies of themselves – is a more successful strategy than the alternative of having reproductive pairs that remain solitary and try to breed successfully on their own.

We can only assume that the southern African termites derive many of the benefits of eusociality discussed for ants, mole-rats and other cooperative breeders. Compared with other eusocial insects it seems that they may, at times, opt for the mole-rat solution – inbreeding and the benefits of the consequential close genetic relatedness between all individuals in the colony. But, unlike the mole-rats, they do also routinely undertake synchronised nuptial swarming after good rains, thereby achieving periodic doses of outbreeding and genetic variability. Perhaps this is their secret to success: cooperative foraging, colony defence, nest building and care of the brood, coupled with a genetic relatedness high enough to justify sterile workers, but also retaining enough genetic variability through outbreeding to have allowed them to track 100 million years of changing climates.

Crammed with fat reserves to provide her with energy for many months until her new offspring can forage, a winged *Macrotermes* termite alate emerges after rain to find a mate and start a new colony.

Apartment robbers and squatters

Although the communal lifestyle of sociable weavers has many advantages, certain aspects of their sociality unfortunately work against them. For instance, the huge nests attract and provide refuge for predators such as the Cape cobra and boomslang (*Dispholidus typus*), which can wipe out the chicks and eggs of a whole colony in a very short time. Fortunately, these catastrophic predation events do not occur all year round, since the snakes are fairly inactive in winter.

Other birds capitalise on the thermal benefits and protection provided by the sociable weaver nests, and may either roost in the compartments at night, or simply annex one or two of the chambers. The pygmy falcon (*Polihierax semitorquatus*), the smallest of the African falcons, smaller than a starling, relies exclusively on the huge nests for roosting and breeding. These raptors live in small family groups

The sociable weaver's nest attracts predators, especiallly Cape cobras and boomslangs (seen here). A resident snake can devour all of the nest's hatchlings within days.

that normally comprise an adult pair and a few subadult offspring. Their diet consists of insects and lizards. It is probably fair to state that their association with sociable weavers is very old – their distribution is identical to that of the weavers and it is unlikely that they would survive the extremes of their desert habitat without their hosts.

A whole family group of pygmy falcons crowd into one compartment in winter, although the birds roost singly in separate compartments in summer. They therefore benefit not only from the thermal buffering of the whole nest structure, but also from the vast amount of heat generated by the resident sociable weavers in winter. Although there is some debate about whether or not the weavers derive any benefit from the falcons, one thing is clear: the falcons do occasionally cheat on their hosts by devouring the odd nestling. One can easily understand why this predation on host birds is limited, for if they did prey upon the birds more extensively, they would simply be turning off their free central heating – a very unwise thing to do in the southern Kalahari Desert in winter. The pygmy falcons do offer some service to the weavers; they aggressively attack snakes at the nest and can be successful at knocking them off the nest.

Pygmy falcons are not the only beneficiaries of the sociable weavers. Kalahari tree skinks (*Trachylepis spilogaster*), which live on the camel thorn trees favoured by the weavers, have learned to 'eavesdrop' on the calls of the weavers and take evasive action from their major predators, the pygmy falcons.[66] It's a tough life in those gorgeous grass nests.

Above left: Cape cobras are excellent tree climbers and often remain resident in trees with sociable weaver nests. **Above centre:** The pygmy falcon is dependent on the nests of sociable weavers for roosting and breeding. **Above right:** Although the routine diet of the pygmy falcon comprises lizards and skinks, it is likely that this bird occassionally snatches one of its hosts' nestlings.

Time out

Gus Mills

Above: Many desert animals are nocturnal, passing hot, stressful daylight hours in dens, warrens or burrows. Largish mammals such as the aardwolf, seen here, and hyena exploit burrows excavated by aardvarks and porcupines.

Left: When conditions deteriorate during the dry season, some large animals seek areas of recent rain or follow well-trodden migration paths to greener pastures, like this one in the NamibRand Nature Reserve.

In their book *Ecology of Desert Organisms*, Gideon Louw and Mary Seely wrote that 'most plants and animals survive in the desert because they do not live in the desert'.[1] Illogical as it may sound, this statement articulates one of the basic truths about desert life: plants and animals avoid its harshest extremes. When conditions become particularly unfavourable organisms begin to lose their grip on their best chances of survival – they struggle to maintain their water or temperature budgets, or they simply cannot find enough food to meet their daily energy needs. If the conditions persist, the organisms will probably be unable to breed or, in the worst cases, they will die, either from dehydration or from lack of nutrition. Also, in their weakened condition they become easy targets for their enemies and predators.

There are few sounds more characteristic of the Arid Savanna and Desert biomes than the metallic 'plinking' calls of the barking gecko (*Ptenopus* species). Beginning at dusk, they signal the geckos' emergence from their daytime retreat.

Exhibiting an escape response to stress, the giant bullfrog has the ability to remain buried underground in its waterproof cocoon for most of the year, emerging only in the rainy season to forage and breed.

Fortunately, many desert organisms are able to avoid this potential disaster by employing physiological, morphological or behavioural escape mechanisms that permit them to take 'time out' from intolerable conditions. Some become inactive, often in an energy-saving state, in safe refuges for time periods ranging from hours to years. Others simply leave the area altogether and return, perhaps, after good rains.

Such 'time out' adaptations should not be regarded as a form of weakness shown by the organism in its attempt to cope with desert life, but should rather be seen as being complementary to the many adaptations concerned with tolerating harsh conditions. The two concepts – tolerance and avoidance – are vital in ensuring an ongoing existence and are certainly not mutually exclusive. For example, a desert organism may be well adapted to tolerate temperature stresses and water scarcity, but the adaptations seldom provide complete protection. At the very extremes of the stress, a logical coordination of the organism's periods of activity is also required to ensure its survival.

Biologists recognise two distinct types of response to extreme stress: 'retreat', which is short-term, and 'escape', a long-term response. The retreat response is the more common and occurs on a day-to-day basis. Typically, it is characterised by patterns of daily activity in which the animal spends the harshest time of day in a refuge, often underground, and remains inactive until conditions improve. The escape response can be divided into two categories: one involves some form of movement out of an area, whereas the other entails a long-term

physiological shutdown of active life. The latter response is found in both plants and animals, whereas movement is obviously undertaken only by animals.

Of all the 'time out' adaptations, those concerning physiological escape are the most impressive, and they can be found in desert organisms throughout the world. Among plants, the annuals are the most proficient at this form of escape; their seeds lie dormant for months or even years, weathering unfavourable periods until conditions are right for germination. Ephemerality, as this response is called, involves morphological as well as physiological adaptations, and in fact it determines virtually every aspect of the plant's life history. It also occurs in animals, as when encysted pupae or larvae lie dormant for long periods. In general, however, the physiological escape responses of desert animals take the form of hibernations of various descriptions, and these, together with many other 'time out' adaptations of a wide variety of desert organisms, are explored in this chapter.

Daily patterns of activity

During the Triassic, about 240 million years ago, mammals became exclusively nocturnal. The reasons remain highly debatable, but my own published hypothesis is that it was related to the problems of offloading heat without having to sacrifice body water for cooling, as archaic mammals (therapsids, see Chapter

Nine) became more endothermic (warm-blooded) and attained higher body temperatures.[2] So, it was not merely a preference for the dark that led animals to be active at night instead of during the day.

Nocturnalism was the default activity in mammals and remains so for the vast majority of mammals to this day.[3] Humans are one of the few exceptions. Nocturnalism shaped mammals more than any other factor, especially during the Triassic: their brains got bigger, which improved sight, smell and hearing, and their eyes changed from a day eye to a night eye.

Whether animals are day-active or night-active is strictly predetermined, for it is important – and more so in deserts than elsewhere – that they conform to reasonable timetables for foraging, grooming, resting or any other daily activity. It would be inappropriate for a bat, for instance, to suddenly go foraging at midday over the Kalahari Desert in search of moths. Not only are the chances extremely remote that it would find any moths – they themselves are nocturnal – but it is far more probable that the bat would either die of thirst or be caught by a bird of prey. Given the huge daily fluctuations in deserts of such factors as temperature and the water vapour saturation

deficit, the differences between daytime and night-time conditions are far too large to permit animals to deviate from the activity time for which they are best adapted. Moreover, they would expose themselves to predators to which they are completely unaccustomed and to which they may not possess appropriate defensive responses. Fortunately, desert animals seldom stray from their activity 'programmes'; when they do, they do so in response to seasonal changes or unpredictable climatic events.

Natural selection has weeded out individual decision-making processes in animals that may lead to ill-timed actions. Instead, the circadian clock, a physiological time-keeping mechanism that is crucial to the biology of all organisms and governs many of the 'time out' practices, regulates each animal. In vertebrates the circadian clock resides in the hypothalamus in the brain, and individuals, having very little control over its settings and how it functions, respond subconsciously to the instructions that it issues. An excellent example of its function in humans is the jetlag experience: after a transatlantic flight from America to Africa a traveller wakes up at midnight feeling bright and ready to start the day. His or her circadian clock is faithfully providing its morning wake-up call as it did the previous morning in America, so the body 'thinks' that it is 07h00 when it is really midnight. It takes the clock about one day for every hour to readjust to what it perceives as a sudden 11-hour shift of the Earth's light-dark cycle.

Typically, desert organisms spend the daylight hours under rocks, in rocky crevices, in well-insulated nests, in holes in trees, or under the loose bark on tree trunks. Alternatively, they seek refuge underground in burrows,

Chantelle Bosch

Bats are strictly nocturnal, but if conditions are adverse they can hibernate for weeks at a time. However, some bats, such as this slit-faced bat of the genus *Nycteris*, which occurs in the Desert Biome, is active throughout winter.

Hennie de Klerk

The larvae of antlions (*Cueta trivirgata*) are active during the day and night. They dig conical pits in the sand, the depth and shape of which protect them from temperature extremes.

Varying activity patterns among silverfish species in the Namib may serve to reduce competition for resources.

showed that these desert insects display a remarkable variety of jigsaw activity patterns within a 24-hour period.[6] The patterns, which seem to have evolved in response to climatic conditions as well as to competition among species for food, can be divided into three basic categories: diurnal, nocturnal and crepuscular. In the crepuscular pattern two activity bouts occur: one in the very early morning, and the other in the early evening. Watson believes that species that seem to share certain dune microhabitats, such as slipfaces and vegetation clumps, reduce competition by being active at different times of the day. For example, of the four species that most heavily exploit the dune slipfaces, two are diurnal: *Mormisma wygodzinskyi* is most active in the morning and *Namibmormisma muricaudata* in the afternoon. The remaining two species, *Sabulepisma multiformis* and *Swalepisma mirabilis*, are mainly crepuscular, although they merge into nocturnal, one being active in the early evening whereas the other restricts its peak activity time to the pre-dawn and early morning hours. Similar patterns can be identified in the three species that most heavily exploit the vegetation clumps. Watson also investigated the water loss rates of silverfish and showed that the diurnal species may be better adapted to withstand desiccating conditions than the nocturnal and crepuscular species.

By no means unique to desert silverfish, crepuscular activity patterns are quite common in many nocturnal mammals. The four-striped grass mouse, one of the most common murid rodents of the Succulent Karoo, Nama-Karoo and Arid Savanna biomes, displays a very marked crepuscular activity pattern.[7] Its peak activity times are from about 05h00 to 08h30 in the morning, and again from about 16h30 to 20h30. There is a theory that the

activity pattern of these omnivorous rodents may be synchronised with the crepuscular emergence of one of their chief food items, harvester termites. However, it can also be argued that in the Karoo and Arid Savanna biomes a crepuscular activity pattern in an omnivorous murid rodent could help to limit competition for food with the desert-specialist cricetid rodents. By foraging at dusk and dawn, the striped mouse avoids the activity period of the large, diurnal otomyid rodents such as Brants's whistling rat and the bush Karoo rat, as well as that of the strictly nocturnal gerbils.

So, the activity pattern of any desert animal, whether it is diurnal, nocturnal or crepuscular, can reveal information about its lifestyle and adaptations. Although climate is certainly important in shaping activity patterns, especially in fine-tuning the hours of daytime activity, factors such as predation, foraging patterns and competition between species are perhaps more powerful evolutionary driving forces. The daily periods of 'time out', as 'programmed' by circadian clocks, are also crucially important to the survival and fitness of all desert organisms because they are invariably fundamental to the successful operation of countless other life-sustaining adaptations. For example, the daily fluctuations in energy expenditure and body temperature, which seem to be universal in all mammals and birds, are closely linked to the animal's circadian clock. The extent and nature of these fluctuations are important to desert organisms for they cost valuable energy reserves on a daily basis. Or do they? They could also save desert organisms energy.

An unusually large number of diurnal rodents occur in the deserts of southern Africa, and the four-striped grass mouse is one of them. These mammals forage during the morning and the evening.

Some economics of activity

Before nocturnal rodents emerge from their nests and burrows at the end of their inactive day, they first undergo a few hours of physiological preparation for the forthcoming night's activity. This is set in motion by the circadian clock, and the animal has no direct control over it. The black-tailed tree rat, a nocturnal, tree-dwelling rodent of the Arid Savanna and Desert biomes, serves as a good basic model.[8] The rat's daily activity commences punctually with the onset of darkness. It emerges from its nest at dusk, usually spends some time at the entrance grooming itself, and then moves off to forage on the branches of its nest tree. The actual onset of activity is sharply defined each night, but preparation for it has been going on for some hours. The rat's body temperature starts to increase about six hours before darkness falls and reaches a peak as activity begins.[9] Later, at dawn, and therefore at the end of the rodent's activity period, its body temperature again decreases a few degrees to the minimum level in its daily cycle.

Humans also display these rhythms, but the daily fluctuations are much smaller. Our limited understanding of the significance or function of these metabolic patterns is one of the remaining barriers to complete insight into energy expenditure in endotherms. The questions that still need to be addressed are quite intriguing. For example, why should endothermic animals – those that maintain, through internal heat production, a more-or-less constant body temperature independent of the environment – require such self-sustained oscillations in their minimal daily energy expenditure over which they have no conscious control? What does it mean in terms of the animal's best chances of survival? Why do desert species show a greater daily decrease in body temperature during their rest phase than non-desert species?[10]

However, genuine torpor, in which the metabolic rate decreases below the level that normally keeps the animal alive and in a wakeful state, certainly does occur in desert animals, notably in Grant's golden mole, as illustrated by its thermal hitchhiking abilities (see Chapter Three). This subterranean mammal exhibits a bizarre form of daily torpor in which its body temperature decreases with that of the sand so that at temperatures below 30°C it becomes comatose.[11] A number of small desert endotherms probably practise daily torpor in response to water and energy stresses, since being both endothermic and small is an expensive existence. However, it is almost certain that the insectivorous, desert-dwelling moles, apart from Grant's golden mole, also employ this daily torpor to save energy. These would include moles such as De Winton's golden mole (*Cryptochloris wintoni*) and Van Zyl's golden mole (*Cryptochloris zyli*) from the coastal sand dunes of the Succulent Karoo Biome, as well as the Cape golden mole (*Chrysochloris asiatica*), a species widespread throughout the Succulent Karoo. By living

The western rock elephant shrew is a member of the Afrotheria clade of mammals, which includes hyraxes, elephants, dugongs, aardvarks, tenrecs and golden moles. It has the ancestral capacity to enter deep daily torpor each day in winter to conserve energy.

Namibia's newest mammal. In 2014 the Etendeka round-eared elephant shrew was described as a new species. It is tiny, weighing a mere 28 grams, the size of a small mouse, and lives on the extremely harsh Etendeka rocky plains of northwestern Namibia. There is a very high likelihood, given its small size, that it employs daily torpor on a regular basis.

Ephemeral plants

Unlike animals, plants, with their sedentary nature, cannot retire underground or to nests every day. Nevertheless, they display impressive seasonal adaptations which serve the same purpose: they weather the bad times in an inactive state, waiting to respond to prime conditions when they do occur. As a growth form group, and in terms of sheer numbers, the annuals, especially those of the Succulent Karoo, are probably the most advanced and certainly the most spectacular in this respect. They are mostly members of the family Asteraceae and include well-known plants such as the Namaqualand daisy (*Dimorphotheca sinuata*) as well as other closely related, daisy-like species. These plants lie dormant from the end of one rainy season to the beginning of the next, or even for a number of consecutive years of low rainfall. This they do in the form of seed, which they produce in enormous numbers at the end of their short growing season.

The seeds lie dormant in the soil wherever they land after dispersal and are well adapted not only to withstand long periods of drought, but also to germinate at specific times. Many of them germinate only after a few years of dormancy. The advantage of this delay is that if the next wet season is a poor one, not all seeds in the soil will have germinated in response to the first rains of that season. If

The diversity of geophytic plants – those with tubers, bulbs or corms – in the Succulent Karoo Biome is quite staggering. The underground storage organs can survive long periods of drought, flowering only when conditions improve. Seen here are *Moraea serpentina* (white and yellow flowers) and *Moraea miniata* (pink flowers), near Kamieskroon in Namaqualand.

all seeds had germinated, the seedlings could easily have failed to reach maturity and set their seeds because of insufficient water, with the result that the entire seed bank in the soil would have been exhausted in one bad season. Although rainfall is, of course, one of the most important stimulants for the seeds to germinate, it is not the only criterion for successful growth. In the Succulent Karoo, a winter-rainfall biome, many seeds possess a 'safety mechanism' that prevents untimely germination. They germinate only when it is both moist and cold, and not in response to an unusual summer rainfall.

The seeds of other Namaqualand annuals possess a greater freedom in the timing of their germination, and do not restrict themselves to winter. This freedom is achieved because the plants are not constrained by photoperiod. Like animals, they possess circadian clocks that 'know' at any time of the year what season it is, based upon the length of the day versus the night, that is, the photoperiod. Normally, winter annuals may only germinate when the daylength falls well below 12 hours, whereas summer annuals may only germinate when the length of the day exceeds 12 hours. In this way, plants germinate at the time of year for which they are best adapted.

Gretel van Rooyen, University of Pretoria, showed that at least three Namaqualand daisies – *Dimorphotheca sinuata*, *Ursinia calenduliflora* and *Heliophila pendula* – are not constrained by photoperiod and can therefore take advantage of early autumn rains.[23] Before the onset of winter the air and soil temperatures are still fairly high, allowing annuals to grow more quickly than they would have done if their seeds had germinated later, during the cold winter. Another advantage of earlier germination is that these annuals can take the first opportunity to capture the soil nutrients that have accumulated during the dry season. The lack of constraint by photoperiod displayed by these three species may therefore have evolved in response to interspecific competition for nutrients with winter-germinating annuals (see Chapter Four).

Of interest here is that this research into the timing of germination is taking place not only because botanists themselves are interested in the subject, but also because of the potential usefulness of the data to the tourism industry. The stunning spring-flower displays in Namaqualand are world famous and, by flocking to Namaqualand to observe them, tourists inject a large amount of money into the local economy each year. However, the business is not without its major problems, the main one being that tourist agents cannot accurately

As pretty as they are, the annuals of Namaqualand are basically pioneering weeds. The seeds of these plants lie dormant for years until suitable rain falls. They are prolific in disturbed areas, as seen here in old ploughed fields at Skilpad in the Namaqua National Park.

Above left: A more typical display of annuals in Namaqualand in undisturbed veld – notice the greater diversity. The species, identified by colour, are: *Felicia australis* (blue), *Grielum humifusum* (pale yellow), *Cleretum papulosum* (yellow flower with spiky petals), *Heliophila lacteal* (white), and *Gazania krebsiana* (orange). **Above right:** Monarch of the veld, the Namaqualand arctotis (*Arctotis fastuosa*) grows in sandy and gravelly flats and washes.

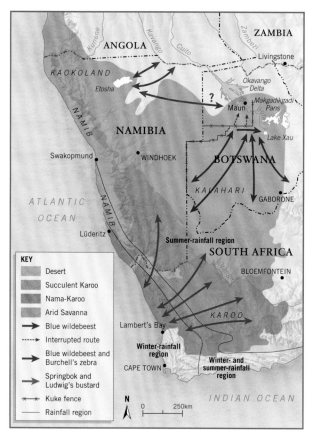

A blue wildebeest slakes its thirst at an artificial waterhole in the Kgalagadi Transfrontier Park.

Migration patterns of blue wildebeest in the central Kalahari (red arrows), blue wildebeest and Burchell's zebra in northern Namibia (blue arrows), and springbok and Ludwig's bustard (green arrows) in southern Namibia and South Africa. The Kuke fence in central Botswana obstructs the wildebeest's migration routes and channels the herds towards Lake Xau. The historic migration routes of springbok, blue wildebeest and Burchell's zebra in other arid regions of southern Africa, before they were fenced, is still a subject of much speculation. It is becoming clear that the mass springbok treks were driven by El Niño-dependent rainfall variability and involved movement between the winter- and summer-rainfall regions of the Nama-Karoo and Succulent Karoo during summer droughts. It is believed that blue wildebeest and Burchell's zebra undertook seasonal migrations between the Etosha Pan region and the Kavango River area. Present-day migration routes of Ludwig's bustard are similar to those shown for the springbok.

Desert. Their successful exploitation of its semi-arid central and southern regions is owed entirely to their superb ability to cover vast distances to water sources and better feeding grounds on a seasonal basis efficiently.[30] For centuries, vast herds have migrated to and from the winter-flooded Lake Ngami and the Boteti River, which are filled by an overflow from seasonal flooding of the

Okavango Delta. The waters of the Boteti flow south past the vast Makgadikgadi Pans, and then into and beyond Lake Xau, where they are eventually swallowed up by the sands of the Kalahari Desert. In the areas surrounding the Okavango complex of pans and rivers these waters, which never reach the sea, stimulate a growth of good-quality grass in the midst of the dry season – a life-supporting supply of food and water for blue wildebeest. The longest ungulate migration in Africa, that of Burchell's zebra, also has the nearby Nxai Pan as its destination during the wet season after migrating from the Chobe River in the north.[31]

The wildebeest migrations continued unhindered until the Botswana government spanned a high tensile steel fence, the so-called Kuke fence, across the traditional migration routes. Their reason for doing so was to prevent the wildebeest from spreading foot-and-mouth disease to Botswana's burgeoning cattle industry. The continuing consequence of the Kuke fence, as well as a tail fence that extends from its eastern end in a southeasterly direction, is that the annual migrations of wildebeest are prevented from ever reaching the Boteti River and what used to be their winter grazing grounds along its banks.

Instead, every year the wildebeest are channelled eastwards in vast herds numbering as many as 100,000 animals, eventually spilling out at Lake Xau, the southernmost terminal of available water in the Kalahari (see map above). But there is a major problem at Lake Xau and its surrounds – pastoralists and their large cattle herds heavily populate the region, and it is severely overgrazed. Today, the closest palatable perennial grasses can only be found about 50 kilometres from the lake. The whole region has been turned into a sand desert: although there is plenty of water, there is no food. Here the weak herds are obliged to walk as many as 100 kilometres every day to find adequate grazing. Typically, blue wildebeest walk daily distances of about 18 kilometres to and from water – 100 kilometres is simply too far. As a result, they die of starvation in their thousands on the shores of Lake Xau and in the surrounding area each year. In addition, they are relentlessly hunted, slaughtered and harassed by the pastoralists and their dogs. Herds are deliberately prevented from reaching water and the authorities make no attempt to control the mass killings. In the winter of 1983 more than 50,000 wildebeest died there[32] as a consequence of one of the strongest El Niño events on record.

The Kalahari population of blue wildebeest cannot withstand losses such as these and is dwindling at an alarming rate. In 1977 it was the second-largest population in Africa, surpassed only by the legendary herds of the Serengeti Plains in Tanzania, and it represented 70 per cent of the world's blue wildebeest population, excluding the Serengeti herds. Today it probably represents less than 35 per cent of that world population. One study estimated that the population was greater than 300,000 in 1980 and declined to less than 30,000 by 2004. Today there are less than 1,000 wildebeest in the central Kalahari.

The most tragic aspect about this well-publicised story is that it has never been proved that the wildebeest are responsible for foot-and-mouth disease in southern Botswana. Since the erection of these fences not one outbreak of the disease has occurred in or on the borders of the central Kalahari Desert. Yet the fences remain. The Botswana authorities face a tremendous challenge in finding a solution to the problem. The interests at stake are those of the pastoralists, the cattle industry, the nature conservation sector and the tourism industry. Boreholes have been sunk in the central Kalahari to provide an alternative water source for the wildebeest. The problem is that, compared to wildebeest without access to water sources, those wildebeest that become reliant upon the water sources lose their 'resilience' and die when the boreholes dry up.[33]

The Okavango complex, being a reliable winter source of water bordered by summer-rainfall deserts to the south and west, must surely have attracted other wildebeest populations. Did these include populations currently restricted by fencing to areas such as the Etosha National Park in northern Namibia and the Hwange National Park in northwestern Zimbabwe? Did they include other populations since decimated, for example, from central Namibia? Unfortunately, we will never know the answers.

We do know, however, that the numbers of wildebeest at Etosha have dropped from 25,000 in 1954 to 2,500 individuals in 1978, and the numbers of Burchell's zebra dropped from 22,000 in 1969 to 5,000 individuals in

Blue wildebeest, Burchell's zebra and gemsbok congregate at a waterhole in the Etosha National Park.

After good rainfall in the Namib Desert, spontaneous congregations of gemsbok, springbok, Hartmann's mountain zebra and ostriches occur as animals move from the fringes of the desert to the gravel plains to exploit the luxuriant flushes of annual grasses. During periods when unusually heavy rains fall for one or two consecutive years, animals breed profusely, and their numbers increase dramatically. First to show these spurts in numbers are the ostriches, followed by the slower-breeding ungulates. Then, as the dry conditions set in once more, the congregations break up again into smaller groups and family units, and disperse throughout the vast expanses of the arid regions neighbouring the Namib.

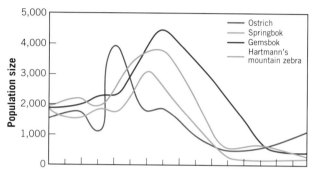

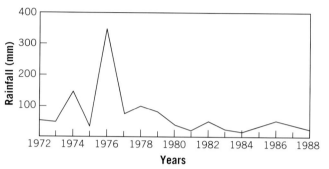

Numbers of ostrich, gemsbok, springbok and Hartmann's mountain zebra show a response to rainfall on the gravel plains of the Namib-Naukluft National Park at Ganab during the period 1972–1988. Records show that prior to 1972 rainfall had been low. After the unusually high rainfall of 355 millimetres in 1976, the populations showed a marked increase that was due primarily to immigration from other desert regions, but also to births in response to the growth of annual grasses. The sharp decline in numbers between 1982 and 1988 resulted partly from emigration and partly from the high death toll caused by persistent lack of rain.[39] The drought that commenced in 1982 was related to one of the strongest El Niño events ever recorded (see Chapter Ten).[40]

Gemsbok are nomadic in the Namib dune sea, where they feed on dune vegetation.

A clutch of young ostriches are accompanied by two adult females in the Kgalagadi Transfrontier Park. Typically, ostriches are the first of the large desert animals to rapidly increase their numbers after good rains.

The trekbokken

The most fascinating historical stories of the Karoo concern those of the massive herds of migratory springbok, known as the trekbokken. No discussion on mass animal movements in the deserts would be complete without them. Today it is difficult to gain any comprehensive perspective of the magnitude and details of the movement patterns of trekbokken before the arrival of Europeans in southern Africa. Their guns and fences have, sadly, changed forever the ancient routes trodden through the Karoo biomes and the Kalahari Desert. At best, we can try to obtain some idea of them from the writings of early travellers and colonists who marvelled at the great springbok 'migrations' and wrote down what they saw.

From the earliest travellers who ventured into what we now know as the Nama-Karoo and Succulent Karoo biomes came the most extraordinary stories of plagues of antelope of a magnitude that, I am sure, nobody can adequately comprehend today. Concerning a migration in 1849, Sir John G. Fraser wrote in his book, *Episodes in My Life* (1922):[41]

> '[W]e were awakened one morning [in Beaufort West] by a sound as of a strong wind before a thunderstorm, followed by a trampling of thousands of all kinds of game – wildebeest, blesboks, springboks, quaggas, elands, antelopes of all sorts and kinds, which filled the streets and gardens, and as far as one could see covered the whole country, grazing off everything eatable before them, drinking up the waters in the furrows, fountains and dams, wherever they could get at them, and as the poor creatures were all in a more or less impoverished condition, the people killed them in numbers in their gardens. It took about three days before the whole of the trekbokken had passed, and it left our country looking as if a fire had passed over it. It was indeed a wonderful sight.'

Although ungulates other than springbok, including sheep, no doubt got carried along with these unstoppable herds, by most accounts this rarely happened – the herds consisted predominantly of springbok. The numbers of animals were quite staggering, and in his book, *The Migratory Springbucks of South Africa* (1925), S.C. Cronwright-Schreiner described his attempts to calculate the number of participants in the trek he witnessed in 1896:[42]

The days of the trekbokken are gone. Today herds of springbok seldom number more than a few hundred, a far cry from the millions reputed to have formed migratory herds 130 years ago.

> 'We alighted from the cart, put our rifles aside and sat down to watch the bucks and take in a sight we most certainly should never see again. We were three farmers; accustomed to estimate numbers of small stock, and we had an excellent pair of field-glasses. I suggested to my friends that we should endeavour accurately to estimate how many bucks were before us. With the aid of field-glasses we deliberately formed a careful estimate, taking them in sections and checking one another's calculations. We eventually computed the number to be not less than five hundred thousand – half a million springbucks in sight at one moment. I have no hesitation in saying that that estimate is not excessive … now, to obtain some rough idea of the prodigious number of bucks in the whole trek, it must be remembered it was computed that they extended twenty-three hours in one direction and from two to three in the other – that is, the whole trek occupied a space of country one hundred and thirty-eight by fifteen miles. Of course, they were not equally dense throughout the area; but, when one says they were in the millions, it is the literal truth.'

According to several experts, Cronwright-Schreiner was not one to exaggerate in his writing.

The springbok herds took massive losses during their treks. In the words of W.C. Scully in his book, *Between Sun and Sand*:[43]

'There is something inexpressibly sad about the fate of these hapless creatures. Beautiful as anything that breathes, destructive as locusts, they are preyed upon by man and brute in the illimitable wilderness ... the unbounded desert spaces, apparently meant for their inheritance, hold for them no sanctuary; the hyaena and the jackal hang and batten on the skirts of their hapless host; the vultures wheel above its rear and tear out the eyes of the less vigorous which lag behind sportsman and pot-hunter, Boer, Half-breed and Bushman, beast of the burrow and bird of the air, slaughter their myriads; but still the mighty mass assembles every year and surges across the desert like a tempest in travail of torture.'

But the mighty masses did not continue to surge. Today, they are gone. With the continued influx of European farmers, the demise of the herds was inevitable. Nobody, it seems, could resist killing as many as they could. The Boers, in particular, were always well prepared for the passing of the herds and slaughtered them in their hundreds of thousands to make biltong (dried meat). To them the springbok, next to locusts, were the vermin of the veld – they competed with their sheep for food, space and water. Cronwright-Schreiner[44] wrote:

'The Dutch farmers were out by the hundred ... we passed several "outspans" where the hunters had encamped for days with their wagons and carts and horses – deserted camps which were marked by ash-heaps and charred bones and the straw of bundles of forage; while offal and heads and lower portions of the legs of the bucks lay about to such an extent as to be quite disagreeable. We constantly saw dead bucks and there were specially large numbers of kids which had perished from starvation, their mothers having been shot. The Dutch farmers made about two shillings and sixpence for the buck – sixpence for skin, two shillings for the "biltong". They enjoyed the sport, made a few sovereigns and did the country a service.'

In the context of what we now know about regional climates and desert vegetation characteristics, there are a few interesting questions that we can ask about these curious migrations. Where did these vast herds come from? Where did they go? Why and how often did they migrate? Were the treks true migrations or merely nomadic movements?

By most accounts, it would appear that the movement was predominantly in a north–south and a northeast–southwest direction. For example, T.B. Davie, a resident of Prieska in the Northern Cape, wrote in *The Cornhill Magazine* of 1921: 'From the year 1887 up to 1896 there were four really great treks over the Prieska District, three with a northern course, and one to the south and west.'[45] And again, about the 1849 migration, Sir John G. Fraser wrote: 'One day a travelling smouse [smous] came to Beaufort [West], and brought tidings that thousands of trekbokken were coming in from the north, devouring everything before them, and there was no means of stopping them.'[46]

Obstacles, such as the Orange River, seemed to pose little problem to the springbok, although they may have incurred high fatalities during the crossings. According to T.B. Davie: '[O]n this occasion they came right through the town of Prieska ... the "boks" trekked on to the banks of the Orange River, and were drowned by the thousands, those behind pushing the front ones into the water.'

Drawing on several sources, I have identified the following characteristics. Firstly, the treks took place between the summer-rainfall regions of the Nama-Karoo Biome and southern Kalahari Desert and the winter-rainfall Succulent Karoo Biome. They were not necessarily restricted to winter, when the vegetation quality in the Succulent Karoo would have been at its best. Secondly, they probably did not take place every year. They seemed to have occurred periodically, every ten to 40 years, but with a marked increase in frequency during particularly severe and prolonged droughts. This would classify the treks as nomadic movements rather than true migrations. Lastly, southbound animals were in a poor physical condition, suggesting that the condition of the veld they had come from was very poor.

Over the years many hypotheses have been advanced to explain why these treks occurred. The general consensus seems to be that the springbok moved between the winter- and summer-rainfall regions of the Karoo, probably for the same reason that Ludwig's bustard today makes seasonal migrations to and from the Nama-Karoo and Succulent Karoo biomes. For animals moving in a southwesterly direction, only a narrow strip of desert, no more than a few hundred kilometres wide, separates the summer-rainfall Nama-Karoo Biome from the winter-rainfall Succulent Karoo Biome – not a large distance to

Boer biltong hunters in the Nama-Karoo shot hundreds of thousands of migrating springbok, leaving the 'worthless', motherless lambs to their fate.

move in order to cross into an entirely opposite rainfall zone! However, whereas Ludwig's bustard migrates every year, the springbok treks may instead have followed something like the natural 18-year rainfall cycle that has now been identified for southern Africa. So, they probably trekked towards the predictable succulent forage of the Succulent Karoo only when veld conditions became particularly poor in the Kalahari Desert and the Nama-Karoo during the drier times of the summer-rainfall cycle.

It is also likely that cyclic fluctuations in the size of the total springbok population, associated with the rainfall cycle, added to the adverse conditions that stimulated the treks. The idea here is that, during the wetter years in the northern deserts, the springbok population would have grown in response to good herbage, but that these greater numbers and the consequent heavy browsing pressures would have taxed all animals during the drier times of the rainfall cycle as good-quality food became scarce. Thus, a combination of poor-quality herbage and high population numbers could have been the stimulus that triggered the mass aggregations and subsequent treks. The activities of the European hunters aside, the population size would again have decreased markedly during the actual treks as a result of starvation, natural mortality and predation.

However, this is merely speculation. It should be noted that observations were made during these treks that make little or no scientific sense at all, and I wonder whether it

is really worth trying to fathom out the causes for these mass movements in terms of a modern understanding of migration. One observation, for example, describes large-scale suicidal behaviour similar in many respects to the well-known lemming migrations during which large numbers of these arctic rodents are reputed to have routinely poured headlong off coastal cliffs into the sea in Norway. We can cite W.C. Scully[47] who was, incidentally, the magistrate at Springbokfontein in Namaqualand, and who witnessed numerous annual migrations across the desert:

'The Springboks as a rule live without drinking. Sometimes, however – perhaps once in ten years – they develop a raging thirst, and may rush forward until they find water. It is not many years ago since millions of them crossed the mountain range and made for the sea. They dashed into the waves, drank the salt water and died. Their bodies lay in one continuous pile along the shore for over thirty miles, and the stench drove the Trek-Boers who were camped near the coast far inland.'

Should we have any reason to doubt the word of the magistrate of Springbokfontein? One thing is certain: if these illogical mass drownings did occur, they cannot be explained in terms of migration, or any other modern ecological theory. I certainly cannot agree that the springbok plunged into the sea because they were thirsty – not in the Succulent Karoo Biome where the vegetation has a very high water content. Can the drownings be compared with the unexplained mass beachings periodically undertaken by whales and dolphins? We may never know. The deserts continue to guard many mysteries, and we may have to accept that the enigma of the springbok treks is one that will never be adequately revealed.

I have not had much cause to revise my understanding of mass migrations of the trekbokken since the first edition of this book, despite the fact that several subsequent studies have added new knowledge.[48–50] However, one aspect that I never considered is the question of why the treks stopped in 1896. Here are the conclusions of Christopher Roche, University of Cape Town, from his excellent thesis on the topic: '[T]he end of springbok treks in the Karoo can … be attributed to a complex combination of factors including the increase in livestock and human populations, the spread of fencing and increasing enclosure, drought and hunting.' Lastly, Ross Couper-Johnson has tied the major treks to the occurrences of El Niño years, which are typically characterised by droughts in southern Africa.[51]

Go forth and multiply

Glenn Pure

Above: The cooperation of birds in social groups frequently enables females to raise more young during favourable breeding seasons. In sociable weaver colonies, the earlier broods help the parents to feed subsequent chicks.

Left: Although ostriches are seasonal breeders, laying their eggs in autumn and winter, they have the ability to breed profusely after above-average rainfall events.

For any organism, the most important time in its life is when it breeds. Indeed, as discussed at the beginning of Chapter Six, the rationale of life for all organisms is to optimise their reproductive output. In the desert environment some plants and animals may have to endure many stressful years before they reach sexual maturity; others may be physiologically capable of breeding, but may still have to wait several years for the appropriate cues – invariably sufficient rain – that would optimise their chances of successful reproduction. And, in the meantime, they have to overcome the problems of water and food scarcity, temperature extremes and predators. This they do by means of various adaptations, some of which have already been discussed.

This unique photograph taken on the edge of the escarpment near Aus, in a strip of the Nama-Karoo Biome in Namibia, shows mesembs flowering in the foreground. There is little vegetation to be seen in the Namib Desert beyond. In desert regions, flowering plants compete with each other – not only for water, but also for pollinators.

The fact that desert organisms are able to withstand the stresses of their environment and reach a reproductive age is testament to millions of years of selection that have resulted in successful combinations of genes from parents and ancestors. Moreover, it is the genes themselves that coordinate desert organisms to breed, ensuring that they, the genes, continue to be passed on into future generations of the particular plant or animal that harbours them.[1] In this respect sexual reproduction plays a crucial role, for by combining genes between unrelated – or even sometimes related – individuals, the variability of genes in the species pool remains high. This high variability ensures that organisms are armed with the blueprints and flexibility upon which natural selection can act in tracking changes in the desert environment.

How, though, does a desert organism optimise its reproductive output? In an arid environment breeding is invariably a risky and expensive undertaking for any organism, whether plant or animal, large or small. This does not imply that desert organisms invest any more heavily in their descendants than do organisms in other ecosystems. However, it is more difficult for them not only to obtain the energy to finance breeding, but also to expend it at just the right time so that their offspring

have the best possible chances of establishing themselves. The adaptations that have evolved to overcome these problems are, not unexpectedly, fascinating and seemingly infinite in number. They serve two principal purposes: firstly, to protect the organism's investment and to optimise the chances of the survival, establishment and future reproduction of its progeny; and secondly, to synchronise the time of breeding with the rare favourable periods that the deserts offer. Such adaptations form the subject of this chapter.

Annuals: desert opportunists

Without question the most spectacular events that occur in the deserts of southern Africa are the flushes of annual flowering plants and grasses that erupt after good rainfalls in the Succulent Karoo Biome and the Namib Desert, respectively. The flowering daisies of the family Asteraceae are particularly good examples of pioneer plants: they are short-lived, they grow extremely quickly, and they produce large amounts of seeds in relation to their size. In response to several appropriate cues, especially rain, the seeds of most asteraceous daisy-like annuals (for example *Arctotis*, *Dimorphotheca*, *Gazania*, *Osteospermum* and *Ursinia* species) germinate and the seedlings grow to maturity and flower rapidly. Soon after flowering, the seeds are dispersed.

In the Namib Desert the annual grasses are the dominant pioneer plants, appearing after single rainfalls of about 20 millimetres or more, and they, too, reproduce with astonishing speed. The role of these grasses in sustaining the food webs of their respective habitats is vital: the Namib simply could not support its remarkable animal diversity were it not for the prodigious numbers of windblown seeds and other material from grasses that form plant detritus.

As pioneer plants, annuals are the first to colonise new open areas or freshly disturbed ground and, since every aspect of their life history is geared towards optimising the colonisation of suitable habitats, they are highly successful organisms in southern African deserts. Some of the factors that stimulate their germination and growth are discussed in Chapter Seven. Concerning ourselves exclusively with annuals of the Asteraceae, let us now pick up the story at the point where the plants flower.

The first step is pollination, the process of fertilisation of the egg in the ovary of the flower with the male gamete carried by pollen. To some extent, plants – especially grasses of the summer-rainfall deserts – rely on wind for pollination, but this method has certain disadvantages. In the first place, vast amounts of lightweight, easily released pollen must be produced if wind pollination is to be effective. This is very expensive for plants. A second downside is that there is no guarantee that the pollen produced by a certain plant will be carried by the wind and deposited on the sticky, receptive stigma of some faraway plant of the same species.

The pollination 'syndromes', as they are called, are highly specialised in southern Africa.[2] This means that, instead of a generalist system in which a large number of insects are involved in pollinating flowers, in southern Africa there is a high degree of specialised plant-pollinator systems, thus limiting the number of insect species that pollinate flowers.

Insects provide a more reliable pollinating service than does wind, and in the deserts of southern Africa it is bees, wasps, flies, butterflies, moths and beetles that do the job of carrying pollen from one plant to another. Insect pollinators are abundant when they are needed, since their larvae or pupae remain in synchronised diapause with the dormant seeds of the annuals, and the emergence of the

In deserts, wind is the most common form of seed dispersal among annual grasses and herbs. The seeds have a variety of lightweight winged structures, such as these *Senecio* seeds show, which facilitate their parachute-like dispersal.

adults coincides with the plants' flowering. Nevertheless, the competition to attract them during the annuals' short flowering periods is intense, especially where dense stands of the plants occur. The enormous variety of colours and flower shapes in desert annuals (and many perennials) bears testimony to this stiff competition, and the mesembs in particular sport some of the brightest, glossiest flowers in the whole plant kingdom. In many studies throughout the world it has been shown that bright colours in flowers serve the principal purpose of catching the attention of insect pollinators. The mesembs can justly be called the neons of the desert.

But advertising is expensive, and so, too, are flowers. Not all the energy invested by the plant goes directly into the production of gametes and their protection. Much is also invested in nectar, oils and extra pollen – rewards for the visiting insects. This additional cost would be completely wasted if annuals did not ensure that the insects were effective at pollination and not merely benefiting from the rewards.

The flowers of the Asteraceae exhibit advanced adaptations for attracting pollinators. They differ from the flowers of other families in that they are highly complex versions of the basic flower, which consists of sepals and colourful petals surrounding the female stigma and the male stamens. Although each head of an Asteraceae flower superficially looks like any other flower, it is actually a composite arrangement of many small individual flowers, called florets, each of which has its own stamens or stigma. The flower head's 'petals' are in fact ray-florets that are highly coloured and, in

A monkey beetle is smothered in the pollen of a Namaqualand *Arctotis* flower.

Marinus de Jager

The members of one group of monkey beetles are known as 'embedders' because they lodge their bodies in the stamen carpet to eat pollen and nectar. Males often copulate with embedded females and use the weaponry on their hind legs to fend off competitors. This photograph shows a female (green coloration) and male blue monkey beetle (*Scelophysa trimeni*) feeding on the pollen of a daisy flower.

most cases, female. Its central part, the disc-floret, is usually yellow and is made up of many small flowers.

From the insect's viewpoint, the attraction – and success – of asteraceous flowers lies in their 'one-stop-shopping' facility. So many flowers are packed onto the disc-floret of one flower head that the insects do not need to fly as much from one flower to another on the plant as they would do on other flowering plants, thereby saving time and energy, and minimising respiratory water losses. Moreover, each of the flowers on the disc-floret produces its own supply of sugar- and oil-rich nectar.

Although there are four basic shapes of asteraceous flowers, the most common in the southern African deserts is the rounded, daisy-like shape, the so-called actinomorphic form. The flat shape of the disc-floret allows virtually all insect types, large and small, to visit the flowers. The ray-florets act as landing pads, and the insects can easily walk over the flat disc-florets as they sample individual flowers for nectar. At the same time, of course, pollination takes place as pollen from their bodies is rubbed off onto the stigmas. Monkey beetles are by far the most efficient pollinators because they carry the heaviest loads of pollen on their hairy bodies.[3]

In addition to ensuring that their insect visitors carry out pollination, annuals must try to promote cross-pollination. This involves pollination with pollen from another plant of the same species, so that high genetic variability may be maintained in the species. In asteraceous annuals, where an insect visits many flowers on a single head, self-pollination to a certain degree seems inevitable, and it does actually occur, but without ill effect. Nevertheless, most plants try to restrict it, although this is no easy task when the flower heads bear receptive stigmas as well as their own pollen. Many asteraceous flowers solve this problem in a very clever way: not only are the florets not all of the same sex, but they also open at different times.

In one common pattern, demonstrated by the Namaqualand daisy (*Dimorphotheca sinuata*), the ray-florets are female, bearing neither anthers nor pollen, and they open before the other hermaphrodite flowers in the centre of the disc-floret. This greatly increases the chances of cross-pollination because the pollen carried by pollinators can only come from another plant. Once the hermaphrodite flowers open, they act as backups; if they have not been cross-pollinated, they can simply self-pollinate.

The next problem that asteraceous plants face is seed dispersal. What are their options? Do they allow their seeds to fall nearby and thus ensure that the habitat that

Beetles are important pollinators of mesembs.

nurtured the parent plant would likewise nurture the seedlings, or do they disperse their seeds far and wide so that new and open habitats can be colonised? Remarkably, most annual daisies and other asteraceous shrubs do both. They produce two – sometimes three – types of seed, each with different dispersal abilities. And again, the highly adaptive asteraceous flower has another advantage: each floret in the flower head produces a single seed, resulting in a high overall seed production. This is an important criterion for pioneer plants, for if they are to capitalise on the short periods of favourable climate and water availability, it is important that they produce large numbers of seeds. Only a small percentage of them are likely to become successfully established since most are eaten by birds and rodents or are collected by ants such as the common harvester ant *Messor capensis*.

For the vast majority of desert annuals of the family Asteraceae the most important option for seed dispersal is anemochory – dispersal by wind. In a study conducted in the Goegap Nature Reserve near Springbok, Gretel van Rooyen, of the University of Pretoria and one of South Africa's foremost specialists on the desert plants of the Succulent Karoo, established that 83 per cent of the annual plants in the reserve are dispersed by wind.[4] Wind-dispersed seeds are the smallest seeds produced by the plant, and they come from the disc-florets. Not surprisingly, they are equipped with a variety of lightweight structures ranging from long, silky hairs to single or multi-veined 'wings' that facilitate their parachute-like flight on the prevailing winds.

Having wind-dispersed seeds does not necessarily mean that the seeds land far from the parent plant. In many species the seeds fall only a few metres away, but

the wind continues to drag them across the ground. In the process, the seed's protective tunic becomes scoured, and this markedly promotes germination because oxygen and water can then freely reach the embryo within. These seeds invariably end up in depressions, such as deep animal tracks, which are favourable for germination because they collect water.

The second type of seed is larger. These seeds are formed from the female ray-florets once flowering is over. They invariably lack any form of wind-dispersal mechanism and often remain in the dried flower head after the winged seeds have dispersed. Because the seeds are bigger, they carry more resources, and this promotes their successful establishment and competition with other seedlings when they eventually germinate, perhaps several years later.

With their different seed dispersal options, these annuals are true opportunists. Their lightweight, wind-borne seeds allow them to colonise new habitats such as freshly disturbed sites where competition is negligible, whereas their larger seeds ensure that they become successfully established in areas where other annuals already exist and competition for water, nutrients and space may be high.

The succulent solution: the vault

Mesembs of the family Aizoaceae, also known as vygies in South Africa, evolved in the Succulent Karoo and today about 1,700 species are estimated to occur there.[5] These succulents' adaptations to water scarcity and temperature stresses have already been discussed, but one may also logically ask whether specialised pollination and seed dispersal adaptations have also played a part in their high species richness. Some mesembs are annuals, so the problems they face are not unlike those described for the asteraceous annuals. Most, however, are perennial dwarf shrubs.

Perennial succulents, and all desert perennials for that matter, face one problem that annuals do not: they cannot rely on an abundance of pollinating insects throughout the year. Despite the fact that they have the option of flowering at any time of the year, most flower in spring and thus join the competition for pollinators. This creates a double-sided problem because when flowering is seasonal, certain pollinators, such as honeybees, which do not enter diapause, are denied a food source throughout the year. Some mesembs do flower at times other than

Of all wasp families, the family Masaridae is one of the most unusual: the adults feed their larvae pollen instead of insects. These wasps, such as this *Quartinia* species, are frequent visitors to mesemb flowers, although a large percentage also favour some asteraceous annuals.

spring and can thus support some pollinators during the dry months, but such species are fairly rare, and the rewards they have to offer may not be sufficient to sustain large colonies of social honeybees. Could this explain why insects other than honeybees pollinate such an unusually high percentage of mesembs?

Fred and Sarah Gess of the Albany Museum in Makhanda (Grahamstown) showed that solitary wasps of the family Masaridae show a clear preference for foraging on mesemb flowers.[6-8] Moreover, they observed that the wasps were frequently the only visitors to the mesembs, even though many other insects were around. Masarine wasps differ from other wasp families in that they collect

oil-rich pollen and form it into 'loaves' that they feed to their larvae; the larvae of other wasps are carnivorous and are supplied with insects and spiders to sustain them.

There is much evidence to suggest that the southern African masarine wasps evolved alongside the mesembs and other flowering plants in the Succulent Karoo and are consequently dependent upon them for their survival. Of 92 species of masarines in southern Africa, 46 per cent show marked preferences for mesembs as forage plants. A high percentage (42 per cent) shows a distinct partiality for certain asteraceous annuals, and 20 per cent single out members of the annual genus *Wahlenbergia*, of the family Campanulaceae.[9] Although the members of most wasp families may be found throughout the world, virtually all southern African genera in the family Masaridae have distributions that coincide with the extent of the Nama-Karoo and Succulent Karoo biomes. Most also have unusually long tongues – certainly much longer than those of other wasps – which enable them to tap hard-to-reach flower nectaries. For instance, the smallest species, *Quartinia parcepunctata*, is a mere 3,6 millimetres long but has a tongue that is nearly one-and-a-half times longer than its body length! On the other hand, wasps of genera such as *Ceramius* are larger (10 to 20 millimetres long), have shorter tongues and seem to favour the larger flowers of the genus.

Although the exact links between flower form and particular wasp species are still emerging, there are various modifications of the basic flower form of mesembs which suggest that some may be promoting pollinator fidelity more than in the asteraceous annuals. Whereas annuals have only one opportunity for pollination during their

A bee fly visits a *Cephalophyllum fulleri* flower.

A *Mylabris* blister beetle and monkey beetle clamber around a *Cephalophyllum spongiosum* flower.

single flowering events and are content to attract any insect to do the job, perennials have many opportunities and can afford to be more selective. In mesembs several distinct flower forms have evolved to encourage pollinator fidelity and thus optimise the chances of successful cross-pollination (see box, page 200). The pollinators of mesembs are insects: bees, flies, wasps, beetles, butterflies, lacewings and moths.

When they have finished flowering, mesembs produce fruits that eventually become woody capsules. Each of these is divided into a number of segmental compartments, or locules, which house the seeds and are protected by valves. Normally closed, the valves open when they become wet or when the relative humidity of the air is high, and how they do so is quite ingenious. At the base of each valve is a keel that is highly hygroscopic and expands rapidly after absorbing water. The expanding keel acts as a lever that lifts the valve, thus exposing the locule and its seed contents to the open air. When the keel dries out again it contracts, pulling the valve down into the closed position once more. The capsule thus automatically opens and closes in response to the moisture content of the air. Some open extremely rapidly, literally within a minute or two, whereas others, such as those of *Lithops* species, may take longer. Warmer temperatures also tend to increase the speed of opening, although some mesembs have an optimal temperature at which the capsules open the fastest. A walk through the veld of the Nama-Karoo and Succulent Karoo biomes during or after rain reveals an intriguing variety of complex forms, sizes and colours of the open, often gaping, seed capsules of the mesembs.

The hydrochastic (water-responsive) seed capsules are one of the features that account for the successful speciation and radiation of the mesembs over the past three million years or less.[10] They have a number of advantages, the most important of which is that the seeds are dispersed at a very appropriate moment – when it is actually raining. At this time, they find themselves in conditions that are favourable for germination, especially if the soil has received a good wetting. Most mesembs produce tiny seeds whose size not only allows for easy dispersal by water, but possibly also makes them unattractive food items to seed-eating birds, rodents and insects. The seeds' smallness can be a disadvantage, however, since it, together with a limited protective coating, is probably a factor in the seeds' rapid decay in the soil if they do not germinate. It is thought that mesemb seeds inside

The flower and seed capsule (left of the flower) of *Cheiridopsis denticulata*. The hydrochastic seed capsule is one of the innovations responsible for the remarkable species diversity of mesembs in Namaqualand.

Mesemb seed capsules are not only tough and woody to protect the seeds from ants and birds, but are also water-responsive, opening their vaults and releasing their seeds only when conditions are perfect for germination – after rain. This photograph shows a dry, closed capsule (left) of *Cheiridopsis denticulata* and a wetted capsule (right) that took about five minutes to open fully.

capsules may remain protected for a year or even longer, until conditions are favourable for germination.

The capsules remain on the parent plant and open and close in response to suitable rainfalls. Capsules may also open in response to fog, but the seeds can only be dislodged from the opened capsule by raindrops. Some mesembs, such as *Drosanthemum montaguense*, release most of their seeds after the first post-flowering rainfall event when the seeds are ripe, whereas others, such as *Malephora latipetala*, release

Pollination adaptations in mesemb flowers

In the Succulent Karoo there are hundreds of different species of succulents belonging to the Mesembryanthemaceae, and each produces its own brightly coloured, glossy flowers. Given this high diversity of species coupled with the enormous numbers of insects that can pollinate the flowers, how does each species ensure that it is successfully pollinated with pollen from another plant of its own kind?

One solution to this problem has been the evolution of several flower adaptations that differ subtly in the arrangement of the stamens, stigmas and petals. Each specific arrangement allows only insects of a certain size and shape to reach into the flower and claim the nectar. It also determines on which part of the insects' body the pollen lands. This increases the chances of pollen reaching the stigma of the next flower of the same species that the insect visits, and thus helps to promote cross-pollination. There are three basic flower types: stamen carpet, central cone (large and small) and recess.

Stamen carpet flowers are very common among mesembs, being found in most species of the genera *Monilaria*, *Mesembryanthemum*, *Cephalophyllum* and *Carpobrotus,* as well as in the only species of the genus *Fenestraria*, *F. rhopalophylla*. They are generally large and flat, and their pollen is harvested by the larger walking insects, such as beetles, which carry it from one plant to the next on their bellies. The flowers produce large amounts of powdery pollen and the plants rely on wind as well as insects for pollination.

To prevent self-pollination, most stamen carpet flowers have two distinct phases: an early 'male' phase when the pollen-bearing stamens are prominent, and a later 'female' phase when the pollen-receptive stigma stands out. For example, one of the most common arrangements is where the stigma is at first shorter than the stamens (**A**). Then, when the stamens have withered and died, the stigma elongates and becomes prominent (**B**).

Cephalophyllum spongiosum

A   B

Small central-cone flowers occur in some species of the genera *Ruschia*, *Leipoldtia* and *Arenifera*. The stamens, forming a small cone in the centre of each flower, surround the equally long stigma (**C**). These flowers are pollinated by bees, which insert their heads through the narrow gap at the top of the cone and reach the nectar at the base of the stamens with their extended probosces. Several of these species have male and female phases, so that pollen collected on the bee's head during the male phase is deposited onto the stigma of another flower in the female phase. The stamens of small central-cone flowers, unlike those of stamen carpet flowers, do not collapse, but retain the shape of the cone to facilitate pollination of the stigma.

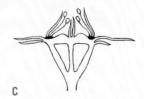

C

Ruschia species

Large central-cone flowers have taller cones with slightly wider entrances that insects have to pass through to reach the nectar. Different flowers of this type cater for different insects. In some species of the genera *Lithops*, *Dinteranthus* and *Dracophilus* pollen is collected along the sides of the insect's body as it enters the ring of stamens (**D**). In species of the genus *Titanopsis* the cone opening is narrower and the insect has to squeeze between the stamens (**E**). In the process, the filaments bend and spring back, scattering pollen onto the insect's back as they do so.

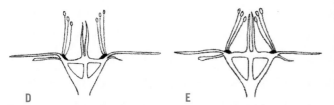

Drosanthemum speciosum

Recess flowers, which conceal both pollen and nectar in a cavity, occur in three main guises. The recess is formed in some flowers by the rim of the underlying hypanthium (**F**), and insects such as bees have to crawl into it to reach the hidden nectar. As they do so, the pollen is scattered all over their bodies. The stigma is very short and often forms a 'cushion' on the floor of the recess. Flowers of this type occur in the genera *Argyroderma*, *Erepsia* and *Stomatium*.

In other flowers the recess consists of a long, narrow tube formed by the petals, stamens and elongated calyx (sepals of the flower) (**G**). The flowers are pollinated by butterflies when they insert their long proboses into the tube to reach the nectar deep within. Species with this kind of recess flower belong to the genera *Berrisfordia*, *Imitaria* and *Conophytum*. Recess flowers of the third type open only at night and, since bright colours are redundant in the dark, they tend to be whitish or greenish in colour. They compensate for their lack of colour by having distinct fragrances that attract the insects. Generally small flowers with finely tapering petal tips (**H**), they are probably pollinated by small moths, probably at night. A good example is *Aridaria noctiflora*.

Argyroderma delaetii

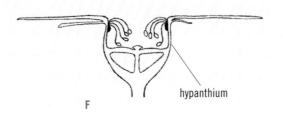

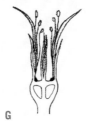

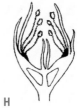

their seeds over several rainfall events, dispersing a number on each occasion; these species can retain as much as 30 to 50 per cent of their seeds after six months.

The way in which water actually disperses the seeds, and the time it takes for all seeds to leave the capsule, depends upon the capsule form, the growth form of the mesemb, and the habitat in which the mesemb is found.[11] Firstly, the seeds can be removed by being washed out or splashed out. This occurs in many mesembs with sunken growth forms, such as *Lithops*, *Conophytum* and *Psammophora* species, in which the fruit capsule is borne close to ground level. Once the capsule is open, it fills up with water, and falling raindrops either splash the seeds out or the seeds are carried out as the water overflows. In the latter case, flowing water may transport the tiny seeds 30 to 50 metres from the parent plant. The washout mechanism of seed dispersal is particularly practical for species that grow in rocky crevices, such as *Conophytum*, since the seeds are transported into the run-off cracks between rocks – ideal places for germination. As a rule, though, the mesemb seeds are not dispersed over great distances. Since suitable habitats are always limited in the deserts, short dispersal distances ensure that the seedling will establish itself in a habitat that has already proved to be favourable.

Some mesemb capsules forcibly eject their seeds, and the forms that enable them to do so, whether simple or quite complex, are all ingenious. The simplest one employs a springboard mechanism formed by a flexible membrane that half covers the seeds. When the valves open and the capsule fills with water, some seeds float up onto the membrane and are catapulted out of the capsule each time the membrane is distorted by impacting raindrops. The most advanced forms of ejection dispersal occur in genera such as *Ruschia*, *Lampranthus* and *Leipoldtia*. In these mesembs the membranes that cover seeds in each locule meet in the middle of the capsule where they form a spout-like opening. These capsules work a bit like tiny floral syringes. Once the valves have opened and the locules have filled with water, raindrops striking the covering membranes cause individual seeds and water to be forcibly squirted out of the spouts. The explosive ejection may propel seeds up to 2 metres from the parent plant. In species such as *Ruschia*, which has relatively deep locules, a membrane prevents all the seeds in each one from floating to the surface at once. Thus only a few seeds are expelled with each rainfall, and as the membrane disintegrates over a period of time the dispersal process is extended. This greatly increases the chances of successful germination of most of the seeds as circumstances may not always be perfect after the first rainfall. Differences in the seed retention and germination times of different mesembs may play a major role in determining how certain plant communities in the Succulent Karoo are structured.

Although dispersal in the mesembs is achieved by hydrochory, that is, by water, this is by no means the only method – wind and animals also play a role. In some mesembs the whole capsule breaks off from the plant and is blown about the desert as a tumble-fruit, the seeds falling out whenever the valves are opened hygroscopically. As it does for the seeds of annuals, the wind can transport the seed capsules of perennials a long way from the parent plant, and certainly further than is ever accomplished by hydrochory. In this case, the disadvantage of leaving a habitat that the parent plant has found suitable may be offset by the chances of the tumble-fruit coming to rest in a drainage line or depression. Both these locations are favourable for germination and the successful establishment of plants as they have higher soil water content than other parts of the desert environment.

Seed dispersal by animals, or zoochory, takes a number of forms, and is without doubt the most plausible means of dispersal of the fleshy fruits of the genus *Carpobrotus*. Known as *suurvye* or sour figs, the multiseeded fruits of these mesembs are delicious and are readily eaten by humans and domestic stock, as well as by animals in the wild. They are remarkably sticky, often adhering to the feet of birds as they are being transported considerable distances from their parent plant.

The delicious seed capsules of the mesemb *Carpobrotus* are favoured by humans and animals alike.

Karoo bossies, camel thorns and others

Since most Karoo shrubs are members of the family Asteraceae, their pollination occurs in much the same way as it does for asteraceous annuals. As far as seed dispersal is concerned, a large percentage (about 61 per cent) also rely on wind as a carrier, and their seeds, like those of the annuals, possess various parachute-like structures. However, in addition to this common form of seed dispersal, desert perennials make use of several other dispersal methods that are quite unusual.

A large number of Karoo shrubs, or *bossies*, rely on animals to disperse their seeds. The sticky fruits of the grey bietou (*Chrysanthemoides incana*), for example, are carried away from the parent plant by birds. Various species of *Eriocephalus*, the common perennial Karoo shrub known as kapokbossie, also rely mainly on birds to disperse their fluffy seeds. Richard Dean and Sue Milton, who specialise in the ecology of the Nama-Karoo and Succulent Karoo biomes, have suggested that kapokbos seeds are adapted for direct dispersal by birds as nest material.[12] They have painstakingly counted more than 28,000 seeds from 55 different plant species in 65 bird nests in the veld near Prince Albert. Although the nest material included seeds of many different plant species, an unusually high percentage (31 per cent) were those of *Eriocephalus* shrubs and a creeper called *Galium tomentosum*. The *Eriocephalus* seeds, which are encased in white, fluffy, cotton-like material, make a soft lining for nests and are much sought after by birds. The seeds of *Galium tomentosum*, on the other hand, are attached to long, fluffy stems that are fine and flexible, and these, too, are used to line the nests, giving structural support.

Dean and Milton argue that the birds may be selecting the kapokbossie's fluffy seeds for their durability and their insulating and water-repelling properties. The benefit to the plant is that its seeds are dispersed varying distances from the parent plant; the birds do not build in the kapokbossies themselves. Moreover, when the nests eventually collapse and fall to the ground several months after the birds have left, the seeds are usually in an ideal position to germinate. Not only are they surrounded by organic material in the form of bird faeces and old nest material, but they also fall into shade, and are thus in a situation that promotes the establishment of the seedlings. Dispersal by animals apart, the fluffiness of the kapokbossie seeds optimises the

Birds are attracted to the fluffy material surrounding the seeds of the kapokbossie, which they use to build or line their nests for waterproofing and insulation.

A nest of the Cape penduline tit (*Anthoscopus minutus*) is built almost entirely of the seeds of kapokbossie plants. When the nest disintegrates, the seeds will fall to the ground, where they stand a good chance of germinating.

Far left: This depiction of a *Hoodia gordonii* by Robert Jacob Gordon shows the plant's foul-smelling flowers and seed pods. This work, along with others by Gordon and his artist, Johannes Schoemaker, provided the first visuals ever of some of the flora and fauna of southern African deserts, all documented on Gordon's five journeys into the southern African interior. His pictures remained hidden from the world, stowed away in a British archive for more than a century until they were bought by the Rijksmuseum in 1914. **Left:** Gordon, born in the Netherlands, and of Scottish descent, was in the employ of the Dutch East India Company when he was commander of the Cape Garrison (1780–1795). Tragically, he committed suicide after the British claimed the Dutch Cape Colony at the Battle of Muizenberg in 1795.

success of dispersal and germination in other ways as well. In the first place, the light, fluffy appendages markedly facilitate dispersal by wind. Secondly, the cotton-like material surrounding the seeds becomes gelatinous when wet, and if the seeds are lying on the ground their sodden mass clings to the soil, creating excellent conditions for germination.

However, the story may not be that simple. The Karoo prinia (*Prinia maculosa*) seems to cheat somehow. An analysis of their nests revealed an average of 6.6 seeds per nest, yet the nests contained fluff from 579 seeds![13] Thus, not all birds that use the fluffy seed material for nests aid in seed dispersal.

In addition to ensuring seed germination by means of dispersal by wind, water and animals, a fair proportion of perennial Karoo shrubs practise autochory, or self-dispersal. These include such well-known species as the granaatbos

(*Rhigozum obovatum*), ertjiebos (*Lessertia incana*), bokhorings (*Microloma sagittatum*) and ghobba (*Hoodia gordonii*). Their seeds are enclosed in pods or capsules, often elongated, which open in response to several factors at certain times of the year. They often explode in the early evening as the temperature drops, or when they have dried out after rain. Each of the released seeds is adorned with long hairs or bladed wings, which greatly facilitate their parachute-like dispersal by wind. As in the case of the seeds of annuals, the objective of wind dispersal is not necessarily to disperse the seeds over great distances, but rather to allow their protective covering to become scoured as they are blown across the desert surface, thus promoting successful germination.

The practice of securing seeds within pods on the parent plant for long periods of time is called serotiny, and in arid regions it has a number of important advantages

Right: The burst seed pod of *Hoodia gordonii* reveals the lightweight, winged seeds of this species. **Far right:** *Rhigozum trichotomum* is a very common shrub in the deserts of southern Africa. Like *Hoodia*, its seeds are enclosed in pods that explode when mature, ready to be dispersed by the wind. Here an African migrant butterfly (*Catopsilia florella*) visits the flowers of the shrub.

relating to the timing of germination, protection of the seeds from herbivores, and keeping the dispersed seeds close to the parent plant. It is particularly well developed on the fringes of the Namib Desert where, studies have shown, the percentage of serotinous plants increases dramatically inland from the coastal Namib, reaching a peak in areas where a high variability of rainfall coincides with the highest amounts of rainfall.[14] The common serotinous genera recorded in the study were *Blepharis* and *Petalidium* (Acanthaceae), *Geigeria* (Asteraceae) and *Rogeria* (Pedaliaceae).

The large perennial trees of the desert regions, although comparatively few in number, face much the same problems as other desert plants do when it comes to pollination and seed dispersal. The majority are confined to drainage lines or dry watercourses, where their long taproots are able to draw water from deep underground throughout the year. Water, therefore, is not as limiting to their growth as it is to the growth of many shrubs and annuals. It is for this reason that some botanists do not consider the larger trees and plants, such as the well-rooted welwitschia, to be typical components of the desert flora.

Desert trees are not exempt from the competition for insect pollinators. Some, such as the sweet thorn, meet the challenge by offering pollinators huge pollen and nectar rewards for anything up to five consecutive months, a bounty that certainly helps to maintain populations of insect pollinators throughout the year. The trees can afford the high cost of these rewards because for them water is less of a limiting factor than it is for annuals and shrubs.

The stink shepherd's tree (*Boscia foetida*), as its species name implies, lures pollinators with evil-smelling flowers that reek of excrement. A ruse such as this is not unique to the smelly shepherd's tree but is found extensively throughout the succulent subfamily Stapelieae, which includes genera such as *Orbea*, *Orbeopsis*, *Pachycymbium* and *Stapelia*. Many of these plants, which also occur in the southern African deserts, give off a smell of rotting meat, attracting flies and other insects which then act as pollinators. However, the plants cheat on the pollinators because no rewards are offered!

After many decades of speculation, it now seems clear that *Welwitschias* are pollinated by various species of flies, especially *Wohlfahrtia pachytyli*, as well as *Oxybelus* wasps and *Allodape* bees.[15] All of these insects have been caught and seen to be carrying welwitschia pollen after visiting male flowers.

About half of all desert tree species rely on the wind for seed dispersal, and another 31 per cent rely on animals. This latter figure represents the highest percentage utilisation of zoochory of all the plant life forms in the southern African deserts. The camel thorn, an outstanding feature of the desert landscape, is a good example. It does not produce as many seeds relative to its size as an average

Above left: An excellent 'bee tree', the sweet thorn produces flowers with prodigious amounts of pollen. **Above right:** The flowers of the stink shepherd's tree smell just like excrement, effectively attracting flies as pollinators.

Welwitschias are pollinated by flies.

annual does, but it certainly invests more energy in each seed pod. Its seeds are borne in large, kidney-shaped pods that, with a protein content of 19 per cent or more, are highly nutritious to many ungulates and are readily consumed by elephants, giraffes, black rhinos, gemsbok, eland and steenbok. The seeds, numbering between eight and 25 in a single pod, are large and rounded, and lie embedded in a spongy, sweet-tasting substance within a fibrous fruit wall that is covered with fine, velvety grey hairs. In the southern Kalahari Desert Michael Knight observed that the greatest number of pods become available to herbivores when they fall off the trees during the hot-wet and early cold-dry seasons, from January to June.

The secret to the successful germination of a camel thorn seed lies, strangely enough, in its extremely hard coating. This protects the seed from being crushed by an ungulate's huge, grinding molar teeth and, being waterproof, prevents water and oxygen from reaching the seed embryo and stimulating premature germination. Fallen camel thorn seeds, like those of most other acacia species, can consequently survive for many years in the soil without germinating, a trait that allows the seed to take advantage of future rainfall events. However, being attractive to herbivores, many seed pods are eaten, and once the seeds have passed through the animal's digestive tract, their germination potential changes dramatically. The hard coating becomes mechanically abraded and is softened and eroded by digestive acids. The mechanical abrasion and the treatment of the seeds with acids increase the germination rates of camel thorn seeds to a considerable degree.[16] Despite what they endure in the digestive tract, most of the seeds that are passed out with the faeces are completely intact and viable, ready to germinate as soon as water becomes available. This dependence on herbivores for seed dispersal and their preparation of the seeds for germination is widespread among acacia trees in Africa and illustrates a long evolutionary association between plants and browsing animals. The major benefits to the acacia seeds are, in the first place, that they are dispersed whatever distance the herbivore moves away from the parent plant before

Above left: About 20 million years of interaction between browsers and the camel thorn tree have given rise to several features of the tree that benefit both plant and animals. The seed pod is one. It is filled with a pulpy material that has a high protein content, which is favoured by large browsers such as gemsbok and elephants. The seeds can germinate only once they have passed through the digestive system of these browsers. **Above right:** Steenbok readily feed on fallen camel thorn seed pods too. The dark spots evident on the animal are flightless louse flies.

it passes the seed. In larger herbivores this represents the distance that the animals move in two to three days, which can be quite considerable, given that in deserts large ungulates need to travel great distances every day in order to meet their daily food demands. Secondly, when the seed is eventually passed, it is deposited with its own 'compost heap', which includes plenty of nutrients such as nitrogen to help the seedling become established. Moreover, the seeds, being large, harbour a good store of energy to invest in the rapid growth of a deep taproot. Thirdly, the seed is likely to be deposited in a habitat similar to the one in which the parent tree grows, simply because the ungulate will continue to browse where conditions are favourable for its food trees. Finally, the passage of the pods through the digestive system kills large numbers of eggs and larvae of bruchid beetles, the most important pest associated with acacia seeds. Throughout Africa bruchid beetles inflict heavy losses on the seeds of all acacia species, and it is believed that the camel thorn's readiness to drop its ripe seed pods shortens the time that the beetles have to attack them, since the pods become more quickly available to ungulates.

The weirdest plant on Earth

When the Austrian doctor Friedrich Welwitsch stumbled on an untidy plant that resembled nothing he had ever seen before, he knew at once that he had discovered the weirdest plant on Earth. His find, made near Cabo Negro in Angola on 3 September 1859, aroused immediate interest among scientists, including Charles Darwin whose description of the welwitschia as the 'platypus of the plant kingdom' is amusingly apt.

All plants are classified as either non-flowering (Gymnospermae) or flowering (Angiospermae). Although the welwitschia has been categorised among the angiosperms, it is more advanced than members of this division, displaying features intermediate between gymnosperms and angiosperms. For instance, the reproductive structures of the male plant bear large 'anthers' similar to those in the flowers of angiosperms, whereas the reproductive structures of the female plant are more like those of gymnosperms. But the strangest of all the plant's characteristics can be seen during fertilisation: instead of the male sperm making its way into the ovary of the female plant to unite with the egg, the egg moves up to the male sperm through a special tube which grows from pollen grains adhering to a sticky substance on the female cone.

Welwitschias are found only in the Namib Desert, where between 5,000 and 6,000 plants occur. Strangely, they do not display the more obvious adaptations to aridity, such as small, wax-covered leaves; instead, two broad leaves grow from the gnarled, stunted stem. Although it is still debatable whether welwitschias can absorb moisture from the

The welwitschia's female cones (above) resemble those of gymnosperms, while the male 'flowers' are similar to those of angiosperms.

frequent fogs in the Namib, it is thought that they balance their high rates of water loss from their broad leaves by means of long, lateral roots, which tap water trapped in underground rocky fissures and gravel deposits. In the extreme west they are found only in washes and run-off areas. It is very rare to find a welwitschia in the Namib Desert that does not harbour several colourful *Probergrothius sexpunctatus* bugs, which feed on its sap. These insects, which often occur in high numbers on a single plant, do not appear to harm them, for some welwitschias have been dated at more than 2,000 years old.

Pollination specials and a Darwinian perspective

Towards the end of his famous journey around the world, Charles Darwin visited Simons Bay (Simon's Town) on 31 May 1836 to take on supplies for his homebound voyage. He spent nearly three weeks in and around Cape Town, but was not enamoured of the Cape.[17] He noted in his dairy about the surrounds of Simon's Town, 'I never saw a much less interesting country.'[18] But he did like the oak trees in Claremont and Rondebosch. He was worn out and homesick and, along with the rest of the HMS *Beagle*'s crew, was eager to get back to England after more than four years away. He had hoped to see the huge herds of springbok, wildebeest and zebra that had been described by William Burchell and others in the Karoo more than a decade earlier, but he barely ventured much beyond Franschhoek, and he most certainly never went to the Karoo or Namaqualand.[19] That was a pity, because he would have seen some of the most specialised orchid-insect pollination relationships long before his interest in orchids was eventually piqued.

After his voyage, Darwin became fascinated by pollination in orchids. Indeed, it was the first time that he showed any interest in plants. He was intrigued by cases of extreme specialisation between plants and their pollinators. Understanding fertilisation in orchids became his biggest passion (and diversion) while struggling to put *Origin of Species* together.[20] He tried to explain why long-tubed flowers, for example, are only successfully probed for nectar by insects that have equally long tongues. He was puzzled about how natural selection might work in these cases. Was selection focused by the plant on the insect to increase tongue length to reach the nectar, or was the selection focused by the insect on the plant to increase tube length to attract long-tongued insects to effect pollination? He even suggested that it may work both ways: selection could focus on both parties, in what he called reciprocal selection, now known as co-evolution, with the end result of near-runaway tube and tongue lengths. The consensus currently seems to suggest that, in deep time, flowers evolved and adapted to the availability of potential pollinators, but that alternative patterns of evolution could follow thereafter.[21–23]

Darwin would have been curious about the relationship between *Pelargonium stipulaceum* and its floral mimic, the orchid *Disa karooica*, and their long-tongued pollinator, *Philoliche gulosa*. The orchid, which does not produce nectar, dupes the long-tongued fly into visiting it by mimicking the nectariferous flowers of its model, the pelargonium. **Above left and centre:** There are several similarities between the two species: the tube of *P. stipulaceum* (top) and the spur (white tubular projection) of *D. karooica* (bottom) are of similar length and the flowers closely resemble one another. **Above far right:** The long-tongued fly shows pollen from *P. stipulaceum* on the underside of its head and thorax, and a pollinarium (mass of pollen grains) of *D. karooica* attached to the base of its proboscis. **Right:** The orchid's pollinarium is visible at the base of the proboscis.

The pollination of the annual plant *Diascia* in the Succulent Karoo would have fascinated Darwin. Gardeners also know the plant as twinspurs, referring to its two downward-pointing, tube-like spurs that secrete oils. *Rediviva* bees have extraordinary long front legs that probe the plant's spurs for oils, and in the process pollinate it.[24–29] The tips of the legs have very fine brush-like hairs that lap up the oils that are then transferred to the back legs for transport back to the underground nest. The oils are mixed with pollen to feed the larvae and are also converted to a wax-like substance used to line the walls of the brood cells of the nest.[30] How did this extraordinary association between plant and bee come about?

One way to investigate *Diascia–Rediviva* relationships is to trace the evolution of both the plant and the insect involved in this form of specialised mutualism. This has been done for the *Rediviva* bees and their closest relatives. Belinda Kahnt, University of Cape Town, and her colleagues started by reconstructing the phylogenetic (family) tree of *Rediviva* and showed that they evolved about 29 million years ago, at the same time as the emergence of the rich Succulent Karoo flora.[31] The common ancestor of *Rediviva* bees had short front legs and did not visit *Diascia* flowers. Moreover, long front legs evolved independently in several lineages. In other words, there was no single common long-legged ancestor that gave rise to all other long-legged *Rediviva* bees. Long-leggedness evolved very rapidly in various *Rediviva* species whenever and wherever there was an opportunity to respond to changing floral resource availability. The study tentatively suggested that the bees might have adapted to the plants, but cautioned that it was too early to know for certain.

In a follow-up study, Kahnt and colleagues matched the phylogeny of *Rediviva* to that of *Diascia* to confirm whether co-evolution occurred in this pollination relationship.[32] In other words, they wanted to confirm whether *Diascia* flowers also showed independent increases in spur length in association with the appearance of long legs in *Rediviva* bees that have visited them in their evolutionary history, and whether these changes occurred at the same time. If this relationship could be found, it might confirm Darwin's notion of reciprocal selection.

As is so often the case in trying to understand the origin of species, especially in biodiversity hotspots, the explanations are seldom straightforward. The Kahnt study found that there was indeed some evidence of co-evolution, but that it occurred rarely, only in about 14 per cent of *Diascia–Rediviva* species interactions. The main evolutionary process that was indentified was pollinator shifting.[33] This concept is not easy to comprehend, but it works something like this. Let's say an insect (A) with a certain tongue length pollinates a plant (B) with a flower spur of matching length. If this relationship were to stay as such, we might suspect co-evolution, that is, Darwin's reciprocal selection. However, a pollinator shift happens in plants when they adapt to another pollinator species (C). This usually happens if plants extend their range beyond that of their pollinators, or if plants compete locally with other plant species for services of a particular pollinator. So, pollinator shifting can result in new floral characteristics and, ultimately, reproductive isolation from the ancestral plant (B), which can lead to the emergence of a new plant species (BB), known as speciation. Pollinator shifting is therefore a powerful evolutionary process.

In orchids, another fascinating evolutionary response is Batesian mimicry, in which some orchids dupe insects into visiting their flowers but do not offer a nectar reward.[34] An example occurs in Namaqualand, involving the orchid *Disa karooica* and its model *Pelargonium stipulaceum*; both species possess long-tubed flowers that are pollinated by the long-proboscid fly *Philoliche gulosa*.[35]

Nectar is expensive to produce, but it is vital for pollination as pollinators would not visit flowers if they

This long-tongued fly (*Prosoeca ganglbaueri*) has been duped into entering an orchid flower that mimics another plant, and has a few pollinaria stuck to its face. Note how the fly tucks its long tongue underneath its body; it is not rolled up like the proboscis of a butterfly.

Michael Whitehead

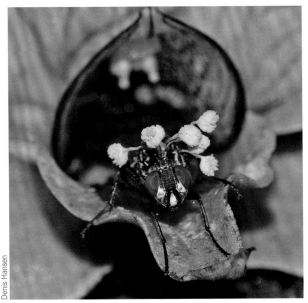

In this marvellous image of deception, a fly exits a *Satyrium* orchid flower, having been attracted by its foul smell, which mimics that of a dead animal. The insect entered the flower with five pollinaria from another plant attached to its back. In trying to get to the depths of its new host flower, its back brushed up against the viscidium (a very sticky pad) on the end of the stalk of a pollinarium, resulting in a sixth stalk attaching to its back. Importantly, one of the attached pollinaria brushed up against the stigma and deposited two bundles of pollen, thus pollinating the plant.

pollinators by producing a scent that mimics the stench of a dead animal, and is highly effective at attracting flies. In Namaqualand the orchid *Satyrium pumilum* attracts flesh flies (Sarcophagidae), which typically feed on small dead mammals, and thus the larger blowflies (Calliphoridae) and houseflies (Muscidae) tend to be excluded. Flesh flies are different from other flies in that they deposit maggots instead of laying eggs. Indeed, they have been observed depositing maggots on the flowers of *Satyrium pumilum*, so deceptive is the carrion odour. The flies are lured deep into the flower where they brush up against sticky pads that are connected to the pollen packages, which then attach to the flies' upper body surface. As the fly reverses out of the flower, the pollen packages are drawn out of the anther sac and then travel with the fly as it visits other flowers – on the same plant or on neighbouring plants. The flies end up self-pollinating the plant that they are on, or cross-pollinating neighbouring plants.[38]

Insects are not the only pollinators of desert plants. Rodents and elephant shrews have been identified as pollinators of certain ground-hugging plants in the Succulent Karoo Biome. The Namaqua rock mouse (*Micaelamys namaquensis*), for example, pollinates *Massonia depressa*,[39] whereas the rock mouse as well as the African pygmy mouse (*Mus minutoides*), the four-striped grass mouse and the pygmy hairy-footed gerbil pollinate two species of ground-flowering *Colchicum* bulbous plants.[40] These plants produce their scent at night to coincide with the times when nocturnal rodents are active. When the rodent pokes its snout into the flowers to lap up the nectar, the snout makes contact with the stigmas and the anthers of the flower, thereby promoting pollination. However, the snout of the Namaqua rock mouse shows no obvious characteristics that might aid it in lapping up nectar. Thus, in the case of rodent species, it is clearly the flower that has evolved in response to ground-dwelling mammalian pollinators.

The Cape elephant shrew (*Elephantulus edwardii*) is known to pollinate at least three ground-hugging plants in Namaqualand: *Hyobanche atropurpurea*, a root parasite, the pagoda lily (*Whiteheadia bifolia*), and the hedgehog lily (*Massonia echinata*).[41–43] Elephant shrews have very long tongues that they use to lick nectar from the flowers of these plants. In so doing, they get pollen on their snout which, when transferred to other plants, facilitates pollination.

A final example is that of the Namaqualand daisy *Gorteria diffusa*, whose flower petals resemble the bee fly

do not obtain a reward. And, if insects did not visit flowers, the flower would not be able to outcross, that is, to transmit its pollen to fertilise other individuals so that the seeds can be set. Yet, pollinators do visit non-rewarding orchids, so how do the orchids manage to fool pollinators without offering something sweet?

As you'd expect from a Darwinian perspective, natural selection is the culprit. Some orchid flowers have evolved to mimic the flowers of completely unrelated plants, or models, which do indeed produce nectar rewards. Orchid mimics fool insects into visiting the flower for just long enough for pollen to attach somewhere on the insect's body, without rewarding the visitor with nectar.

In addition to orchids, there are probably many more examples of Batesian mimicry to be discovered because there are about 14 species of long-tongued flies in southern Africa.[36] Moreover, Batesian mimicry is not limited to long-tongued flies: it occurs in bees and butterflies that visit orchid mimics and their models.

In addition to many well-known stinky plants that attract flies as pollinators,[37] some orchids also fool their

It is now known that rodents act as pollinators of several ground-hugging plants in Namaqualand. The Namaqua rock mouse has been documented pollinating the pagoda lily (*Whiteheadia bifolia*).

The Cape elephant shrew (*Elephantulus edwardii*) laps up the nectar of the parasitic plant *Hyobanche atropurpurea* in Namaqualand.

The first recorded example of sexual mimicry outside of the Orchideae involves *Gorteria diffusa* daisies found in Namaqualand. Sexual mimicry occurs when a plant mimics an insect, in this case female bee flies, to entice a male to mate with the floral mimic and, in so doing, to pollinate the plant. Notice the elevated, darkened petals with reflective spots that mimic the thorax of the female bee fly.

Megapalpus nitidus. The ray-florets sport dark spots to which male flies in search of potential mating partners are strongly attracted. The cells of the ray-florets are raised into bumps, which reflect an ultraviolet pattern that is similar to that of the black thorax of the bee flies. Similar dark spots occur on other Namaqualand daisies, such as *Gazania* and *Dimorphotheca*, and also in pelargoniums, probably to attract the same bee flies.[44]

These are some of the recently described specialised relationships, or mutualisms, as biologists call them, which occur in Namaqualand, the flower capital of Africa. What has been described so far, though, is probably the tip of the iceberg, and we can expect many more fascinating 'pollination specials' to be described in the future.

Insect plagues

Most desert insects endure unfavourable dry periods in the larval or pupal stages of development. During this time, diapause may or may not occur, but rainfall is the most common cue for the emergence of the insects. Many of them display pioneer-like traits. Periodic outbreaks of brown locusts (*Locustana pardalina*) are characteristic of many regions of the Nama-Karoo Biome, especially following extended droughts. A fascinating aspect of the Acrididae, the family to which the brown locust belongs, is that its members have two distinct forms or phases: a grasshopper or solitaria phase, and a typical locust or gregaria phase. In the solitaria phase small eggs are laid; these often go into diapause and produce hoppers that are relatively small and cryptically green or brown in colour. Adults are also small and, like the hoppers, sluggish and anti-social. On the other hand, gregaria-phase eggs are large, extremely drought-resistant, and do not go into diapause. The hoppers are large and conspicuously brightly coloured, and both hoppers and adults are active, moving together in large swarms.

Within about ten days of their last moult, adult female brown locusts become sexually mature, and about eight weeks after mating they lay about 400 eggs, depositing 40 or so at a time in 'pods' 10 centimetres deep, which they excavate in the bare soil with their highly expandable ovipositors. Gregaria eggs may hatch between 11 and 14 days later if the soil is wet and the

Piotr Naskrecki

A brown locust swarm in the Nama-Karoo. Locust swarms illustrate the explosive reproduction pattern after good rainfalls. En masse, these insects can cause extensive damage to cereal crops.

Yathin S Krishnappa / CC BY-SA 3.0, Wikimedia Commons

Gerrie van Vuuren / CC BY-SA 4.0, Wikimedia Commons

Locusts, especially when they swarm, make up a large component of the diet of several small desert carnivores, including the black-backed jackal (above left), the bat-eared fox (above centre) and the Cape fox (above right).

temperatures are high enough, or they may remain in the soil for three years or more, waiting for sufficient rains to wet the earth and initiate hatching. Solitaria eggs may hatch within a few weeks, but eggs laid towards the end of the previous summer tend to go into diapause during the subsequent winter months. When the tiny locusts hatch after rain they undergo five 'instar' nymph, or 'hopper', stages, during which they grow from nine to 30 millimetres in six to eight weeks.

The association between the solitaria and gregaria phases is fascinating and was first observed in the laboratory during the 1920s. All hoppers start off in the solitaria phase. When solitaria hoppers were

raised in captivity in low numbers or in isolation, they maintained solitaria characteristics. However, if the hoppers were raised together in high densities, they developed gregaria characteristics. Thus, the density of hoppers around any one individual determines the physiological, behavioural and morphological characteristics of the hopper phase.

In the field, solitaria hoppers turn into gregaria forms wherever local accumulations of hoppers become very high. This may occur for a number of reasons. For example, high numbers of hoppers may emerge in areas that are very suitable for egg laying. Whereas solitaria locusts are fairly sedentary, once large aggregations of gregaria locusts have formed they take to the air in enormous swarms that can move considerable distances each day. These are the spectacular periodic 'locust outbreaks' so dreaded by farmers, especially in the Nama-Karoo. Although the locusts do inflict some damage on the natural Karoo vegetation, the damage is particularly severe when the swarms move out of the Nama-Karoo and into agricultural areas where maize crops occur.

Scientists do not properly understand why two such different life-history patterns should have evolved in the same species of locust. Moreover, they understand even less the factors that might explain the periodicity of locust outbreaks, and where the alternative life-history patterns may be involved in these outbreak cycles. The locust outbreak 'problem' continues to generate heated debate between entomologists, farmers and government agencies responsible for monitoring and controlling local locust outbreaks.

The principal predators of the brown locust in the Nama-Karoo are birds, especially white storks (*Ciconia ciconia*), mammals such as black-backed jackals, bat-eared foxes and Cape foxes, and also lizards, robber flies (Asilidae), solpugids and scorpions. The impact that some of these predators may have on locusts can be quite considerable. For example, it has been estimated that white storks alone could eat as many as 80 million locusts a day in areas where high densities of these insects occur.[45]

Another pest insect that periodically irrupts after rainfall in the Nama-Karoo Biome is the Karoo caterpillar (*Loxostege frustalis*). It feeds almost exclusively on relatively unpalatable *Pentzia* shrubs which, with the advent of overstocking and intense browsing pressures by livestock, have come to dominate the Nama-Karoo at the expense of palatable shrubs and grasses. This implies that large populations of these insects may again be a human-made problem, a consequence of poor veld management. Despite their limited palatability, *Pentzia* shrubs are valuable fodder plants, helping to sustain the 8 million or so sheep in the Karoo today. Not only do the caterpillars voraciously consume vast quantities of forage, their silken webs often cover individual plants and render them unpalatable to sheep. The reproduction of these insects, like that of the brown locust, is well tuned to the unpredictable nature of the Karoo climate. The pupae persist for many years in waterproof cocoons, waiting to emerge as nondescript grey moths as soon as favourable rainfall conditions occur.

'Perennial' insects and desert lizards

Although the majority of adult desert insects live for less than a year, ensuring continuity in the form of larvae and pupae during the dry season, there are some insects which do not, and these display certain traits of long-lived insects. Good examples are several tenebrionid beetles of the Namib dune sea. Beetles such as *Onymacris plana* can live for longer than three years – a surprisingly long time for an insect of its body size. In contrast, the brown locust, a much bigger insect, lives for no more than about two months. Tenebrionid beetles sustain a moderate but constant reproductive output throughout even the driest of months, periodically laying small batches of eggs in the sand of the dune sea.

The beetles of the Namib dune sea utilise a reliable source of food in the form of windblown detritus, and water in the form of coastal fog. Therefore, food and water are not limited to intermittent periods of plenty, and the beetles can afford to breed throughout the year.

Scorpions also display a number of long-lived traits. They are well known for the parental care that they afford their progeny – behaviour not seen in arthropods. Scorpions are born live, and soon after birth they clamber onto the back of their mother. They remain with her if escape from predators is necessary and can rely on her to defend them. This is particularly useful in desert-dwelling scorpions such as *Parabuthus granulatus*, whose stings can be fatal. Like most desert scorpions, *P. granulatus* takes several years to reach sexual maturity

Species of *Parabuthus* are the most venomous of the African scorpions. This species is from the Kalahari Desert.

and is also extremely long-lived for its size. Its longevity can be related to its remarkably waterproof body surface and exceptionally low rate of water loss, for it can survive for longer than a year without food, which is also its only source of water.

Among desert lizards there are also some marked differences in life-history patterns, but not much is known about the ecological circumstances that might explain them. For example, one of the most beautiful lizards in southern Africa is the Cape flat lizard, a species that can be observed at very close quarters at one of southern Africa's popular tourist attractions, the Augrabies Falls. With their stunning blue, red, brown and yellow colour patterns, the males are conspicuous throughout the year, but when they need to hide from predators their wide and flat shape allows them to find refuge in very narrow cracks in rocks. These lizards are long-lived, and are recorded as having survived for more than 14 years in captivity; they take three years to reach sexual maturity; and they lay only two eggs per year. The last-named trait is in marked contrast to the seven to 12 eggs laid twice a year during the rains by the southern rock agama, which occurs in the same habitat. Finally, the Cape 'flatties' appear to be social, living in dense colonies overseen by territorial males. Sociality is another trait common among long-lived animals. Perhaps the longevity of the Cape 'flatties' is made possible by a reliable source of insect food – mostly flies, mayflies and mosquitoes – which is available in their extremely limited

The southern rock agama lays seven to 12 eggs per year.

distributional range along the lower Orange River in the Nama-Karoo and Succulent Karoo. The proximity of a large perennial water source – the Orange River – to their habitat may ensure a year-round supply.

The shovel-snouted lizard of the Namib dune sea has been the subject of intensive study, and much more is known about its reproduction than about the reproduction of Cape 'flatties'.[46, 47] Like the tenebrionid beetles, shovel-snouted lizards display some long-lived traits and for the same reasons: a fairly reliable year-round food and water supply. They feed on grass seeds in the detritus as well as on insects, many of which also rely on the detritus for food. Males vigorously defend their territories in the sand dunes, the best of which have reliable accumulations of detritus on the dune slipfaces. Each male's territory supports about three females, which each year lay up to four clutches of either one or two eggs, depending on rainfall.[48] This aseasonal breeding is very rare in non-tropical lizards, especially in desert species, and is made possible by moderate winter temperatures that do not retard egg development, and by the reliability of resources in the Namib dune sea.

Zeitgebers and small mammals and birds

The timing of most vertebrate reproduction in desert ecosystems differs from that in other ecosystems in a number of ways. Most importantly, the physiological state of readiness required for reproduction is often triggered by more than one environmental cue. In the vast majority of cases – humans being an obvious exception – vertebrates give birth to young on a seasonal basis from year to year. The timing of this process is exquisitely controlled by a *Zeitgeber* (an environmental 'time-giver') based on photoperiod and its effect on the pineal gland in the brain. The pineal gland releases variable doses of a hormone called melatonin in response to a cessation of light cues received from the eyes via the optic nerves. The daily timing of the doses of melatonin depends on whether it is dark or light. The melatonin in turn can markedly influence reproductive potential, such as the size and function of the testes and the development of eggs in the ovaries. In the Northern Hemisphere, for instance, where vertebrates such as rodents breed during the long days of the productive summer months, the onset of autumn, and hence daylength shorter than about 12 hours, is sufficient to trigger the complete regression of the testes.

One can readily appreciate that such total dependence on photoperiod would be quite inappropriate in a desert ecosystem where seasonality does not necessarily spell good conditions for breeding. Rainfall patterns, and therefore food supplies, are simply too unreliable. Although seasonal reproduction does occur in some of the larger desert vertebrates, this is the exception rather than the rule. In addition to the 'primary' *Zeitgeber* that is determined by photoperiod, desert animals wait for an additional 'secondary' *Zeitgeber* before they launch into the reproductive process. More often than not this is a good rainfall, but it may be something else, such as the protein content of the food. So, although desert animals are physiologically prepared for breeding by photoperiod, they wait for a second cue that will confirm good chances of successful breeding before they proceed.

Consider the four-striped grass mouse, whose highly flexible social system I discuss in Chapter Six. In the Succulent Karoo Biome, apart from the influence of population size (density dependence), the secondary *Zeitgeber* seems to be the quality of the winter annuals, especially the protein content which stimulates dispersal from the natal nest. In the Desert Biome, in the vicinity of the Gobabeb Research Institute on the Kuiseb River, the primary *Zeitgeber* is temperature and rainfall, but the secondary *Zeitgeber* is also food quality, especially that of the flowers of the nara plant.[49] The males of the four-striped mice, however, remained reproductively active throughout the year. It was only the females that responded to the secondary *Zeitgeber*. The same situation occurs on the eastern fringes of the Nama-Karoo Biome, in the Mountain Zebra National Park, which is a summer-rainfall desert. There the male four-striped mice also remained reproductively active throughout the cold, unproductive winters, whereas the females became reproductive in response to plant quality.[50] These two examples have been described as 'opportunistic reproduction', a not uncommon reproductive system in unpredictable deserts.

On the other hand, some desert rodents that feed on perennial vegetation, such as the black-tailed tree rat, are seasonal breeders and rely only on the primary photoperiod *Zeitgeber* for breeding preparedness. A female I kept in captivity under light conditions similar to those in the Kalahari Desert in summer (that is, daylength of 14 hours) continued to breed throughout the year,

Two playful pups. Reproduction in four-striped grass mice depends not only on temperature and population size but also on the quality of available food.

Carsten Schradin

producing five litters of three pups each! She immediately stopped breeding when the daylength was shortened to ten hours of light.

Small desert birds are also excellent examples of desert vertebrates that rely indirectly on rainfall as the secondary *Zeitgeber* for breeding. This is best illustrated in several species of insect- and seed-eating larks that inhabit the deserts of southern Africa. Gordon Maclean, University of KwaZulu-Natal, showed that, in the southern Kalahari Desert, larks lay their first eggs within a week or so after a good rainfall, especially in summer, and continue to raise subsequent broods for as long as favourable conditions remain.[51–54] In the hot summer months the breeding periods after rain tend to be short because the food supply deteriorates rapidly, but in winter they last longer because the reduced evaporation in autumn allows the vegetation to stay greener longer than in summer.

The fact that many larks in summer-rainfall zones are able to breed opportunistically after rain in winter shows that photoperiod does not completely control a seasonal gonadal cycle. In fact, in many of these larks, the testes reach a completely regressed state for only a few weeks of the year. Even if there is no prevailing secondary *Zeitgeber* – which in these larks is thought to be the protein content of insects and seeds – the larks maintain a 'ticking over' hormonal level in the blood that would allow the gonads to develop very rapidly should the secondary *Zeitgeber* arrive.

Many desert larks, such as Stark's lark and the grey-backed sparrow-lark, are highly nomadic, and we would perhaps expect them to display certain pioneer-like traits

The 'primary' factor or cue that prepares the gonads of many animals for breeding is seasonal daylength. In the unpredictable desert habitat, however, many smaller animals wait for a 'secondary' cue. In the case of the highly nomadic grey-backed sparrow-lark, a good rainfall is the signal to breed. The birds lay as many clutches as possible in favourable conditions but restrict the clutch to two eggs.

Sclater's lark breeds opportunistically. On the exposed rocky flats of the northwestern Nama-Karoo, it lays a single egg that is slightly larger than the eggs of other desert larks of the same size.

such as large clutch sizes. Yet they don't. Most lay only two eggs, very rarely three. In the most extreme case, Sclater's lark, which also breeds opportunistically after rain, lays a single egg that is slightly larger in size than the eggs of other larks. Instead, larks seem to hedge their bets by laying as many clutches as possible during the favourable periods. The eggs are laid on the ground, and the losses of eggs and nestlings to predators are enormous. Rather than produce single clutches with many fledglings, they produce as many small clutches as possible, thereby optimising the chances of successfully raising their chicks.

In regions of extreme aridity, such as the Namib Desert, resident desert birds revert once more to seasonal breeding. This is the case in Namib endemics such as the dune lark and Rüppell's korhaan. In these instances, it is

thought that rainfall, or some resource consequence of it, is too unpredictable and unreliable to act as a secondary *Zeitgeber*. The birds therefore breed during the season with the maximum probability of rainfall, that is, summer. Seasonal breeding is also found in two other large, ground-dwelling birds, the Karoo korhaan and Ludwig's bustard, which are nomadic visitors to the Namib Desert.

The sociable weaver is perhaps the best example of a small, opportunistic desert bird that displays long-lived traits. It responds indirectly to rainfall, breeding throughout the year if conditions are favourable. As discussed in Chapter Six, the sociality of these birds and the huge nest structure they build permit them to be independent of the thermal stresses faced by small birds in the deserts. Gordon Maclean showed quite clearly that they are independent of a *Zeitgeber* based on photoperiod.[55] Instead, they quickly start breeding after rainfalls greater than 20 millimetres at any time of the year. One pair of birds may raise as many as four broods following a single, good rainfall event. When the offspring in the first brood have been raised, they help the parents to feed the subsequent broods. This is an important adaptation that ensures that sufficient food will be found for the last of the broods when insects, the birds' major food item, become scarce again.

The smallest and most bizarre members of the long-lived club are undoubtedly the social mole-rats. While on the one hand these strange rodents exemplify longevity to the extreme, at times one is almost led to believe that two species may have carried pioneering-like traits to unusual lengths. The Damara mole-rat and the naked mole-rat are two of the most social mammals in the world (see Chapter Six). They are in fact eusocial, like bees, ants and termites,

Peter Steyn

The Karoo korhaan (*Eupodotis vigorsii*) is a seasonal breeder that usually lays a single egg on the bare ground.

having one queen per colony and castes of workers and soldiers. In mole-rat colonies the pups are meticulously tended, protected and fed by the workers and soldiers in the colony for many months after their birth. Moreover, these small animals are extremely slow-growing and long-lived for their body size, especially the most social ones, the naked mole-rats.

Life-history patterns such as these can, however, be easily explained by the fact that mole-rats have carved out a niche in the most stable and predictable habitat to be found anywhere in a desert – the underground realm. In reality, these animals do not live in the desert, but under it. Temperatures and food supplies remain remarkably constant underground from day to day and, in the case of the naked mole-rat, from year to year. There is one proviso if the mole-rats are to benefit from these constant conditions: they themselves must conform more or less to one rule of constancy and maintain a certain minimum colony size. Although their chief food items – tubers, bulbs and corms – are constant in terms of their abundance, they are difficult and expensive to find underground by burrowing. As discussed in Chapter Six, the more widespread the food items become in a habitat, the larger the colony size that is required to minimise foraging risks. In the most extreme cases, naked mole-rat colonies can be as large as 300 animals. In order to maintain the minimum colony size the single queen must

produce huge litters to replace losses through predation, disease and natural mortality. And indeed, she does; a productive naked mole-rat queen bears litters of as many as 20 pups every 80 days! Naked mole-rats take good care of their slow-growing pups. To facilitate regular, aseasonal breeding, the naked mole-rat, along with humankind, seems to be one of the very few mammals whose preparation for breeding does not require any form of environmental *Zeitgeber*.

Large desert ungulates

Large desert-dwelling mammals face one constraint that limits their ability to respond rapidly to rainfall – long gestation periods. For this reason, we cannot expect them to breed opportunistically after rain. It would be quite pointless for springbok, for example, to conceive en masse after a good rainfall on the Namib's gravel plains because by the time their lambs would be born, 24 weeks later, the annual grasses would almost certainly have disappeared. Typically, therefore, the *Zeitgeber* that controls reproductive activity is more dependent on photoperiod than on rainfall. The best that they can do is to remain seasonal breeders and to drop their young at the time of year with the best chances of rainfall.

The majority of large vertebrates are seasonal breeders, although some display interesting variations that increase the young's chances of survival. Female blue wildebeest, for example, come into oestrus in early winter and their calves are born sometime in December, a month or so before the summer rains can be expected. However, despite the fact that they use photoperiod (in this case, the shorter days of autumn) as the primary *Zeitgeber* for readiness for mating, the secondary *Zeitgeber* comes from the herd itself. It is not known precisely what this may be: it could be courtship display, a secondary male characteristic, or a sex-pheromone (an airborne hormone). Whatever it may be, the outcome is that all receptive females conceive and calve within a week or two. This is an important adaptation because it serves the principal purpose of 'flooding' the predator market with an abundance of food. Since most predators, such as lions and spotted hyenas, maintain fixed territories, 'foreign' predators cannot move into the calving zone to exploit the easily caught calves – these are the prey of the resident predators. Synchronised calving works on the simple basis

Certain desert-dwelling ungulates such as blue wildebeest respond to synchronised mating cues – perhaps a courtship display – within the herd. This results in most calves being born within a period of a few days. Overall loss to the herd is minimised because predators can only eat a certain proportion of the calves available during their vulnerable early weeks of life. Within such a short time the predators cannot increase their own numbers to take full advantage of the glut of food.

Gemsbok females show synchronised breeding, as seen here in the similar age of the calves.

that there is a limit to how much food a fixed population size of predators can consume in the month or so that it takes the calves to grow enough to start keeping up with the herd. The wildebeest certainly lose a percentage of the calves to the predators, but they would lose many more if the calving time were staggered.

Gemsbok have a polygynous breeding system in which one male mates with a group of females. The females also show synchronous breeding such that all calves within the herd are of the same age.

Springbok, one of the most arid-adapted of all desert ungulates in southern Africa, display reproductive patterns that have had biologists arguing for decades. In the southern Kalahari Desert springbok typically occur in herds numbering several hundred. While undertaking research in the region, Gus Mills observed that the peak in springbok births usually occurred in January. However, he noted that in some years it occurred earlier, and in 1981 there was no peak at all, the ewes dropping their lambs over a period between January and April.[56] Lambs were also born at other times of the year, particularly in April–May and September–October.

Neil Fairall, University of Pretoria, and his colleagues observed similar strange lambing times in the Nama-Karoo biome.[57] For two consecutive years the springbok dropped their lambs over an extended spring–summer period, then switched to autumn lambing the following year. Unfortunately, that study was terminated at the end of autumn, so there is no record of what happened during the following spring and summer. Extended lambing times such as these cast serious doubt on the role of photoperiod as a *Zeitgeber*. John Skinner, University of Pretoria, plotted lambing times from 3,000 records from all over the deserts of southern Africa and established that springbok drop lambs in every month of the year.[58] This pattern contrasts sharply with the definite seasonal three-month lambing period of impala (*Aepyceros melampus*), the ecological counterpart of the springbok in non-arid habitats, which drop their young immediately before the onset of the summer rains.

Skinner argued that the *Zeitgeber* for the stimulation of oestrus behaviour in non-lactating, post-pubertal springbok lambs is the 'flush of green forage' following rainfall. Although this may be so, I have yet to see any convincing data in support of this assertion. From an ecological perspective, a vegetation-quality *Zeitgeber* makes no sense at all because it does not guarantee good-quality vegetation when the lambs are born six months later.

What we do know is that a certain degree of synchronisation of lambing occurs within particular herds. This is not surprising considering the large numbers of lambs that are taken by spotted hyena clans at night. I once followed a clan of foraging hyenas throughout the night in the company of Mike Knight, University of Pretoria, and observed the hyenas catch and eat a dozen or so lambs within a few hours until all the animals were satiated. It could be argued that a secondary *Zeitgeber* may come from within the herd itself, in much the same way as it does for blue wildebeest. The evidence of synchronised lambing can be seen on a regular basis in the Kgalagadi Transfrontier Park. Once the lambs are three to four weeks old and are able to run with the herd, they form 'nursery herds' attended by a few females. From these it often appears that all the lambs within the herd are about the same age.

What is the springbok's secret? We know they have an uncanny ability to detect rainfall several hundred kilometres away over flat desert plains, so perhaps they simply trek to wherever it has rained, and the vegetation is abundant enough to feed their young. They may even be playing the fickle and unpredictable desert environment at its own game, by being equally unpredictable in their lambing times and thereby confusing predators. Perhaps they are champion bet-hedgers. Whatever the case, springbok have come to epitomise the fascinating, and the mysterious, in southern Africa's deserts.

Evidence from the Kgalagadi Transfrontier Park shows that synchronised lambing in springbok herds occurs there on a regular basis.

The Ancient Karoo

Gerhard Marx / Albany Museum

Above: Swamp forests grew along the northern shore of the vast Karoo Sea during the Permian. This plant material accumulated over time, eventually developing into South Africa's vast coal deposits.

Left: A reconstruction of the Ancient Karoo when it was a swampy basin – about 250 million years ago. A mother *Thrinaxodon*, a cynodont, keeps an eye on her young. Although this reconstruction shows the animals with fur, there is no fossil evidence for this.

John Sibbick

The Nama-Karoo has a fascinating history of life recorded in its rocks. Of particular interest is the vertebrate life that occurred there between the Middle Permian, around 270 million years ago, and the Early Jurassic, about 190 million years ago. The unbroken 80-million-year fossil record of the ancestors of mammals and birds that lived in the Karoo during this period tells the dramatic story of the extinction events at the boundary of the Permian and the Triassic, about 252 million years ago, and at the end of the Triassic, about 201 million years ago. The end-Permian extinction was the greatest extinction event ever to have occurred

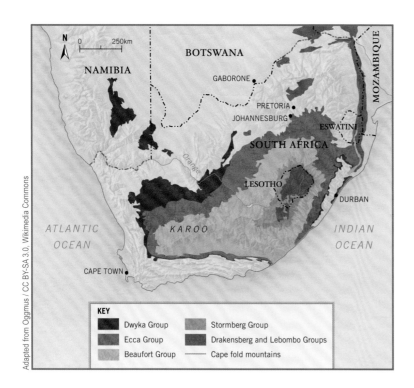

KEY

Dwyka Group	Stormberg Group
Ecca Group	Drakensberg and Lebombo Groups
Beaufort Group	— Cape fold mountains

The shale and sandstone strata of the Karoo Supergroup. The oldest deposits are represented by the Dwyka Group, with the overlying rock layers getting progressively younger towards the Drakensberg Mountains. The Beaufort Group is particularly rich in archaic mammals (therapsids) and in the reptilian progenitors of the bird lineage.

on them. Therapsids are often incorrectly called 'mammal-like reptiles'; they are not reptiles, but the ancestors of the true mammals. Their fossils are recorded today, in stunning diversity, in the rock layers that cover the Ecca rocks, namely the Beaufort and the Stormberg groups. Younger rocks, the Drakensberg Group, which overlay the Stormberg Group, are not considered part of the Karoo Supergroup, but they contain fossils that nevertheless represent the most recent chapter of the story of mammal and bird evolution.

The Permian Period extended from 299 to 252 million years ago. The climate during the Early Permian was cool and dry, an ice-age condition inherited from the Late Carboniferous Period. The giant glacier that covered those parts of Pangaea that lay over the South Pole essentially captured much of the Earth's water, causing sea levels to subside and the interior of the enormous continent to become arid. By the Late Permian, about 260 million years ago, the Karoo Basin had drifted north to approximately 60 degrees south. Following the cooler,

on Earth, and the Karoo fossils provide better insight into what happened than any other fossil site on Earth.[1] It also tells part of the story of how true mammals evolved from their synapsid ancestors – the stem synapsids ('pelycosaurs') and the therapsids – and how birds evolved from dinosaurs.

The Karoo Basin was formed about 320 million years ago when there was still only one giant continent on Earth: Pangaea. At that time the Karoo lay over the South Pole, so it was a very cold place covered with a giant glacier. The glacier deposited tillites (unsorted debris) on the basin floor, which became the basement of the Karoo Supergroup formation, known today as the Dwyka Group. The Karoo Basin was formed about 290 million years ago when, through continental drift, the Falklands Plateau crashed into the African continent in the south and threw up the Cape fold mountains, isolating the Karoo Basin from the Paleo-Pacific Ocean. Africa started to drift northwards into warmer latitudes and the Karoo Basin turned into a vast inland sea with extensive swamps on its northern shores.

The plant material surrounding the swamps, especially that of the tree *Glossopteris*, eventually became the coal deposits of the Ecca Group, which today overlays the Dwyka Group. *Glossopteris* was a very important food source for the large herbivores of the Permian. These herbivores were therapsids and they roamed the shores of the Karoo swamps with therapsid carnivores that preyed

Glossopteris was the most important food plant for the herbivorous therapsids, or large herbivores, of the Permian. *Glossopteris* trees, and the herbivores that fed on them, were the victims of the mass extinction at the boundary of the Permian and the Triassic about 252 million years ago.

wetter conditions of the Early Permian, the climate had shifted to a variation of hot and cold, with arid woodlands and deserts becoming a feature of the landscape. By this time, Pangaea had yet to split into the southern continent Gondwana and the northern continent Laurasia – an event that occurred later, during the Triassic, and which eventually led to the formation of the modern continents.

Glossopteris trees dominated the woodland areas of the Late Permian, and plants such as horsetails (*Phyllotheca*), creeping ground covers such as *Trizygia*, and cycads and ferns formed the understorey. Unlike the vegetation that characterises the Nama-Karoo today, no grasses existed during the Late Permian.

'Pelycosaur' stem synapsids

The Early Permian climate favoured the emergence of land-based vertebrates from their slimy, aquatic stem amphibian ancestors that dominated the Carboniferous swamps. These were the stem synapsids, also known as pelycosaurs; they were the earliest members of the mammalian lineage. Adaptations that allowed tetrapods (four-legged vertebrates) to inhabit dry land evolved for the first time in the stem amphibians, and were passed on to the stem synapsids via a common ancestor. These were the critical first steps towards 'mammalness'.[2] Stem synapsids possessed a waterproof body, which was made possible by keratin-lipid complexes in the outer layers of the skin. Their eggs – bigger than stem amphibian eggs – were also waterproof and could be laid on land. They could walk on land in a sprawling gait with forward-pointing hands and feet, the gait facilitated by the ossification and modification of the bones in the hands and feet. They could do push-ups. Some were herbivorous (Caseidae), a trend that originated in the stem amphibians (Diadectidae). Eating land-based plants required a large vat-like space somewhere in the digestive tract for fermentation to take place. The Caseidae had small heads perched upon huge barrel-like bodies with expanded ribs to accommodate the fermentation chamber that probably resided in the large intestine – as it does today in hindgut fermenters such as horses.

Most stem synapsid fossils occur in Europe and North America, but the youngest ones are found in the Karoo Basin. The Varanopidae were another family that looked very much like modern-day monitor lizards. *Elliotsmithia*

Matt Celeskey/Studio 252MYA / 252mya.com

Heleosaurus was a slender, lizard-like varanopid from the Middle Permian. It had bone deposits in the skin, presumably to serve as body armour. Fossils of this lizard were found in the Abrahamskraal Formation (deposited 268 to 259 million years ago) near Victoria West.

was a small carnivorous varanopid discovered in 1917 near the Karoo town of Prince Albert. This stem synapsid was one of the few that co-existed with the earliest therapsids, the descendants of the stem synapsids, in the Middle Permian. The therapsids evolved from a sister stem synapsid group, the Sphenacodontidae. Another varanopid, *Heleosaurus*, was collected from the same rock layer near Fraserburg in 1995. It occurred as an aggregation of an adult and four juveniles, which Jennifer Botha-Brink and colleague Sean Modesto have suggested provides the earliest evidence of parental care in the synapsids.[3]

The therapsids

As the climate of the Permian became warmer and more arid, the therapsids started to dominate the landscape, driving most stem synapsid families to extinction. One of the earliest therapsid suborders was Dinocephalia, which included herbivorous, omnivorous and carnivorous species. The herbivorous and omnivorous species were enormous. Some herbivores, such as *Tapinocephalus* ('tumble head'), recovered from the lower Beaufort beds of the Karoo, weighed as much as 2,000 kilograms, about the same as a black rhino. These head-butting beasts were so common that the geological (stratigraphic) layers in which their remains occur were named the *Tapinocephalus* Assemblage Zone. The common carnivorous dinocephalian in the Karoo was *Titanosuchus* ('fierce Titan crocodile').

As large as a black rhino, 'tumble heads' (*Tapinocephalus*) were among the first giant herbivorous proto-mammals to emerge in the Permian. They dominated the Karoo landscape – so much so that a geological stratum is named after them, the *Tapinocephalus* Assemblage Zone (deposited between 265 and 259 million years ago).

Ultimately, the Late Permian herbivorous dicynodonts (Dicynodontia) replaced the dinocephalian herbivores. These therapsids are so named because they exhibited two canine-like teeth, with some species having had an arrangement of post-canine grinding teeth too. They possessed tough, bony beaks, much like those of tortoises and turtles, which they used to tear off mouthfuls of their plant food before passing it backwards to the grinding teeth. They occurred in an extraordinary diversity of sizes, from small and mole-like to giants the size of an elephant. They survived from the Middle Permian and throughout the Triassic, but had their heyday during the Late Permian. However, some dicynodonts, such as *Lystrosaurus*, are well known for having survived the Permo–Triassic extinction and having gone on to numerically dominate the Karoo Basin during the Early Triassic.

Dicynodonts shared their dominance of the Late Permian with other therapsids, the gorgonopsids, which preyed upon them and the last of the dinocephalians. The gorgonopsids had teeth, and very impressive ones too. The meanest and most powerful gorgonopsid, though not the biggest, was *Rubidgea*, which exhibited canines that were apparently longer than the teeth of *Tyrannosaurus rex*. *Rubidgea*, along with all other gorgonopsids, did not survive the Permo–Triassic extinction event.

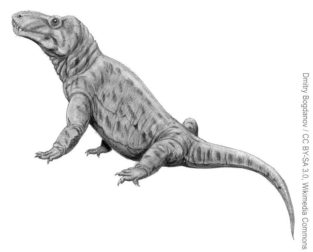

An early therapsid, *Titanosuchus* was the largest dinocephalian carnivore of the Permian in the Karoo Basin.

The herbivorous *Lystrosaurus* (Dicynodontia), an iconic Karoo therapsid, survived the mass extinction at the end of the Permian 252 million years ago. Four species have been described from the Karoo Basin: two larger-bodied species from the Late Permian and two smaller-bodied species from the Early Triassic. So common was it in the Early Triassic that the *Lystrosaurus* Assemblage Zone (deposited between 251 and 249 million years ago) bears its name.

Moschorhinus kitchingi was a carnivorous therapsid from the Late Permian that, like *Lystrosaurus*, survived the Permo–Triassic mass extinction and also underwent a size reduction in the process – from the size of a lion in the Late Permian to a much smaller size in the Early Triassic.

The therocephalians (Therocephalia), another carnivorous therapsid group, also emerged in the Middle Permian. They resembled the gorgonopsids in a number of ways, and many species sported large canines. Most, however, also went extinct at the Permo–Triassic boundary. This group is highly significant in terms of the evolutionary history of mammals because it gave rise to a sister therapsid group, the cynodonts (Cynodontia), which in turn led to the emergence of the true mammals. One species that did survive the mass extinction event was *Moschorhinus kitchingi*, and its fossils have provided valuable insights into how some therapsids persisted into the Triassic. To tell this story, though, we need to understand what happened to the climate during and towards the end of the Permian, and how it fuelled the extinction event and life thereafter.

The Rubidge legacy

The nucleus of Karoo palaeontological research in South Africa at the turn of the twentieth century centred on the activities of a sheep farm in the Karoo, close to Nieu Bethesda. A descendant of 1820 British settler stock, Richard Rubidge developed the farm Wellwood, which has gone on to become an outstanding merino stock farm. In addition to farming, his son Sidney Rubidge maintained a life-long passion for vertebrate palaeontology. Today, Sidney's grandson Bruce Rubidge continues that legacy, as the director of the Evolutionary Studies Institute at the University of the Witwatersrand.

It is not surprising that Sidney and Bruce Rubidge became interested in the remains of prehistoric animals: Wellwood and the surrounding farms are literally built on the fossils of the ancestors of mammals and birds – the archaic synapsids (therapsids) and sauropsids (archosauriforms).

The farm's most famous frequent visitor was the palaeontologist Robert Broom (see box, page 229). Although Broom collected many fossils in the region, he was not permitted by Sidney Rubidge to remove any remains found on Wellwood. Today, the fossils unearthed on the farm are neatly catalogued and

Dinogorgon rubidgei

arranged in a farm barn. This collection is the largest and most valuable private collection of archaic mammal fossils in the world.

In recognition of Sidney Rubidge's contribution to vertebrate palaeontology, Broom named many species in his honour, including three species of gorgonopsids – *Dinogorgon rubidgei*, *Clelandina rubidgei* and *Rubidgea atrox* – in the subfamily Rubidgeinae, which he described. This subfamily includes the genus *Rubidgea*. It is an apt homage to this remarkable family.

Clelandina rubidgei

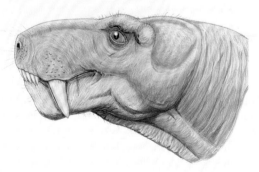

Rubidgea atrox

Besides the proto-sauropods, early representatives of the ornithischian dinosaurs occur in the Early Jurassic Elliot formations. The most notable of these is *Heterodontosaurus tucki*. As its name infers, this small, turkey-sized bipedal dinosaur had different teeth. Unlike most dinosaurs that tend to have had homodont teeth, that is, similar, peg-like teeth, *Heterodontosaurus* displayed distinct cone-shaped front teeth, similar to incisors in the upper jaw, canine-like tusks in the upper and lower jaws, and chisel-like hind teeth in both jaws. These teeth were lined with thick enamel on their inner surfaces to withstand wear associated with a vegetarian diet. The front of the jaws was covered with a keratinous 'beak'. *Heterodontosaurus* may also have been one of the earliest dinosaurs to display structures that resemble spines on the head and back; these may have been the precursors of the feathers seen in later theropod dinosaurs. Two other small, bipedal heterodontosaurids from the Upper Elliot Formation are *Lycorhinus* and *Abrictosaurus*.

Other non-heterodontosaurid ornithischian dinosaurs that have been unearthed in the Upper Elliot Formation include *Eocursor* and *Lesothosaurus*, two fast-running herbivorous/omnivorous small dinosaurs, both of which weighed less than 40 kilograms each.

Fossils of the third major dinosaur lineage, the Theropoda – bipedal, carnivorous dinosaurs that gave rise to the modern birds – also occur in the Upper Elliot Formation. *Dracovenator* takes its name from the Drakensberg Mountains near which it was found. The word *draken* means 'dragon' in Afrikaans. *Dracovenator* was a medium-sized dinosaur that weighed about 400 kilograms and would have preyed on the high diversity of proto-sauropods of the Early Jurassic.

The most famous theropod dinosaur, though, is *Coelophysis*, as it was one of the first dinosaurs to be described more than a hundred years ago. It was a fast runner and weighed up to 20 kilograms. Apart from the fossils discovered in the Elliot Formation, fossils of this dinosaur have also been found in New Mexico.

The third major group of dinosaurs is the Theropoda, the bipedal lineage that gave rise to the birds. One theropod from the Stormberg Group is *Dracovenator regenti*, a medium-sized carnivorous, bipedal dinosaur that weighed about 400 kilograms. It is named after the Drakensberg Mountains. Here it is depicted hunting *Heterodontosaurus*.

Another theropod discovered in the Karoo Stormberg Group is *Coelophysis*, one the earliest-known dinosaur genera also found extensively in North America. It was a small, highly nimble, fast, bipedal dinosaur, and it bore the ground plan for what was to become the modern bird.

Mammals and dinosaurs of the Karoo Basin

In summary, in the mammalian lineage, the fossils of the Karoo Basin tell the unbroken story of the evolution of mammals, from the earliest stem synapsids of the Permian right up until the emergence what was almost a true mammal, *Megazastrodon*. They explain how the stem mammals successfully invaded dry land after evolving from their slimy, stem-amphibian, swamp-dwelling ancestors of the Carboniferous. They reveal how the stem synapsids and large-bodied therapsids that dominated the landscapes of the Permian became more waterproof, showed vast improvements in locomotion and feeding efficiency, could digest plants for the first time, and possibly displayed the first signs of the ability to produce their own internal heat (endothermy). The mammal story traverses the Permo–Triassic extinction, documenting how large-bodied therapsids went extinct, and how the smaller generalist dicynodont therapsids such as *Lystrosaurus* went on to dominate the hot, dry Early Triassic. After the early dominance of small dicynodonts, larger species evolved in lower diversity in the Middle Triassic and managed to survive until the end of the Triassic when the elephant-sized *Lisowicia bojani* went extinct in Poland. But the success story of the mammals is the cynodonts; it was this group that persisted throughout the Triassic to give rise to the mammaliaforms, such

as *Megazastrodon,* one of our immediate mammalian ancestors, and took the mammalian lineage into the Jurassic to compete with the dinosaurs. Had they not, we would not exist.

The evolution of the sauropsid lineage that led to the birds is not as dramatic in the Permian, merely because of the supreme dominance of the therapsids. Nevertheless, the large-bodied anapsid pareiasaurs did make an impression in the Permian. However, the diapsid sauropsids made their mark only after the extinction of so many large-bodied herbivorous and carnivorous therapsids at the Permo–Triassic and Triassic–Jurassic boundaries. These extinctions allowed archosauromorphs and archosaurs to occupy the niches vacated by extinct therapsids and to go on to completely dominate the Jurassic and the Cretaceous. The Triassic–Jurassic boundary dramatically documents how the Early Jurassic favoured the radiation of the progenitors of the sauropod, ornithischian and theropod dinosaurs.

So, the Karoo Basin tells the story of the early evolution of the lineages that led to the birds and mammals better than anywhere else on the planet. It is such a pity, though, that South Africa has been so sluggish in recognising and promoting this unique assemblage of life in the Ancient Karoo outside of the palaeontological literature. Its dramatic story has, unfortunately, been eclipsed by the intense international interest in the rich collection of South African hominids that date back only six or so million years.

The future of the deserts

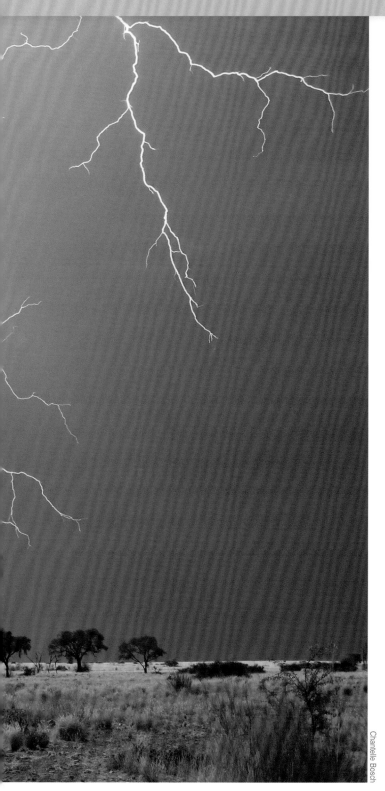

Above: The crimson-breasted shrike (*Laniarius atrococcineus*) typifies the many birds that will be affected by global heating in the Kalahari Desert.

Left: A rare, spectacular thunderstorm broke out over the Namib Desert in the late summer of 2021. The above-average rainfall recorded during this time, which ended a nine-year drought, was probably due to a strong La Niña.

When I wrote this chapter in the first edition of *Living Deserts* there was minimal public awareness about global heating and El Niño. But in the 27 years since its publication it is astonishing how much has been learned and observed about these two devastating climate effects. Global heating is destined to change the deserts of southern Africa in the future more than any other factor.

There is no doubting the unique nature of southern Africa's four desert biomes, but the Succulent Karoo, in particular, is the only recognised desert diversity hotspot in the world. It is the origin of the succulent mesembs, some of which have spread naturally to other continents.[1, 2]

Yet, as we shall see, this is a desert that faces the greatest threats from global heating. I never thought that I would live to see the predictions of climate change models come true, but in the Succulent Karoo I have seen it happening, and it is stupefying. However, before I discuss the impacts of climate change, let us focus first on the conservation status of the region's deserts.

Conservation

Southern Africa's four desert biomes harbour an unusually high richness of plant and animal species, so it is important to enquire whether this wealth is being adequately conserved. In essence, we need to ask whether sufficient conservation areas have been identified and acquired in each biome to preserve the greatest possible diversity of organisms that live there. While pundit conservationists may claim that the question is too simplistic, arguing that the preservation of biodiversity is overemphasised at the expense of ecosystem form, structure and function, we still need to know more about the biomes to be able to identify what to protect and for what reason. Initially, we had little option but to use the geographical distribution of species as a basis for conservation management, whereby priorities were determined by the percentage area of the veld type or distribution range conserved and the number of threatened species per unit area.[3] However, the techniques

Community game guards at the Otjimboyo Conservancy in Namibia play a pivotal role in protecting local wildlife.

used today are much more holistic in their approach to identifying those biodiversity hotspots that can feasibly be acquired and conserved. Moreover, there is the additional challenge of deciding whether conservation areas will be able to accommodate distribution shifts – probably latitudinal and altitudinal – of plants and animals in response to climate change. An area that may adequately conserve a suite of species now may no longer do so by the end of the century. Today there are two trends to conservation in southern Africa: state effort and growing private involvement. Let us examine how these responses are unfolding in southern Africa's desert biomes.

Desert Biome

The Desert Biome enjoys an above-average conservation status with more than 44 per cent of its land area under state, community or private conservation management. This is a remarkably high percentage by any standards, and reflects the low productivity and unsuitability for agriculture of much of the biome, which spans a zone that receives less than 100 millimetres of rainfall per year.

The largest areas of conserved land in the biome are the Namib-Naukluft National Park, which was officially proclaimed in 1979, and the Tsau ‖Khaeb National Park, which was established in 2004. The Tsau ‖Khaeb, which lies to the south of the Namib-Naukluft park, incorporates the large expanse known as Diamond Area No. 1, or the *Sperrgebiet* ('forbidden area' in German). Public entry into the *Sperrgebiet* is strictly controlled. The other conservation area in the Namib Desert is the Skeleton Coast National Park, a strip of coastal desert about 40 kilometres wide that stretches from about 180 kilometres north of Swakopmund to the Kunene River at Namibia's border with Angola.

Not only do these conservation areas provide sanctuary to vulnerable and rare mammals such as the brown hyena, Hartmann's mountain zebra and the black rhino, but their continued existence and management also protect one of the world's oldest and most remarkable deserts.

There are vast regions of the Namib Desert – and other biomes in Namibia – over which conservation management has been devolved to local communities following Namibia's establishment of the Community-based Natural Resource Management programme (CBNRM) in 1996. In the Desert Biome, the most well known of these are the vast wilderness areas of Damaraland and Kaokoland bordering the eastern flank of the Skeleton Coast National Park in the northwestern Namib Desert. Here, populations of desert black rhinos and elephants still roam free and there is no controlled access to most of the area. Poaching in this remote corner of Namibia was rife during the South African border war in the 1980s and elephant and rhino populations were decimated. However, the populations have since recovered, mostly due to the tireless efforts of two nongovernmental organisations: Save the Rhino Trust, a public charity organisation founded by Blythe Loutit and established in 1982, and the Integrated Rural Development and Nature Conservation (IRDNC) scheme, initiated through the dedicated efforts of Garth Owen-Smith, Margaret Jacobsohn and others.

In 1998 the 3,522-square-kilometre Torra Conservancy was established and has become, arguably, a successful model for community-based conservation globally. The scheme follows the philosophy that the future preservation of wildlife in Damaraland and Kaokoland is only possible if the regions' natural resources are exploited to the benefit of local communities. Garth Owen-Smith argued that the local people can derive financial reward from sustainable initiatives, mostly in ecotourism but also trophy hunting and controlled hunting for meat, the latter driven by their own efforts to eradicate poaching and their expert knowledge of the terrain and the animals that live there. In this respect, he suggested that local inhabitants should play the primary conservation roles in their immediate regions in order to safeguard their own resources and futures. The scheme claims that the 'IRDNC exists to facilitate and empower rural communities in Namibia and adjacent countries to manage and utilize wildlife and other natural resources sustainably, as the foundation of rural economies, biodiversity conservation and strong local governance institutions. This has been done primarily through community conservancies, a unique Namibian system that grants communities legal rights over wildlife, including all revenues generated by tourism and sustainable utilization.'[4]

Today the Torra Conservancy employs and coordinates the monitoring activities of dedicated trackers from the local communities who know virtually every individual rhino that wanders throughout the conservancy. There are 82 such community conservancies

Viktoria Keding

Based at the NamibRand Nature Reserve, the Namib Desert Environmental Education Trust introduces schoolchildren to the world of conservation.

throughout Namibia, not only in the Desert Biome. As mentioned later, another important community conservancy in the Arid Savanna Biome in Namibia is the Nyae Nyae Conservancy on the southern border of the Khaudum National Park.

In addition to the state reserves and community conservancies, there are two new, privately owned reserves that have been established since the last edition of *Living Deserts*: the NamibRand Nature Reserve and the Oana Nature Reserve.

NamibRand Nature Reserve conserves 2,021 square kilometres of the Pro-Namib and is continuous with the Namib Sand Sea, a UNESCO World Heritage Site, within the Namib-Naukluft National Park. It is an indescribably beautiful place, perhaps my favourite of all southern African desert landscapes, embracing dunes and sandy plains, inselbergs and mountains, gravel plains, and the interface between sand and gravel plains. It is an exclusive reserve, committed to high-quality, low-impact tourism. However, it does offer a valuable service to the Namibian community in the form of a very active environmental education centre where schoolchildren are introduced to conservation and sustainable living.

Hot-air ballooning is one of the exclusive activities available in the NamibRand Nature Reserve, a vital grazing corridor for wildlife in the Pro-Namib to the west of the Namib dune sea.

The conservation management plan of NamibRand includes yearly game counts and, when necessary, the capture and sale of live game. For example, the 2019 census counted 3,200 gemsbok and 12,400 springbok in the reserve, which is also home to Burchell's zebra (reintroduced), Hartmann's mountain zebra, red hartebeest, giraffe (reintroduced), and all of the smaller desert ungulates, as well as all major desert-dwelling carnivores except lions. The NamibRand Nature Reserve is also a member of the Greater Sossusvlei-Namib Landscape (GSNL) association, whose vision is to conserve the landscape and biodiversity of the Pro-Namib. This type of protection is important, not only because of the sand dune sea, but also because the region's gravel plains provide the annual grasses that sustain its herbivores after rains. For the most part, remember, fog-dependent plants are the only alternative sources of herbage in the region.

Another interesting new reserve in the very early stages of development, currently with minimal infrastructure, is Oana Nature Reserve on the northern bank of the Orange River in Namibia, close to the town of Warmbad. Although I have yet to see a formal biological assessment of Oana, from my visit there I would probably describe it as ecotonal, that is, a zone of transition – where biomes meet and overlap – between the Desert, Nama-Karoo and Succulent Karoo biomes. Like NamibRand Nature Reserve, it was once a series of

Located along the Orange River's northern bank is the rugged and extremely arid Oana Nature Reserve.

sheep farms whose fences have been taken down. It is an extremely arid reserve of 1,100 square kilometres and is exposed to an ensemble of highly unpredictable and limited winter and summer rains. With the increasing manifestation of climate change, especially the demise of the winter rainfall in the northerly parts, sheep farming has become unprofitable in the region, and neighbouring farmers are being encouraged to add their farms to the reserve. The vision of Oana is that wildlife and adventure tourism can provide economic stability

Newly established, Oana Nature Reserve is run from a temporary tented centre of operations.

The banks and the islands of the Orange River are badly invaded by mesquite trees.

to both local farmers and the local community in nearby Warmbad. At the moment the reserve harbours herds of Hartmann's mountain zebra, gemsbok, hartebeest, and the smaller desert-dwelling ungulates. It has a healthy population of leopards and smaller desert carnivores. One of Oana's major challenges will be the eradication of the highly invasive mesquite (*Prosopis*) trees that have formed an impenetrable wall along the banks of the Orange River and have smothered the indigenous riverine trees.[5, 6]

Succulent Karoo Biome

Much progress has been achieved in identifying and acquiring conservation areas in the florally diverse Succulent Karoo Biome since the first edition of *Living Deserts*. Moreover, the various approaches have been groundbreaking, innovative and scientifically astute.

The Richtersveld National Park (now part of the Ai-|Ais/Richtersveld Transfrontier Park) was established in 1991 after many decades of negotiation between the local Nama farmers and the then National Parks Board (now South African National Parks, or SANParks). Situated on the southern bank of the Orange River in Namaqualand, the park plays a crucial role in the conservation of many mountain succulent endemics, the most conspicuous of which are the halfmens, bastard quiver tree, maiden's quiver tree (*Aloidendron ramosissima*) and *Aloe pearsonii*.[7] Excluding azonal riverine vegetation units, the park conserves nine vegetation units* within the Richtersveld Bioregion: Central Richtersveld Mountain Shrubland (SKr 1), Northern Richtersveld Scorpionstailveld (SKr 7), Rosyntjieberg Succulent Shrubland (SKr 8), and Tatasberg Mountain Succulent Shrubland (SKr 9). In addition, it conserves five vegetation units within the Gariep Desert Bioregion of the Desert Biome: Noms Mountain Desert (Dg 1), Richtersberg Mountain Desert (Dg 2), Richtersveld Sheet Wash Desert (Dg 3), Kwaggarug Mountain Desert (Dg 4), and Kahams Mountain Desert (Dg 5).

The transfrontier park was unique in its original conceptualisation because for the first time in South African conservation history local inhabitants and their domestic livestock were *not excluded* from land set aside for protection. There is good evidence that the Nama people have been living in the area for at least 2,000 years, practising what is called a transhumant lifestyle.[8, 9] This nomadic lifestyle involves the annual movement of livestock – usually three or four times a year – between summer and winter grazing areas and the erection of seasonal camps.

---

* The codes provided in this chapter correspond with the vegetation units identified in *The Vegetation of South Africa, Lesotho and Swaziland* by Ladislav Mucina and Mike Rutherford (2006), referred to in Chapter One. The book can be downloaded at www.sanbi.org/news/national-vegetation-map-chapters-available-for-download/. Readers can use it to identify and read more about vegetation units wherever they may find themselves.

Andrew Hall / CC BY-SA 3.0, Wikimedia Commons

Left: Nama herders have occupied the northern regions of South Africa for more than 2,000 years. This cave at the mouth of the Spoeg River in Namaqualand has served as a shelter for transhumant Nama. **Above:** A characteristic Nama hut made with reed mats, known as a |*haru oms*, and a sheep enclosure in the shade of a shepherd's tree typify a temporary Nama herder's camp in the Richtersveld Cultural and Botanical Landscape.

Established in 1999, the Namaqua National Park protects the Strandveld vegetation of the Succulent Karoo Biome.

In 2003 the Ai-|Ais/Richtersveld Transfrontier Park was established jointly by South Africa and Namibia. The existing Richtersveld National Park was amalgamated with vast tracts of land surrounding the Fish River Canyon in southern Namibia, including the Ai-Ais hot springs. A new river border crossing in the form of a floating pontoon was established at Sendelingsdrif, the entrance to the old Richtersveld National Park.

About 1,600 square kilometres in size, the Richtersveld Cultural and Botanical Landscape is a large, mountainous region to the south of the Ai-|Ais/Richtersveld Transfrontier Park in South Africa. It is communally owned and managed by the Nama people. In recognition of the unique culture of the Nama people, the conservancy has been designated a UNESCO World Heritage Site.

The Succulent Karoo Biome has benefited from the establishment of four critically important conservation areas over the past few decades: Namaqua National Park, Goegap Nature Reserve, Oorlogskloof Nature Reserve, and the budding Knersvlakte Nature Reserve.

The Namaqua National Park (1,300 square kilometres) was gazetted in 1999 and today stretches from the Kamieskroon area, near the main highway running from South Africa to Namibia (N7), to the Atlantic Ocean coast. It was centred originally on the farm Skilpad, whose old ploughed fields produce fantastic displays of annuals during winter. Farms to the west of Skilpad were added to create a corridor to link up with a relatively unspoilt coastal strip, between the mouths of the Groen and Spoeg rivers, which is leased by SANParks from the De Beers Group. The park now also conserves Coastal Strandveld (SKs 7, SKs 8), Namaqualand Heuweltjieveld (Skn 4) and Klipkoppe Shrubland (SKn 1). The component of Strandveld that has been included is important because, prior to the establishment of the park, a mere 9,43 square kilometres was conserved, representing less than one percent of the area covered by Sandveld.

Perhaps the most botanically important of all reserve initiatives in Namaqualand concerns the massive effort that has been involved in identifying and acquiring land to conserve the Knersvlakte, just north of Vanrhynsdorp. At present, the Knersvlakte Nature Reserve covers 850 square kilometres and conserves about 1,500 species of which 190 are endemic. These are extraordinary statistics of floral biodiversity for such a relatively small parcel of Namaqualand. The reserve is owned by the South African branch of the World Wide Fund for Nature (WWF) and is managed by CapeNature. It conserves several vegetation units in the Knersvlakte Bioregion, especially Northern Knersvlakte Vygieveld (SKk 1), Central Knersvlakte Vygieveld (SKk 2), Knersvlakte Quartz Vygieveld (SKk 3), Knersvlakte Shale Vygieveld (SKk 4) and Vanrhynsdorp Gannabosveld (SKk 5). The reserve was established in 2014 but, at the time of writing, was yet to be opened to the public. Sadly, 155 species within the reserve are threatened with extinction, in part from climate change and very active poaching.

The Knersvlakte Nature Reserve in Namaqualand is dominated by light-coloured quartz stones that reflect radiation from the sun, helping to keep ground temperatures a few degrees cooler than in other parts of the region. This has contributed to the extraordinarily high diversity of ground-hugging mesembs, such as *Lithops,* and *Argyroderma,* found on the Knersvlakte.

A gemsbok lingers in the ancient Nossob riverbed in the Kgalagadi Transfrontier Park.

Sara & Joachim Huber-Schwegler

Burchell's zebra slake their thirst at a waterhole in Etosha National Park.

an area of nearly 100,000 square kilometres and was the largest natural reserve in the world. However, in 1967 its size was dramatically reduced to make way for tribal trustlands, and today it covers an area of about 23,000 square kilometres surrounding the vast Etosha Pan. The park provides refuge to most of the large predators, including lion, spotted hyena, cheetah and leopard, as well as large herbivores such as elephant and black rhino. It is the only reserve in southern Africa in which the Damara dik-dik is protected, and is also home to the subcontinent's second largest population of blue wildebeest. When the pan contains sufficient water, it is one of the few breeding grounds in southern Africa for greater and lesser flamingoes.

The Etosha National Park and the Kgalagadi Transfrontier Park complement each other well as representatives of the Arid Savanna Biome: the former's broad-leaved mopane vegetation and the latter's fine-leaved acacia woodland are both typical of the biome. Unfortunately, the Etosha National Park, large as it is, cannot embrace all of the unusually high number of vertebrates that are endemic to the ecotone between this broad-leaved savanna and the Desert and Nama-Karoo biomes (see Chapter One). For example, no fewer than

eight bird species – violet wood hoopoe (*Phoeniculus damarensis*), rockrunner (*Achaetops pycnopygius*), Rüppell's parrot (*Poicephalus rueppellii*), Carp's tit (*Parus carpi*), bare-cheeked babbler (*Turdoides gymnogenys*), white-tailed shrike (*Lanioturdus torquatus*), Monteiro's hornbill (*Tockus monteiri*) and Herero chat (*Melaenornis herero*) – are found only in this northern arid region of Namibia, but not all necessarily occur within the park. At least two – the white-tailed shrike and the Herero chat – are found more typically in arid mountainous regions rather than in the flat woodland that surrounds the Etosha Pan. There is also a total of 21 reptile species that are endemic either to the broad-leaved savanna or to the northwestern corner of Namibia, a region that encompasses sections of the Desert, Nama-Karoo and Arid Savanna biomes.

The huge 52,800-square-kilometre Central Kalahari Game Reserve (CKGR), the second-largest game reserve in the world, was established in 1961 in Botswana, primarily to preserve the hunter-gatherer lifestyle of the San who have lived there for thousands of years. Its northern border is the Kuke veterinary fence, responsible for the ongoing deaths of thousands of migrating wildebeest (see Chapter Seven). The management of the reserve has been extremely controversial, especially following the forced removal of three-quarters of the San population and the withdrawal of vital services such as water in 1997 by the Botswana government.[11] In terms of its ecology and species composition, the reserve is very similar to the Kgalagadi Transfrontier Park.

There are several community conservancies in the Arid Savanna in Namibia, of which the Nyae Nyae Conservancy, mentioned earlier, is unquestionably the most newsworthy. Nyae Nyae was established to provide a sanctuary for the Ju/'hoan San. It is the oldest conservancy in Namibia; its origins can be traced to the 1950s, but it was only gazetted in 1998. The Botswana border constitutes its western boundary, whereas other community and conservation areas form its borders to the south (Ondjou Conservancy, 8,729 square kilometres), west (N≠a-Jaqna Conservancy, 9,120 square kilometres), and north (Khaudum National Park, 3,842 square kilometres). There is very limited fencing between these big-five conservation areas and eight other neighbouring community conservation areas, so collectively they potentially conserve a vast region of game-rich Arid Savanna Biome. Trophy hunting is an important activity as the region is well known for the large size of its elephant bulls.

The biggest privately owned reserve in the Arid Savanna is Tswalu Kalahari Reserve (1,140 square kilometres) near Van Zylsrus in the Northern Cape. It conserves three Arid Savanna vegetation units: Olifantshoek Plains Thornveld (SVk 13), Gordonia Plains Shrubland (SVk 16) and Gordonia Duneveld (SVkd 1). The park has an interesting history. Stephen Boler was an English entrepreneur who turned his attention to conservation in South Africa towards the end of his business career. He bought dozens of farms and amalgamated them into a single reserve that is now the Tswalu reserve. Boler died quite unexpectedly of a heart attack in 1998 at the early age of 55. In his will he specified that the South African businessman Nicky Oppenheimer should have first refusal on the purchase of Tswalu. Nicky did not hesitate. Today the Oppenheimer family – led by the vision of Nicky's wife, Strilli, his son Jonathan, and Jonathan's late wife, Jennifer – has developed Tswalu into the most important privately owned game reserve in Africa, certainly in terms of conservation and research. Tswalu has an excellent management plan carried out by a well-trained staff of managers, rangers, guides and researchers. One unique aspect of Tswalu is its excellent medical clinic, which serves not only the reserve's 200 employees, but also the wider community, at no charge.

Euphorbia avasmontana grow on the quartz hills of Tswalu Kalahari Reserve, adding to the diversity of the duneveld.

The privately owned Tswalu Kalahari Reserve conserves a unique combination of Kalahari dune fields and ancient quartz hills.

Tswalu's *Terminalia sericea* trees grow predominantly on dune crests, demonstrating their preference for deep sandy soils.

One important consequence of the easterly trade winds generated by the Hadley cells is that they blow surface seawater from the west coast of southern Africa towards the west, that is, towards South America, across the Atlantic Ocean. The surface waters are replaced by cold water from the deep in a process, known as upwelling. Indeed, upwelling occurs along the west coasts of all Southern Hemisphere continents. These upwelled waters are very rich in nutrients, so when the water gets exposed to sunlight as it approaches the sea surface, massive phyto- and zooplankton blooms are generated. These feed some of the richest fisheries in the world. However, when the easterly trade winds weaken, or even reverse their direction, the surface waters that were blown westwards, now well heated by the tropical sun, slosh back again across the Atlantic towards the west coast and suppress the upwelling. The sea temperature increases dramatically, causing large changes in atmospheric pressure across the Atlantic Ocean. These are called El Niño events, and their consequences for inter-annual patterns of rainfall in southern Africa are profound and severe. The resulting fluctuations in atmospheric pressure across the Atlantic are called the El Niño Southern Oscillations (ENSO). It is the key warning index used to predict El Niño and La Niña events in the Southern Hemisphere. La Niña is the cold phase of these oscillations.

With the seasonal movement of the Intertropical Convergence Zone (ITCZ) (the low-pressure equatorial rainbelt), as the Earth circles the sun on its tilted axis, the position of the southern Hadley cell moves south in summer and north in winter. The high-pressure subtropical ridge of the Hadley cells is what makes Cape summers so charming and the east coasts wet and humid. It displaces the westerly storm tracks to the south, terminating winter rainfall. But the southward shift of the Hadley subtropical ridge in summer also allows moist air to be carried into the interior of southern Africa from the Indian Ocean by the southeasterly trade winds to generate summer rain over the eastern parts of southern Africa. During winter, though, the Hadley cells are displaced to the north, allowing the westerly storm tracks to brush the southwestern tip of the African continent and supply winter rain, whereas the subtropical ridge sits over the interior of southern Africa, sustaining dry winter conditions.

There is a lot of natural variation in these patterns on decagonal scales (for example, changes caused by El Niño) and longer timescales (for example, changes

caused by the Ice Ages and Glacial Periods). Currently, though, anthropogenic global heating is having a profound effect on the Hadley cells, causing them to expand southwards as the Antarctic Ice Sheet gets smaller. In other words, the high-pressure subtropical ridge is being displaced to the south. This shift displaces the westerly storm tracks to the south as well, even in winter, bringing less winter rainfall to southwestern Africa, especially in southern Namibia and Namaqualand. Moreover, the southward displacement of the westerlies causes what is called 'Agulhas leakage', in which parcels of warm water from the Agulhas Current, which flows down the east coast of southern Africa, 'leak' into the west coast current system and elevate sea temperatures.[27] This supresses the upwelling of cold water, thus mimicking El Niño events.[28]

An Ice Age is a long period within a Glacial Period during which the Earth's temperature is reduced and ice sheets at the poles and alpine glaciers expand. During the Last Glacial Maximum, about 26,500 years ago, the last time that the Earth was covered by much ice at the poles and in glaciers, the climate was vastly different to what it is today. On average, it was about 6°C colder, the sea level was 125 metres lower, and it was a lot more arid. The deserts of the world, including those in southern Africa, were more expansive.

Forsaken: floral consequences for the Succulent Karoo

It was the new combination of winter rainfall and aridity that sparked the rapid diversification of the succulent Aizoaceae – the ice plants that glorify the Succulent Karoo – into 127 genera and 1,750 species from ancestral stock in the surrounding arid areas.[29] But it was one clade, in particular, that really stood out in spectacular

The floppy leaves of *Conicosia pugioniformis* may subject this mesemb to excessive heating as global temperatures rise.

fashion: the Ruschioideae, or mesembs. Between 1.5 and 8.7 million years ago, the Ruschioideae, comprising 101 genera of 1,563 species – that is, 85 per cent of the Aizoaceae – underwent the most rapid diversification and rate of speciation known in the plant kingdom.[30–32] The Succulent Karoo is host today to a remarkable assemblage of plants with unique shapes, sizes, growth forms and physiologies, testament to the Glacial Periods and the Ice Ages, winter rainfall and aridity. The innovations that allowed the Ruschioideae to explode in diversity were the wide-band tracheids that prevent the collapse of the primary cell wall when a plant is water-stressed, similar in function to that discussed for *Welwitschia* plants (see box, page 45), and the smaller, rounder leaf shapes, which help to reduce water loss.[33, 34] The unique seed capsule that protects the seeds and releases them only when it is raining has also played a crucial role in their success.

Today the winter rainfall region is shrinking, in southern Africa and in southern Australia as well.[35] Not only is it getting smaller in distributional range, but it is also heading south, and so abandoning the unique Richtersveld flora and that of the *Sperrgebiet* in southern Namibia. With global heating and the ongoing southward retraction of the Antarctic sea ice, the westerly storm tracks are again shifting southwards so that the westerly weather fronts that sweep across the southwestern Cape now barely brush southwestern Namibia. They also seldom reach my hometown, Pietermaritzburg, anymore. When a particularly strong front does penetrate into the South African interior, it may blanket high-lying ground in snow for a few weeks. But these events, too, are becoming rare. If global heating is not contained, the winter rainfall might disappear from southern Africa altogether.

Let's focus now on how these climate change patterns will affect the fate of succulents in the Succulent Karoo Biome. Let's start by focusing on one widespread genus, *Conophytum*, which is supposedly very well adapted to the climate conditions under which the genus evolved during the past Glacial Periods.

A common climate change model, or General Circulation Model (GCM), is ECHAM5, which was used in the Fourth Assessment Report of the Intergovernmental Panel on Climate Change (IPCC). This model is typical of so-called niche models that predict changes to vegetation patterns based purely on changing climate. Andrew Young, Liverpool John Moores University, and his colleagues used

The diverse genus *Conophytum*, including *Conophytum ficiforme*, seen here, is widespread throughout the Succulent Karoo and a good 'model' group for predicting climate change effects on succulent mesembs.

Lampranthus is typical of the shrubby mesembs that are unlikely to escape the impact of climate change.

The future of mesembs such as *Jordaaniella spongiosa* in the Sandveld will depend on how climate change influences the occurrence of fog on the west coast.

ECHAM5 to predict the future of the diverse genus *Conophytum* in the Succulent Karoo, home to 90 per cent of the *Conophytum* species of which 96 species are endemic.[36] The predictions are quite bleak: 'significant projected reductions in the habitable bioclimatic envelope are very likely to increase risk of extinction of around 80 percent of taxa even under a partly mitigated emissions [of greenhouse gases, especially CO_2] scenario', they concluded.

Much of the problem with *Conophytum* is the high degree of point endemism of so many species. Point endemics are plants that occur within a single small range of less than about 100 square kilometres and nowhere else. Changes in the growing conditions within this restricted area and the poor dispersal ability of many of them – seeds are dispersed by water – make point endemics highly vulnerable to extinction. This problem applies not only to *Conophytum* but also to many other mesembs that bear their seeds in capsules.

One good indicator of climate change is what is happening to the iconic long-lived tree of the Succulent Karoo and Desert biomes, the quiver tree (*Aloidendron dichotomum*). There are greater mortalities and population declines in the northern parts of this plant's distribution. In the south of its distributional range, though, botanists describe 'good evidence for positive population growth trends in pole-ward populations'.[37] This is good news because it is what we'd expect an organism to do when its habitat starts to change, that is, to show signs of the capacity to 'migrate' to where the growing conditions are more suitable. In the majority of organisms, both plants and animals, this involves poleward shifts in the Southern Hemisphere, most typically because the south is cooler. Moreover, winter rainfall is more reliable in the south.

Guy Midgley, University of Stellenbosch, and his colleague W. Thuiller, Université Joseph Fourier (now part of the Université Grenoble Alpes) in France, are principal researchers on the effects that climate change is

Quiver trees show signs of positive growth at the southern end of their distribution range – as seen here by the number of young plants near Kamieskroon in Namaqualand. This poleward 'migration' is a result of the plants searching for a more suitable environment as temperatures in their traditional range rise.

likely to have on the flora of southern Africa. Their study of the fate of the Succulent Karoo provides a broader perspective rather than just a focus on point endemics and a widespread, long-lived tree.[38] A very important point that these authors make is that succulents, despite their amazing capacity to tolerate heat and drought, actually evolved during the cooler Pleistocene and Miocene 23 to 2.58 million years ago, and indeed even more recently.[39] Since the Earth's climate is now stuck in a stubborn Interglacial Period, and additional heat is being added through anthropogenic greenhouse gas emissions, succulents are being pushed well beyond their thermal tolerance limits. The authors, too, emphasise the vulnerability of point endemics in the face of declining winter rainfall, especially since the fate of coastal fogs is uncertain.

One bioregion in the Succulent Karoo that deserves mention is the Knersvlakte because it is a truly unique hotspot of biodiversity. Why is this seemingly barren region of Namaqualand so rich in miniature, ground-dwelling mesembs? The answer has to do partly with the prevalence of quartz stones. Being of a light colour and other surface properties, quartz has a high reflectance-to-absorbance ratio compared with other ground surfaces in Namaqualand. In essence, it reflects more of the incident radiation of the sun. The consequence is that the ground temperatures are about 3°C cooler in the Knersvlakte than they are in the surrounding areas of Namaqualand. So, during the Interglacial Periods, when air temperature attained maximum levels during the last 5 million years, the Knersvlakte temperatures would always have been lower. The Knersvlakte is typical of a dissected landscape that supports a mosaic of habitat types which differ in altitude, soil type, and rockiness of the terrain.[40] Microhabitats such as the Knersvlakte tend to limit gene flow and promote species diversity in a system subject to changing climate.

The fate of the Nama-Karoo and Arid Savanna biomes

While there is little argument about the fate of the Succulent Karoo, the same cannot be said for the Nama-Karoo and Arid Savanna biomes. Niche-based models suggest that the Nama-Karoo and Arid Savanna biomes are destined to show a vegetation decline and an eastward expansion, yet alternative models predict other responses. Understanding how these two biomes will respond, or have already responded, to climate change cannot be

Environmental disturbances, such as fires, may significantly alter the vegetation in the Nama-Karoo and Arid Savanna.

entrusted to niche-based climate change models only. This is because these biomes are *disturbance-driven* ecosystems in which fires and mega-herbivores alter the vegetation significantly.

William Bond, from the University of Cape Town and South Africa's foremost plant ecologist, and Guy Midgley have synthesised how these two biomes are likely to respond to climate change in the face of current disturbance patterns.[41] They insist that dynamic global vegetation model (DGVM) approaches must be adopted because they take into account the role of disturbance in association with increasing carbon dioxide levels.

The C_4 grasses in these biomes evolved in the Miocene at a time when the carbon dioxide levels were lower, and the climate was cooler (see box, page 52). Low carbon dioxide levels retarded the growth of C_3 trees at that time, allowing the C_4 grasslands to spread dramatically in warm, arid regions throughout the world. Grasslands are very prone to fires, caused, for example, by lightning strikes. Grass fires kill tree saplings – called topkill – and in so doing they retard the spread of woodlands.

But what is happening now, given increasingly higher carbon dioxide levels, is that the shrubs and trees are growing faster than grasses in the absence of fire.[42] In the Arid Savanna Biome, in particular, this problem is being exacerbated by bush encroachment caused by overgrazing because there is less grass to fuel fires. Predictions made by the IPCC in 2007, based upon DGVM approaches, suggest a greening of the aridlands of southern Africa. Clearly these predictions are the opposite of what niche-based climate models suggest. Predicting the response to climate change in DGVM approaches is more challenging because it involves the complex interplay between the physiological performances of grasses, shrubs and trees under carbon dioxide fertilisation, fire regimes and their intensity, and grazing patterns from domestic and wild herbivores.

In the first edition of *Living Deserts* I devoted seven pages to desertification, covering a predicted eastwards spread of the shrubby Nama-Karoo, driven by commercial small-stock overgrazing. Well, now, 27 years later, the perception and observations seem to have changed completely: the Nama-Karoo, it seems, is not advancing on the eastern biomes of southern Africa. Instead, it seems that the grasslands are spreading westwards into the Nama-Karoo.[43–45]

Much of the Arid Savanna is a vegetated dune system. When sand dunes are at least 14 per cent vegetated, they do not move in response to prevailing winds. In the southern Kalahari, *Terminalia* trees and *Stipagrostis* grasses grow on dune crests, thereby stabilising the dunes. However, should the vegetation on the dunes be compromised, for example, by overgrazing or in response to global heating, then the dunes will become de-vegetated and mobilised – a process known as 'aeolian sediment mobilisation'. David Thomas, University of Oxford, and his collaborators have employed general climate models to predict the responses of the Kalahari dunefields to global heating.[46] Using three different models, they forecast that, following global heating, moisture depletion in the dunes and enhanced windiness, 'the general trend and the magnitude of possible changes in the erodibility and erosivity of dune systems suggests that the environmental and social consequences of these changes will be drastic'.

Again, we might ask how the same predictions would emerge from DGVM approaches. If these models predict increased greening with global heating, might we not expect an increase in the 14 per cent plant cover threshold for sand mobility?

Kalahari birds and mammals

At the time of writing, a serious prolonged drought in the Kalahari Desert was having a devastating effect on mammals that specialise in eating ants and termites, namely aardvarks and pangolins. We are fortunate enough to know about this courtesy of the long-term research projects on these animals being conducted in the Tswalu Kalahari Reserve. However, given the lack of research

Andrea Fuller

In response to drought conditions in the Kalahari Desert, an aardvark in poor condition forages during the day so that it can draw energy from the sun rather than use its own to maintain its body temperature at night – its usual foraging period. An extremely high number of aardvarks died during a nine-year drought that eventually ended in 2021.

Wendy Panaino

The ground pangolin is another large ant-eating mammal whose numbers declined during the prolonged drought in the Kalahari Desert. The extent of the mortality has yet to be published.

elsewhere, it is not known how widespread the mortalities of these two species are in the rest of the Kalahari Desert.

Aardvarks were captured and surgically implanted with body temperature telemeters that measure and record body temperatures continuously over long periods of time. These are very valuable data that reveal important behavioural and physiological patterns in free-ranging animals. Following a drought in 2012, 84 per cent of the study animals as well as 11 other aardvarks died at the study site from starvation.[47] As their condition deteriorated, the animals adopted desperate behaviours in an attempt to save energy, such as basking in the sun to maintain a body temperature instead of using their own energy to do so. Moreover, although aardvarks are normally nocturnal, the study aardvarks switched to foraging during the day, again, to conserve energy that would have been used to maintain a constant body temperature.

The demise of the aardvarks was attributed to climate change, not necessarily because of global heating, but because of the indirect consequence of reduced rainfall and the resultant extreme reduction of grasses.[48] Grasses are the main food resource of harvester termites, on which the aardvarks feed, and the termite populations crashed during the drought.

The severity of the potential loss of aardvarks from the Kalahari Desert cannot be underestimated. Aardvarks are the ecosystem engineers of the Kalahari. Their burrows provide shelter during the day, especially from the climate-change increases in temperature, for at least 27 species of other animals.[49] The burrows also have a higher relative humidity that acts to minimise respiratory water losses (see Chapter Two).

In a very similar scenario, pangolins are facing the same fate in the Kalahari Desert. However, at this time, data have yet to be published, although the animals have been well studied.

Climate change in the Kalahari is also affecting birds. The first findings of a collaborative research project by the universities of Cape Town and Pretoria called 'The Hot Birds Project' is not good news. The study, designed to evaluate the impact of climate change on the desert birds of southern Africa, examined so-called sublethal fitness costs, such as progressive body mass loss, reduced nestling growth rates, and increased breeding failure, in response to global heating. All of these costs will expand dramatically. For example, it was predicted that, by the 2080s, 'the region will experience 10–20 consecutive

The reproduction of many bird species in the Kalahari Desert, including this southern yellow-billed hornbill, is being seriously impaired by global heating.

days per year in which southern pied babblers (*Turdoides bicolor*) will lose ~4% of body mass per day, conditions under which this species' persistence will be extremely unlikely'.[50] You do the sums – the maximum body weight of the babblers is 96 grams. The study also emphasises increased breeding failures in species such as southern yellow-billed hornbills (*Tockus leucomelas*)[51] and southern fiscals (*Lanius collaris*).[52] Overall, the study predicts 'large declines in avian diversity in the southern African arid zone by the end of the century'.[53, 54]

Other threats to the Desert Biome

Despite its pristine nature and enormous extent, the Namib-Naukluft National Park continues to face the serious threat of the water table dropping along the Kuiseb River. This is caused primarily by the extraction of groundwater from two sites near Walvis Bay. The extracted water is used for domestic consumption by the growing population of the town. Because of the extreme aridity of this region, very little water replenishes the exploited alluvial aquifer, so the water table continues to drop.

The Kuiseb River – a linear oasis and the Namib's lifeline – is threatened by the extraction of groundwater for use in Walvis Bay. A Topnaar settlement can be seen at bottom left in the photograph.

It takes little imagination to understand the devastating consequences of the continuation of this exploitation. Many ecologically important desert plants, such as the camel thorn and the ana tree, rely exclusively on this deep groundwater, and already severe deterioration in the riverine vegetation has been recorded. The dense growth in the Kuiseb riverbed acts as a windbreak to the southerly winds, retarding the northward movement of the dune sea onto the Namib's gravel plains. The destruction of this natural barrier to sand movement would have serious ecological consequences in this part of the Namib Desert.

The indigenous Topnaar community, and the nara plants on which they depend, rely on groundwater for their existence. The wildlife, too, depends on it, and has been able to endure very dry seasons in the past by digging deep holes in the Kuiseb riverbed to reach the water table. Their survival is directly threatened if the subsiding of the water table cannot be halted. The good news, though, is that the Kuiseb River Basin now has a Basin Management Committee, which monitors and manages the water inputs and extractions from the basin.

Topnaar pastoralists graze goats, sheep, cattle and donkeys along the middle and lower reaches of the basin. Today, about 350 Topnaars live in 14 settlements along the Kuiseb. Biologists and conservationists have expressed concern at the consequences of uncontrolled grazing in this linear oasis, a life-support system that traverses the Namib dune sea, providing vital resources to the desert fauna. Already the livestock have severely overgrazed the understorey plant growth and fallen acacia seed pods. The animals compete for food with ungulates such as gemsbok, which browse on the riverine vegetation, and they destroy the vegetation cover in habitats used by the rich insect fauna that is endemic to the Kuiseb. The competition is not restricted to the

Topnaar pastoralists keep sheep, goats, cattle and donkeys, which are heavy browsers of riverine and dune vegetation.

In addition to their livestock, Topnaar people depend heavily on nara fruit for food. The nara is an edible, melon-like fruit that grows in sand dunes within the Namib's coastal fog belt and depends on groundwater for survival.

Nara fruit have a high water content, and when ripe are sweet and juicy. The seeds can be eaten fresh or roasted, or ground into flour for cooking. The pulp is usually boiled and dried to make flat cakes. Herbivores browse the flowers and tips of young stems of the nara plant.

riverbed either. Topnaar donkeys, horses, goats and cattle graze on the limited grasses and nara plants at the edge of the dune sea. Unlike other arid biomes, the Namib simply cannot sustain high levels of relatively sedentary stock if its unique plant and animal life is to be preserved.

In his book *Pastoral Nomads of the Central Namib Desert: The People History Forgot*, anthropologist John Kinahan, formerly of the National Museum of Namibia in Windhoek, showed that the Topnaars and their stock have inhabited the Kuiseb riverbed and its environs on a nomadic basis for many thousands of years.[55] Queen Victoria granted them use of the riverbed at a time when there was no interest in the unproductive desert zones. Consequently, today they are the only people who enjoy uncontrolled access to the Namib-Naukluft Park and the Kuiseb riverbed. The Topnaar question is sensitive politically as well as ecologically, and a suitable agreement between the Topnaars, the Namibian Ministry of Environment and Tourism, and concerned environmentalists remains a matter of some urgency.

Other problems of concern to conservationists include the impact of off-road driving in the Namib, particularly on the gravel plains, and the surface diggings of mining prospectors.

Diamonds of Namaqualand

The Orange River, which wends its way through the arid northern parts of South Africa, enters the sea at Oranjemund, on the border between South Africa and Namibia. Forming a natural boundary between the two countries, its greater claim to fame is the thousands of diamonds it has transported from the interior to the frigid waters of the Atlantic Ocean. But the river did not always enter the sea at its current location, and geological research shows that the mouth of the original Orange River changed several times over the millennia. It is these changes, combined with upliftment and erosion, that help to explain the distribution pattern of diamonds along the west coast – both on land and offshore. Although there are slightly different ideas about the ancient origins of the Orange River,[67] here I discuss the reconstruction of this water system suggested by Michiel de Wit, formerly of De Beers Consolidated Mines.[68]

During the Cretaceous Period tropical conditions predominated: rainfall was considerably higher than it is today, and conditions were warm and humid. The ancient Karoo River, which no longer exists, carried water from the interior of the Nama-Karoo along its southern boundary, and the ancient Kalahari River drained the northern parts of the interior, including the southern Kalahari Desert. The Karoo River flowed into the Atlantic Ocean somewhere near the present-day mouth of the Olifants River, and the Kalahari River debouched into the sea in the vicinity of the current Orange River mouth.

Rates of erosion were high at this time, and it is estimated that about 1,4 kilometres of ground (strata), which overlay the diamond-bearing kimberlite pipes in the interior, were carried down the ancient Karoo River to the Atlantic Ocean. Diamonds, too, were swept along to their southernmost distribution along the Namaqualand coast – at the mouth of the present-day Olifants River. Then, during the Miocene, which commenced 23 million years ago, the Karoo River was 'captured' by the ancient Kao River that flowed northwards to become a tributary of the Orange River. This resulted in water-borne diamonds being deposited at the mouth of the Orange River. These were 'reworked' stones that had originally been deposited along the Karoo River terraces during the Cretaceous.

The mouth of the Olifants River today. During the Cretaceous this was approximately where the diamond-carrying Karoo River flowed into the Atlantic Ocean.

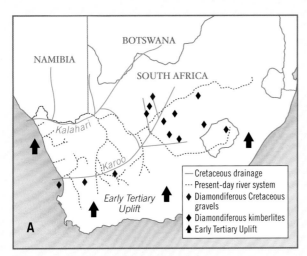

Cretaceous drainage 100 million years ago.

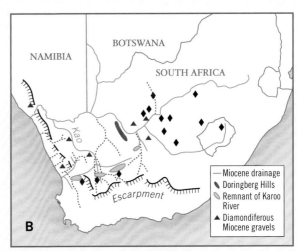

Miocene drainage 20 million years ago.

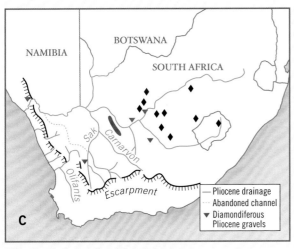

Pliocene drainage 5 million years ago.

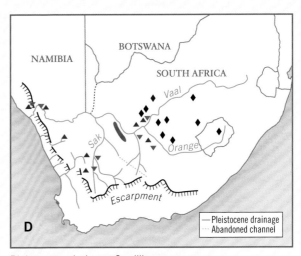

Pleistocene drainage 2 million years ago.

This series of maps shows how the river drainage system has changed over the past 100 million years as a result of the uplifting of the escarpment, and how the water route changes have influenced the distribution of diamonds in Namaqualand. In maps A and B the dotted river courses show the routes illustrated in map D.[69]

About 5 million years ago the Kao River silted up, and the Sak and Carnarvon rivers became the new tributaries of the Orange River. Then, about 2 million years ago, the Carnarvon River dried up, leaving the Sak River as the sole remnant of the ancient Karoo drainage system. In general, the shift from a southern (Karoo River) to a northern (Orange River) drainage system in the region was driven by the uplifting of the escarpment.

Today, diamonds lie scattered all along the west coast of southern Africa, from the mouth of the Olifants River in South Africa to Lüderitz in Namibia. They may be found offshore, in the intertidal zone, and for several kilometres inland, lying in sand-covered potholes and rocky gullies in the bedrock. Since most of the river-borne diamonds on land have already been extracted, current mining operations are mainly focused offshore.

Despite disruptive mining on the coast, the vast expanse of the forbidden *Sperrgebiet* in Namibia remains a pristine preserve of Succulent Karoo and Desert flora and fauna.

expensive windbreaks.[70] Many overburden dumps also have slopes that are too steep for successful rehabilitation. But perhaps the biggest problem is that the original thin 5-centimetre film of topsoil is never properly restored, regardless of attempts to do so.[71] Despite the best efforts at rehabilitation, the species diversity of plants is never restored to its former state.[72]

The positive side of diamond mining in the Succulent Karoo involves the large, restricted *Sperrgebiet* – now incorporated into the Tsau ‖Khaeb National Park – in southern Namibia. The park plays an extremely important role as a conservation area. The destructive mining activities in the *Sperrgebiet* are now mostly limited to within a few kilometres of the coast, and further inland there are many thousands of hectares of Succulent Karoo habitat in which all plants and animals enjoy protection from human disturbance. Further south, the region between the mouths of the Groen and Spoeg rivers in Namaqualand has been incorporated into the Namaqua National Park, and is thus protected from strip mining.

Although fracking has yet to commence in the Nama-Karoo Biome, the South African Environmental Observation Network (SAEON) has initiated the Karoo Shale Gas Ecology Project to monitor and study the effects of fracking on Karoo ecosystems. Surprisingly

little is known about the effects of fracking on ecosystems in the world, but what has been published has been employed to identify the main impacts that will occur in the Nama-Karoo.[73] Obvious impacts include noise and light pollution; habitat loss; the direct and indirect effects of constructing road networks, for example, habitat fragmentation; the risks of open waste-water ponds; the construction of pipelines; and the generation of dust.

The Succulent Karoo is presently experiencing an unprecedented increase in succulent poaching. The huge overseas demand for and online trading of these fascinating plants have created a lucrative poaching industry. Much the same applies to a number of reptile species, especially *Cordylus* lizards, which are highly prized by overseas collectors. One species in particular, the armadillo girdled lizard, is heavily targeted by Japanese poachers to satisfy a huge demand in the pet trade in Japan. This lizard is popular because it has an endearing behaviour of biting its tail and rolling into a ring when threatened.

Although South Africa is a signatory to the CITES agreement, which controls the world trade of threatened species, poor policing has failed to stem the flow of plants and reptiles out of the Succulent Karoo. Encouragingly, although all too few, those poachers that have been apprehended (currently Europeans and Asians) have received jail terms as well as severe fines. Hopefully, these cases will be a deterrent and will help to stem the plundering of the Succulent Karoo's precious biota.

In the southern African subcontinent, a region which is to a very large extent covered by arid land, the topic of desertification inspires a great deal of discussion and debate. But what exactly does 'desertification' mean? According to a United Nations conference on the subject, held in 1978, desertification can be defined as the 'diminution or destruction of the biological potential of the land'.[74] In the simplest practical terms, it means a conversion from a more productive state to a less productive one.

The members of the government-appointed Drought Investigation Commission expressed the first views on the process of desertification in South Africa in 1923. They warned that, unless farming practices changed dramatically in the arid regions of South Africa, it would not be long before the country became 'the Great South African Desert uninhabitable by Man'.[75] More warnings, especially concerning the deterioration of the Karoo vegetation, have followed, but none has been so comprehensive and graphically explicit as that presented by John Acocks in 1953 with the publication of his 'Advancing Karoo Hypothesis'.[76, 77]

The process underlying Acocks's prediction that the area covered by desert in South Africa is increasing in size involves changes in the ratios between grass cover and shrub cover. The Karoo, Acocks argues, used to be a perennial palatable grassland (sweet veld) prior to and during the early period of habitation by European farmers. Today it is not. The overgrazing and trampling that have occurred over two to three centuries of cattle, sheep and goat farming have been so heavy that the grasses and palatable shrubs have thinned out dramatically and have been replaced by the unpalatable shrubs that characterise the Nama-Karoo today. Selective grazing, whereby stock eat only the more palatable grasses in the case of cattle, and palatable shrubs and forbs in the case of small stock – and ignore the less palatable ones – has played perhaps the most important role. Persistently grazed or browsed to ground level, the grasses and shrubs were not able to grow to maturity and set seed. The result is that the unpalatable shrubs have taken over the spaces that the palatable shrubs and grasses once occupied. The most valuable of the grasses that were replaced was the highly palatable rooigras (*Themeda triandra*), an excellent grazing grass.

The percentage of grass cover in relation to shrub cover in the Karoo biomes increases from west to east in response to the increased rainfall gradient, and to the increased amount of this rain which falls in summer (see maps, page 15). Summer rainfall has considerable influence on the proportion of grasses in the Karoo because most of the grasses employ C_4 metabolism and are thus adapted to rapid growth during the hot, wet season (see map, page 52). So, when the grass cover in the eastern Karoo decreases and the shrub cover takes over, the overall impression is that the landscape is more similar to the drier, less productive western regions. This in turn creates the impression that the Nama-Karoo is spreading eastwards.

Handré Basson / CC BY-SA 3.0, Wikimedia Commons

The armadillo girdled lizard is highly threatened because of poaching for the pet trade.

The dire consequence of this desertification process is that it is accompanied by very serious soil erosion. Acocks maintains that traces of topsoil that could still be seen in the Karoo indicate that the region was not always the eroded wilderness it has become. As the grass climax retreats, there is a certain stage when the topsoil is no longer protected by grass; once this stage has been reached it is not easy to regain the grass climax, even if grazing is completely halted, since the grasses can no longer re-establish themselves in the absence of sufficient topsoil. Invasion by unpalatable Karoo bushes does not check the erosion because their growth habit does not protect the topsoil. Moreover, the bushes can exist in very poor conditions, where topsoil is not a prerequisite for their survival.

Over the years the majority of ecologists have supported and reinforced Acocks's theories. For example, Piet Roux of the Department of Agriculture (Karoo region) in Middelburg, an acknowledged expert on grazing problems in the Karoo, corroborated Acocks's predictions in a 1983 publication in which he equated changing vegetation patterns with desertification.[78] He observed that change can be seen in the thinning of the vegetation, in the decrease or destruction of perennial grasses, and in the increase in undesirable Karoo bush and woody species. Roux also maintained that vegetation changes in the Karoo have proceeded through five identifiable stages: primary degradation, denudation, re-vegetation, secondary degradation and, finally, desertification.

However, in 1990 two botanists from the Department of Botany at the University of Cape Town, Timm Hoffman and Richard Cowling, published a strong challenge to Acocks's ideas.[79] They suggested that perennial grasses before the advent of European farmers may not have dominated the eastern Karoo, and that the effect of seasonal rainfall may be responsible for much of the perceived vegetation change in the region. They employed three separate lines of evidence to support their claim: firstly, the records of early travellers; secondly, before-and-after photographic evidence over the past 60 to 70 years; and thirdly, experimentally measured vegetation changes in ungrazed plots between 1962 and 1989.

Concerning travellers who explored the Karoo between 1777 and 1843 – men such as Robert Jacob Gordon, John Barrow, William Burchell and John Campbell – Hoffman and Cowling point out that most of the earliest written accounts that describe the landscapes of the eastern Karoo reported either a dominance of Karoo shrubs frequently with 'not a blade of grass' to be seen, or a mixture of grasses and Karoo shrubs. This by no means corresponds with Acocks's description of palatable grassland – a description that is, however, corroborated by Gordon, who recorded his observations in the eastern Karoo as early as 1777, sometime before European farming practices began there. Gordon referred to the landscape near Hofmeyr as being 'mostly completely grassveld', while near Noupoort the terrain was 'for the most part sweet grassveld, here and there Caroo patches and gebroken veld'. However, concerning these reports, Hoffman and Cowling emphasise that during Gordon's 56-day expedition through this area in summer, he recorded rain on 24 days. They suggest that it was likely that Gordon experienced a particularly wet Karoo summer. This point has a bearing on the importance of the quantity of summer rain for grass dominance.

It is the photographic evidence, however, which seems to provide the most compelling visual support for Hoffman and Cowling's challenge. In a series of 13 matched photographs taken 60 to 70 years apart, no clear evidence of desertification can be seen. In fact, if anything, the grass component seems to be very much improved in all areas that were meant to have already reverted to 'near desert', as predicted by Acocks. Two of these matched pairs are presented on the opposite page. The two photographs in the first sequence were taken 23 kilometres north of Hofmeyr along the Steynsburg road by the ecologist Illtyd Buller Pole-Evans in 1925 and by Hoffman in 1989. Acocks maintained that the vegetation in this region had deteriorated into 'eroded Karoo', yet the evidence in the photographs seems to deny this emphatically. Indeed, when Hoffman took his photograph, he recorded at least five grass species, of which *Aristida curvata* and *Eragrostis lehmanniana* were dominant, with percentage canopy covers of 20 to 30 per cent and 15 to 20 per cent, respectively. The Karoo shrub ankerkaroo had a five to ten per cent canopy cover. The difference between the two photographs is truly striking – notice the absence of grasses at the site in 1925.

Pole-Evans took the first picture in the second sequence in 1928, and the later corresponding picture was taken by Hoffman in 1989. The photographs were taken 15 kilometres east of Britstown on the De Aar road. This site is also in a region that Acocks predicted would have deteriorated into desert by the year 2050.

Are the Nama-Karoo's dwarf shrubs spreading eastwards at the expense of grasslands of the Free State as originally thought? These matched photographs, taken between Steynsburg and Hofmeyr in 1925 by Illtyd Pole-Evans (left) and in 1989 by Timm Hoffman (right) suggest the opposite – the grasslands seem to be invading the Nama-Karoo, which is indeed what is presently happening.

A second matched pair of photos, taken near Britstown in 1928 by Illtyd Pole-Evans (left) and in 1989 by Timm Hoffman (right), confirm that, if anything, the grass component is higher, and the shrub component possibly lower, than it was in the 1920s. The different vegetation patterns shown are undoubtedly also linked to long-term rainfall variability cycles and El Niño events in the summer-rainfall areas of the Nama-Karoo Biome.

Here Hoffman and Cowling conclude that there seems to have been little vegetation change at the site in the 60 years between 1928 and 1989, apart from the increase in *Aristida congesta*, the grass species seen. Hoffman recorded the co-dominance of the grass *Aristida congesta* and the driedoring shrub, each with a 15 to 20 per cent canopy cover.

Finally, the authors resurveyed 11 eastern Karoo sites in the southern Free State in 1989 that were originally surveyed by Piet Roux between 1961 and 1963. Roux was in attendance in 1989 for the resurveying of the first

site to ensure that similar procedures were adopted. This study revealed that from the early 1960s to 1989 all sites showed an increase in total percentage canopy cover which was attributed largely to an increase in the cover of grasses. Hoffman and Cowling believe that much of the misconception of an advancing Karoo may be due to a lack of appreciation and understanding of the influence of the natural cycles of rainfall in the summer-rainfall regions of South Africa. No understanding of changing vegetation patterns in the Karoo is possible, they argue, without a better appreciation of the long- and short-term influence that these rainfall cycles may have on the physiology and composition of Karoo vegetation.

Whatever the effect of the natural rainfall cycle, the process of grass replacement by Karoo shrubs would have been, and probably still is, accelerated by selective grazing. In any attempt to understand Karoo vegetation changes, and the general functioning of this ecosystem, the difficulty seems to lie in how to separate environmental influences, such as rainfall and temperature cycles, from biotic influences, such as grazing patterns and intensities.[80]

John Acocks and Piet Roux could not have factored in climate change as a potential future driver of a mobile Karoo. The knowledge was simply not available. Today we know that the eastern Karoo has greened up and become grassier as the easterly trade winds more readily penetrate the interior of South Africa as a result of the southward displacement of the high-pressure subtropical ridge of the Hadley cell, as discussed earlier.

In the Tankwa Karoo, probably the most degraded of all Karoo regions, the problem is not one of shrubs replacing grass, nor one of the loss of succulent plants. There the number of all plant species, particularly Karoo shrubs, is decreasing, and the consequence is massive ongoing erosion by wind and water. The vegetation cover is simply too sparse to check the process, and many thousands of tons of valuable topsoil are being carried into the Atlantic Ocean each year by the Tankwa and Olifants rivers, or blown there by the strong seasonal offshore winds.

To summarise, it would seem that the potential for desertification exists wherever an imbalance in Karoo vegetation is created by sustained and excessive grazing, browsing and trampling, resulting in unpalatable shrubs taking over niches previously occupied by grasses or palatable shrubs. Such an imbalance does appear to have occurred in certain parts of the Nama-Karoo, where centuries of overgrazing may have changed forever the shrub components of the vegetation, and where certain shrubs and grasses cannot be replaced because of a lack of soil-stored seed banks. Clearly, though, the Karoo is not spreading eastwards and posing any threat to the Free State grasslands.

Abused by overgrazing for centuries, the Tankwa Karoo is probably the most degraded of all Karoo habitats. The Tankwa Karoo National Park was established in 1986 to conserve this corner of the Succulent Karoo Biome.

Although the rugged Ai-IAis/Richtersveld Transfrontier Park is one of the most inhospitable regions in southern Africa, it is a biodiversity hotspot, containing a rich variety of succulents. Like many parts of the Succulent Karoo Biome, its unique plant life is under threat from global heating.

Endnotes

Preface

1. South African National Biodiversity Institute. *National Vegetation Map*. (South African National Biodiversity Institute, 2018).
2. Lovegrove, B.G. *Fires of Life: Endothermy in Birds and Mammals*. (Yale University Press, 2019).
3. Kyalangalilwa, B., Boatwright, J.S., Daru, B.H., Maurin, O. & van der Bank, M. Phylogenetic position and revised classification of *Acacia* s.l. (Fabaceae: Mimosoideae) in Africa, including new combinations in *Vachellia* and *Senegalia*. *Botanical Journal of the Linnean Society* 172, 500–523, doi:10.1111/boj.12047 (2013).

Chapter One

1. Noy-Meir, I. Desert ecosystems: environment and producers. *Annual Review of Ecology and Systematics* 4, 25–51 (1973).
2. Schulze, R. & McGee, O. Climatic indices and classifications in relation to the biogeography of southern Africa in Werger, M.J.A. & van Bruggen, A.C. (eds), *Biogeography and Ecology of Southern Africa*: 19–52. (Springer, 1978).
3. Ibid.
4. Cowling, R.M., Rundel, P.W., Lamont, B.B., Arroyo, M.K. & Arianoutsou, M. Plant diversity in Mediterranean-climate regions. *Trends in Ecology & Evolution* 11, 362–366 (1996).
5. Cowling, R.M., Pressey, R.L., Rouget, M. & Lombard, A.T. A conservation plan for a global biodiversity hotspot – the Cape Floristic Region, South Africa. *Biological Conservation* 112, 191–216 (2003).
6. Linder, H.P. The radiation of the Cape flora, southern Africa. *Biological Reviews of the Cambridge Philosophical Society* 78, 597–638 (2003).
7. Mucina, L. & Rutherford, M.C. (eds). *The Vegetation of South Africa, Lesotho and Swaziland*. (South African National Biodiversity Institute, 2006).
8. Linder, *Biological Reviews of the Cambridge Philosophical Society* 78, 597–638.
9. Cowling, Rundel, Lamont, Arroyo & Arianoutsou, *Trends in Ecology & Evolution* 11, 362–366.
10. Wolf, A. *The Invention of Nature: Alexander von Humboldt's New World*. (Alfred A. Knopf, 2016).
11. Cain, S.A. Life-forms and phytoclimate. *The Botanical Review* 16(1), 1–32 (1950).
12. Mucina & Rutherford, *Vegetation of South Africa, Lesotho and Swaziland*.

13. Mucina, L. Biome: evolution of a crucial ecological and biogeographical concept. *New Phytologist* 222, 97–114 (2019).
14. Ibid.
15. Mucina & Rutherford, *Vegetation of South Africa, Lesotho and Swaziland*.
16. The desert biomes map is based on the latest release of the National Vegetation Map of South Africa (South African National Biodiversity Institute, 2018).
17. Klak, C., Reeves, G. & Hedderson, T. Unmatched tempo of evolution in southern African semi-desert ice plants. *Nature* 427, 63 (2004).
18. Ibid.
19. Klak, C., Hanacek, P. & Bruyns, P.V. Out of southern Africa: origin, biogeography and age of the Aizooideae (Aizoaceae). *Molecular Phylogenetics and Evolution* 109, 203–216, doi:10.1016/j.ympev.2016.12.016 (2017).
20. Hartmann, H.E.K. Mesembryanthema. *Contributions from the Bolus Herbarium* 13, 75–157 (1991).
21. Cowling, Pressey, Rouget & Lombard, *Biological Conservation* 112, 191–216 (2003).
22. Klak, Reeves & Hedderson, *Nature* 427, 63.
23. Klak, Hanacek & Bruyns, *Molecular Phylogenetics and Evolution* 109, 203–216.
24. Cowling, R., Esler, K. & Rundel, P. Namaqualand, South Africa – an overview of a unique winter-rainfall desert ecosystem. *Plant Ecology* 142, 3–21 (1999).
25. Valente, L.M., Britton, A.W., Powell, M.P., Papadopulos, A.S.T., Burgoyne, P.M. & Savolainen, V. Correlates of hyperdiversity in southern African ice plants (Aizoaceae). *Botanical Journal of the Linnean Society* 174, 110–129, doi:10.1111/boj.12117 (2014).
26. Mucina & Rutherford, *Vegetation of South Africa, Lesotho and Swaziland*.
27. Ibid.
28. Klak, Reeves & Hedderson, *Nature* 427, 63.
29. Valente, Britton, Powell, Papadopulos, Burgoyne & Savolainen, *Botanical Journal of the Linnean Society* 174, 110–129.
30. Mucina & Rutherford, *Vegetation of South Africa, Lesotho and Swaziland*.
31. Ibid.
32. Goudie, A. & Eckardt, F. The evolution of the morphological framework of the central Namib Desert, Namibia, since the early Cretaceous. *Geografiska Annaler: Series A, Physical Geography* 81, 443–458 (1999).
33. Ibid.
34. Pickford, M., Senut, B., Mocke, H., Mourer-Chauviré, C., Rage, J. & Mein, P. Eocene aridity in southwestern Africa:

timing of onset and biological consequences. *Transactions of the Royal Society of South Africa* 69, 139–144 (2014).

35. Ibid.

36. Hartley, A.J., Chong, G., Houston, J. & Mather, A.E. 150 million years of climatic stability: evidence from the Atacama Desert, northern Chile. *Journal of the Geological Society* 162, 421–424 (2005).

Chapter Two

1. Henschel, J.R. Wassenaar, T.D., Kanandjembo, A., Louw, M.K., Neef, G., Shuuya, T. & Soderberg, K. Roots point to water sources of *Welwitschia mirabilis* in a hyperarid desert. *Ecohydrology* 12, e2039 (2019).

2. Kartusch, B. & Kartusch, R. Stem anatomy of *Acanthosicyos horridus* (Cucurbitaceae). *South African Journal of Botany* 74, 647–650 (2008).

3. Felger, R. & Henrickson, J. Convergent adaptive morphology of a Sonoran desert cactus (*Peniocereus striatus*) and an African spurge (*Euphorbia cryptospinosa*). *Haseltonia* 5, 77–85 (1997).

4. Robinson, M.D. Summer field energetics of the Namib Desert dune lizard *Aporosaura anchietae* (Lacertidae) and its relation to reproduction. *Journal of Arid Environments* 18, 207–215 (1990).

5. Krüger, G.H.J., Jordaan, A., Tiedt, L.R., Strasser, R.J., Kilbourn Louw, M. & Berner, J.M. Opportunistic survival strategy of *Welwitschia mirabilis*: recent anatomical and ecophysiological studies elucidating stomatal behaviour and photosynthetic potential. *Botany* 95, 1109–1123, doi:10.1139/cjb-2017-0095 (2017).

6. Eller, B.M. & Ruess, B. Water relations of *Lithops* plants embedded into the soil and exposed to free air. *Physiologia Plantarum* 55, 329–334 (1982).

7. Oddo, E., Veca, R., Morici, G. & Sajeva, M. Water recycling in leaves of *Lithops* (Aizoaceae). *Plant Biosystems – An International Journal Dealing with all Aspects of Plant Biology* 152, 161–165 (2018).

8. Young, A., Suarez, L.P., Kapralov, M. & Opel, M. Leaf epidermal structure in the dwarf succulent genus *Conophytum* NE Br. (Aizoaceae). *Bradleya*, 217–237 (2017).

9. McClain, E., Seely, M.K., Hadley, N.F. & Gray, V. Wax blooms in tenebrionid beetles of the Namib Desert: correlations with environment. *Ecology* 66, 112–118 (1985).

10. McClain, E., Hanrahan, S.A. & Gernecke, D. Extracuticular secretion on a Namib Desert tenebrionid *Onymacris plana*: an indicator of aridity. *Madoqua* 14(4), 363–368 (1986).

11. Lillywhite, H.B. Water relations of tetrapod integument. *Journal of Experimental Biology* 209, 202–226 (2006).

12. Young, Suarez, Kapralov & Opel, *Bradleya*, 217–237.

13. Barthlott, W., Mail, M., Bhushan, B. & Koch, K. Plant surfaces: structures and functions for biomimetic innovations. *Nano-Micro Letters* 9, 23 (2017).

14. Krüger, Jordaan, Tiedt, Strasser, Kilbourn Louw & Berner, *Botany* 95, 1109–1123.

15. Vogel, J.C. & Fuls, A. The geographical distribution of Kranz grasses in South Africa. *South African Journal of Science* 74, 209–215 (1978).

16. Krüger, Jordaan, Tiedt, Strasser, Kilbourn Louw & Berner, *Botany* 95, 1109–1123.

17. Young, Suarez, Kapralov & Opel, *Bradleya*, 217–237.

18. Felger & Henrickson, *Haseltonia* 5, 77–85.

19. Kartusch, B. & Kartusch, R. Stem anatomy of *Acanthosicyos horridus* (Cucurbitaceae). *South African Journal of Botany* 74, 647–650 (2008).

20. Lighton, J.R.B. Discontinuous gas exchange in insects. *Annual Review of Entomology* 41, 309–324 (1996).

21. Lighton, J.R. Slow discontinuous ventilation in the Namib dune-sea ant *Camponotus detritus* (Hymenoptera, Formicidae). *Journal of Experimental Biology* 151, 71–82 (1990).

22. Zachariassen, K.A. Routes of transpiratory water loss in a dry-habitat tenebrionid beetle. *Journal of Experimental Biology* 157, 425–437 (1991).

23. Schmidt-Nielsen, K. *Animal Physiology: Adaptation and Environment.* (Cambridge University Press, 1983).

24. Withers, P.C., Siegfried, W.R. & Louw, G.N. Desert ostrich exhales unsaturated air. *South African Journal of Science* 77, 569–570 (1981).

25. Ibid.

26. Buffenstein, R., Cambell, W.E. & Jarvis, J.U.M. Identification of crystalline allantoin in the urine of African Cricetidae (Rodentia) and its role in their water economy. *Journal of Comparative Physiology B* 155, 493–499 (1985).

27. Korine, C., Vatnick, I., Tets, I.G.V. & Pinshow, B. New observations on urine contents in water-deprived Negev Desert rodents. *Canadian Journal of Zoology* 81, 941–945 (2003).

28. Warren-Rhodes, K.A., McKay, C.P., Boyle, L.N., Wing, M.R., Kiekebusch, E.M., Cowan, D.A., Stomeo, F., Pointing, S.B., Kaseke, K.F., Eckardt, F., Henschel, J.R., Anisfeld, A., Seely, M. & Rhodes, K.L. Physical ecology of hypolithic communities in the central Namib Desert: the role of fog, rain, rock habitat, and light. *Journal of Geophysical Research: Biogeosciences* 118, 1451–1460 (2013).

29. Ibid.

30. Rumrich, U., Rumrich, M. & Lange-Bertalot, H. Diatomeen als 'Fensteralgen' in der Namib-Wüste und anderen ariden Gebieten von SWA/Namibia. *Dinteria* 20 (1989).

31. Adriaenssens, E.M., van Zyl, L., de Maayer, P., Rubagotti, E., Rybicki, E., Tuffin, M. & Cowan, D.A. Metagenomic analysis of the viral community in Namib Desert hypoliths. Environmental Microbiology 17, 480–495 (2015).

32. Ibid.

33. Seely, M.K., de Vos, M.P. & Louw, G.N. Fog imbibition, satellite fauna and unusual leaf structure in a Namib Desert dune plant *Trianthema hereroensis*. *South African Journal of Science* 73, 169–172 (1977).

34. von Willert, D.J., Eller, B.M., Werger, M.J.A., Brinckmann, E. & Ihlenfeldt, H-D. *Life Strategies of Succulents in Deserts: With Special Reference to the Namib Desert*. (Cambridge University Press, 2012).

35. Martin, C.E. & von Willert, D.J. Leaf epidermal hydathodes and the ecophysiological consequences of foliar water uptake in species of *Crassula* from the Namib Desert in southern Africa. *Plant Biology* 2, 229–242 (2000).

36. Ibid.

37. Vogel, S. & Müller-Doblies, U. Desert geophytes under dew and fog: the 'curly-whirlies' of Namaqualand (South Africa). *Flora – Morphology, Distribution, Functional Ecology of Plants* 206, 3–31 (2011).

38. Berry, Z.C., Emery, N.C., Gotsch, S.G. & Goldsmith, G.R. Foliar water uptake: processes, pathways, and integration into plant water budgets. *Plant, Cell & Environment* 42, 410–423 (2019).

39. von Willert, Eller, Werger, Brinckmann & Ihlenfeldt, *Life Strategies of Succulents in Deserts*.

40. Berry, Emery, Gotsch & Goldsmith, *Plant, Cell & Environment* 42, 410–423.

41. Ibid.

42. Ibid.

43. Ebner, M., Miranda, T. & Roth-Nebelsick, A. Efficient fog harvesting by *Stipagrostis sabulicola* (Namib dune bushman grass). *Journal of Arid Environments* 75, 524–531 (2011).

44. Vogel & Müller-Doblies, *Flora – Morphology, Distribution, Functional Ecology of Plants* 206, 3–31.

45. Ibid.

46. Hamilton, W.J. III. Fog basking by the Namib Desert beetle, *Onymacris unguicularis*. *Nature* 262, 284–285 (1976).

47. Nørgaard, T. & Dacke, M. Fog-basking behaviour and water collection efficiency in Namib Desert darkling beetles. *Frontiers in Zoology* 7, 23 (2010).

48. Barthlott, Mail, Bhushan & Koch, *Nano-Micro Letters* 9, 23.

49. Comanns, P. Passive water collection with the integument: mechanisms and their biomimetic potential. *Journal of Experimental Biology* 221, jeb153130 (2018).

50. Guadarrama-Cetina, J. Mongruel, A., Medici, M.-G., Baquero, E., Parker, A. R., Milimouk-Melnytchuk, I., González-Viñas, W. & Beysens, D. Dew condensation on desert beetle skin. *European Physical Journal E* 37, doi:10.1140/epje/i2014-14109-y (2014).

51. Robinson, M.D. & Hughes, D.A. Observations on the natural history of Péringuey's adder, *Bitis peringueyi* (Boulenger) (Reptilia: Viperidae). *Annals of the Transvaal Museum* 31, 187–196 (1978).

52. Couthie, P.A. & Crowe, J.H. Absorption of water vapor from subsaturated air by tenebrionid beetle larvae. *American Zoologist* 15, 802–802 (1975).

53. Selebatso, M., Bennitt, E., Maude, G. & Fynn, R.W. Water provision alters wildebeest adaptive habitat selection and resilience in the Central Kalahari. *African Journal of Ecology* 56, 225–234 (2018).

54. Knight, M.H., Knight-Eloff, A.K. & Bornman, J.J. The importance of borehole water and lick sites to Kalahari ungulates. *Journal of Arid Environments* 15, 269–281 (1988).

55. Brain, C. Water gathering by baboons of the Namib Desert. *South African Journal of Science* 84, 590–591 (1988).

56. Knight, M.H. Ecology of the gemsbok *Oryx gazella gazella* (Linnaeus) and blue wildebeest *Connochaetes taurinus* (Burchell) in the southern Kalahari. PhD thesis, University of Pretoria (1991).

57. Maclean, G.L. Water transport by sandgrouse. *BioScience* 33, 365–369 (1983).

58. Cade, T.J. & Maclean, G.L. Transport of water by adult sandgrouse to their young. *The Condor* 69, 323–343 (1967).

59. Williamson, D.T. Plant underground storage organs as a source of moisture for Kalahari wildlife. *African Journal of Ecology* 25, 63–64 (1987).

60. Lovegrove, B.G. & Knight-Eloff, A. Soil and burrow temperatures, and the resource characteristics of the social mole-rat *Cryptomys damarensis* (Bathyergidae) in the Kalahari Desert. *Journal of Zoology, London* 216, 403–416 (1988).

61. Cooper, P.D. & Robinson, M.D. Water balance and bladder function in the Namib Desert sand dune lizard, *Aporosaura anchietae* (Lacrtidae). *Copeia*, 34–40 (1990).

Chapter Three

1. Lovegrove, B.G. *Fires of Life: Endothermy in Birds and Mammals*. (Yale University Press, 2019).

2. Sinclair, B. & Chown, S. Climatic variability and hemispheric differences in insect cold tolerance: support from southern Africa. *Functional Ecology* 19, 214–221 (2005).

3. Duman, J.G. Antifreeze and ice nucleator proteins in terrestrial arthropods. *Annual Review of Physiology* 63, 327–357 (2001).

4. Graham, L.A., Walker, V.K. & Davies, P.L. Developmental and environmental regulation of antifreeze proteins in the mealworm beetle *Tenebrio molitor*. *European Journal of Biochemistry* 267, 6452–6458 (2000).

5. Eller, B.M. & Nipkow, A. Diurnal course of the temperature in a *Lithops* sp. (Mesembryanthemaceae Fenzl) and its surrounding soil. *Plant, Cell and Environment* 6, 559–565 (1983).

6. Eller, B. & von Willert, D. Optical properties and succulence of plants in the arid Richtersveld (Cp., Rep. South Africa). *Botanica Helvetica* 93, 47–55 (1983).

7. Valente, L.M., Britton, A.W., Powell, M.P., Papadopulos, A.S.T., Burgoyne, P.M. & Savolainen, V. Correlates of hyperdiversity in southern African ice plants (Aizoaceae). *Botanical Journal of the Linnean Society* 174, 110–129, doi:10.1111/boj.12117 (2014).

8. Eller, B. & Grobbelaar, N. Diurnal temperature variation in and around a *Lithops lesliei* plant growing in its natural habitat on a clear day. *South African Journal of Botany* 52, 403–407 (1986).

9. Krüger, G.H.J., Jordaan, A., Tiedt, L.R., Strasser, R.J., Kilbourn Louw, M. & Berner, J.M. Opportunistic survival strategy of *Welwitschia mirabilis*: recent anatomical and ecophysiological studies elucidating stomatal behaviour and photosynthetic potential. *Botany* 95, 1109–1123, doi:10.1139/cjb-2017-0095 (2017).

10. Opel, M.R. Leaf anatomy of *Conophytum* nE Br. (Aizoaceae). *Haseltonia* 2005, 27–53 (2005).

11. Eller, B.M., von Willert, D.J., Brinckmann, E. & Baasch, R. Ecophysiological studies on *Welwitschia mirabilis* in the Namib Desert. *South African Journal of Botany* 2, 209–223 (1983).

12. Midgley, G. & van der Heyden, F. Form and function in perennial plants in Richard, W., Dean, J. & Milton, S.J. (eds), *The Karoo: Ecological Patterns and Processes*: 374. (Cambridge University Press, 1999).

13. Lovegrove, *Fires of Life*.

14. Nicolson, S.W., Bartholomew, G.A. & Seely, M.K. Ecological correlates of locomotion speed, morphometrics and body temperature in three Namib Desert tenebrionid beetles. *South African Journal of Zoology* 19, 131–134 (1984).

15. Curtis, B.A. Temperature tolerances in the Namib Desert dune ant, *Camponotus detritus*. *Journal of Insect Physiology* 31, 463–466 (1985).

16. Marsh, A.C. Thermal responses and temperature tolerance in a diurnal desert ant, *Ocymyrmex barbiger*. *Physiological Zoology* 58, 629–636 (1985).

17. Sommer, S. & Wehner, R. Leg allometry in ants: extreme long-leggedness in thermophilic species. *Arthropod Structure & Development* 41, 71–77 (2012).

18. Harris, D.J., Arnold, E.N. & Thomas, R.H. Rapid speciation, morphological evolution, and adaptation to extreme environments in South African sand lizards (*Meroles*) as revealed by mitochondrial gene sequences. *Molecular Phylogenetics and Evolution* 10, 37–48, doi:10.1006/mpev.1997.0463 (1998).

19. Lovegrove, *Fires of Life*.

20. Lovegrove, B.G., Heldmaier, G. & Knight, M. Seasonal and circadian energetic patterns in an arboreal rodent, *Thallomys paedulcus*, and a burrow-dwelling rodent, *Aethomys namaquensis*, from the Kalahari Desert. *Journal of Thermal Biology* 16, 199–209 (1991).

21. Ibid.

22. Ibid.

23. Zduniak, M., Pillay, N. & Schradin, C. Basking African striped mice choose warmer locations to heat up: evidence from a field study. *Journal of Zoology* 309, 133–139 (2019).

24. Schradin, C., Krackow, S., Schubert, M., Keller, C., Schradin, B. & Pillay, N. Regulation of activity in desert-living striped mice: the importance of basking. *Ethology* 113, 606–614, doi:10.1111/j.1439-0310.2007.01361.x (2007).

25. Fielden, L.J., Waggoner, J.P., Perrin, M.R. & Hickmann, G.C. Thermoregulation in the Namib Desert golden mole, *Eremitalpa granti namibensis* (Chrysochloridae). *Journal of Arid Environments* 18, 221–237 (1990).

26. Scantlebury, M., Lovegrove, B.G., Jackson, C.R., Bennett, N.C. & Lutermann, H. Hibernation and non-shivering thermogenesis in the Hottentot golden mole (*Amblysomus hottentottus longiceps*). *Journal of Comparative Physiology B* 178, 887–897 (2008).

27. Müller, E.F. & Lojewski, U. Thermoregulation in the meerkat (*Suricata suricata* Schreber, 1776). *Comparative Biochemistry and Physiology* 83A, 217–224 (1986).

28. Fick, L.G., Kucio, T.A., Fuller, A., Matthee, A. & Mitchell, D. The relative roles of the parasol-like tail and burrow shuttling in thermoregulation of free-ranging Cape ground squirrels, *Xerus inauris*. *Comparative Biochemistry and Physiology A* 152, 334–340 (2009).

29. Bennett, A.F., Huey, R.B., John-Alder, H. & Nagy, K.A. The parasol tail and thermoregulatory behavior of the Cape ground squirrel *Xerus inauris*. *Physiological Zoology* 57, 57–62 (1984).

30. Hetem, R.S., de Witt, B.A., Fick, L.G., Fuller, A., Kerley, G.I.H., Meyer, L.C.R., Mitchell, S. & Maloney, K. Body temperature, thermoregulatory behaviour and pelt characteristics of three colour morphs of springbok (*Antidorcas marsupialis*). *Comparative Biochemistry and Physiology A* 152, 379–388 (2009).

31. Hofmeyr, M.D. & Louw, G.N. Thermoregulation, pelage conductance and renal function in the desert-adapted springbok, *Antidorcas marsupialis*. *Journal of Arid Environments* 13, 137–151 (1987).

32. Ibid.

33. Ibid.

34. Louw, G.N. & Seely, M.K. *Ecology of Desert Organisms*. (Longman, 1982).

35. Mitchell, D., Maloney, S.K., Jessen, C., Laburn, H.P., Kamerman, G.M. & Fuller, A. Adaptive heterothermy and selective brain cooling in arid-zone mammals. *Comparative Biochemistry and Physiology B* 131, 571–585 (2002).

36. Maloney, S.K., Fuller, A., Mitchell, G. & Mitchell, D. Brain and arterial blood temperatures of free-ranging oryx (*Oryx gazella*). *Pflügers Archiv* 443, 437–445 (2002).

37. Strauss, W.M. Hetem, R.S.,Mitchell, D., Maloney, S.K., O'Brien, H.D., Meyer, L.C.R. & Fuller, A. Body water conservation through selective brain cooling by the carotid rete: a physiological feature for surviving climate change? *Conservation Physiology* 5, doi:10.1093/conphys/cow078 (2017).

38. Ibid.

39. Hetem, R.S., Maloney, S.K., Fuller, A. & Mitchell, D. Heterothermy in large mammals: inevitable or implemented? *Biological Reviews of the Cambridge Philosophical Society* 91, 187–205 (2014).

40. Lubbe, N., Czenze, Z.J., Noakes, M.J. & McKechnie, A.E. The energetic significance of communal roosting and insulated roost nests in a small arid-zone passerine. *Ostrich* 89, 347–354 (2018).

41. Ferguson, J., Nijland, M. & Bennett, N. Simple roost nests confer large energetic savings for sparrow-weavers. *Journal of Comparative Physiology B* 172, 137–143 (2002).

42. Conradie, S.R., Woodborne, S.M., Cunningham, S.J. & McKechnie, A.E. Chronic, sublethal effects of high temperatures will cause severe declines in southern African arid-zone birds during the 21st century. *Proceedings of the National Academy of Sciences*, 201821312 (2019).

Chapter Four

1. Lovegrove, B.G. The zoogeography of mammalian basal metabolic rate. *American Naturalist* 156, 201–219 (2000).

2. Hölldobler, B. & Wilson, E.O. *The Ants*. (Belknap Press, 1990).

3. Midgley, G. & van der Heyden, F. Form and function in perennial plants in Richard, W., Dean, J. & Milton, S.J. (eds), *The Karoo: Ecological Patterns and Processes*: 374. (Cambridge University Press, 1999).

4. Ibid.

5. van Breda, P.A.B. & Barnard, S.A. *Veld Plants of the Winter Rainfall Region: A Guide to the Use of Veld Plants for Grazing*. (Department of Agricultural Development, 1991).

6. Ibid.

7. Marsh, A.C. The foraging ecology of two Namib Desert harvester ant species. *South African Journal of Zoology* 22(2), 130–136 (1987).

8. Marsh, A.C. Checklist, biological notes and distribution of ants in the central Namib Desert. *Madoqua* 14(4), 333–344 (1986).

9. Marsh, A.C. Ant species richness along a climatic gradient in the Namib Desert. *Journal of Arid Environments* 11, 235–241 (1986).

10. Marsh, A.C. Forager abundance and dietary relationships in a Namib Desert ant community. *South African Journal of Zoology* 20(4), 197–203 (1985).

11. Lovegrove, B.G. & Siegfried, W.R. Distribution and formation of Mima-like earth mounds in the western Cape Province of South Africa. *South African Journal of Science* 82, 432–436 (1986).

12. Slabber, M.H. 'n Grondopname van die Malmesbury–Piketberg streek. DSc thesis, Stellenbosch University (1945).

13. Lovegrove & Siegfried, *South African Journal of Science* 82, 432–436.

14. McAuliffe, J.R., Hoffman, M.T., McFadden, L.D. & Jack, S. Whether or not *heuweltjies*: context-dependent ecosystem engineering by the southern harvester termite, *Microhodotermes viator*. *Journal of Arid Environments* 163, 26–33 (2019).

15. Midgley, G.F. & Hoffman, M.T. *Heuweltjies*: nutrient factories. *Veld and Flora* Sept, 72–75 (1991).

16. Moore, J.M. & Picker, M.D. *Heuweltjies* (earth mounds) in the Clanwilliam district, Cape Province, South Africa: 4000-year-old termite nests. *Oecologia* 86, 424–432 (1991).

17. Coaton, W.G.H. Fossilised nests of Hodotermitidae (Isoptera) from the Clanwilliam district, Cape Province. *Journal of the Entomological Society of Southern Africa* 44(2), 79–81 (1981).

18. Lovegrove & Siegfried, *South African Journal of Science* 82, 432–436.

19. Lovegrove, B.G. & Siegfried, W.R. Spacing and origin(s) of Mima-like earth mounds in the Cape Province of South Africa. *South African Journal of Science* 85, 108–112 (1989).

20. Cox, G.W., Lovegrove, B.G. & Siegfried, W.R. The small stone content of Mima-like mounds in the South African Cape region: implications for mound origin. *Catena* 14, 165–176 (1987).

21. Cramer, M.D., von Holdt, J., Khomo, L. & Midgley, J.J. Evidence for aeolian origins of *heuweltjies* from buried gravel layers. *South African Journal of Science* 112, 114–123 (2016).

22. Knight, R.S., Rebelo, A.G. & Siegfried, W.R. Plant assemblages on Mima-like earth mounds in the Clanwilliam district, South Africa. *South African Journal of Botany* 55(5), 465–472 (1989).

23. Esler, K.J. & Cowling, R.M. The comparison of selected life-history characteristics of Mesembryanthema species occurring on and off Mima-like mounds (*heuweltjies*) in semi-arid southern Africa. *Vegetatio* 116, 41–50 (1995).

24. Lovegrove, B.G. Mima-like mounds (*heuweltjies*) of South Africa: the topographical, ecological and economic impact of burrowing animals. *Symposia of the Zoological Society of London* 63, 183–198 (1991).

25. Armstrong, A.J. & Siegfried, W.R. Selective use of *heuweltjie* earth mounds by sheep in the Karoo. *South African Journal of Ecology* 1(2), 77–80 (1990).

26. Zhao, X., Dupont, L., Schefuß, E., Meadows, M.E., Hahn, A. & Wefer, G. Holocene vegetation and climate variability in the winter and summer rainfall zones of South Africa. *The Holocene* 26, 843–857 (2016).

27. Lim, S., Chase, B.M., Chevalier, M. & Reimer, P.J. 50,000 years of vegetation and climate change in the southern Namib Desert, Pella, South Africa. *Palaeogeography, Palaeoclimatology, Palaeoecology* 451, 197–209 (2016).

28. Chase, B.M., Boom, A., Carr, A.S., Meadows, M.E. & Reimer, P.J. Holocene climate change in southernmost South Africa: rock hyrax middens record shifts in the southern westerlies. *Quaternary Science Reviews* 82, 199–205 (2013).

29. Carr, A.S., Thomas, D.S., Bateman, M.D., Meadows, M.E. & Chase, B. Late Quaternary palaeoenvironments of the winter-rainfall zone of southern Africa: palynological and sedimentological evidence from the Agulhas Plain. *Palaeogeography, Palaeoclimatology, Palaeoecology* 239, 147–165 (2006).

30. Schuller, I., Belz, L., Wilkes, H. & Wehrmann, A. Late quaternary shift in southern African rainfall zones: sedimentary and geochemical data from Kalahari pans. *Zeitschrift für Geomorphologie* 61, 339–362 (2018).

31. Meyer, J.J.M., Schutte, C.E., Hurter, J.W., Galt, N.S., Degashu, P., Breetzke, G., Baranenko, D. & Meyer, N.L. The allelopathic, adhesive, hydrophobic and toxic latex of *Euphorbia* species is the cause of fairy circles investigated at several locations in Namibia. *BMC Ecology* 20, 23, doi:10.1186/s12898-020-00313-7 (2020).

32. Mills, M.G.L. *Kalahari Hyaenas: Comparative Behavioural Ecology of Two Species.* (Unwin Hyman, 1990).

33. Ibid.

34. Mills, M.G.L. & Gorman, M.L. The scent-marking behaviour of the spotted hyaena *Crocuta crocuta* in the southern Kalahari. *Journal of Zoology, London* 212, 483–497 (1987).

35. Ibid.

36. Mills, *Kalahari Hyaenas*.

37. Watson, R.T. Niche separation in Namib Desert dune Lepismatidae (Thysanura: Insecta): detrivores in an allochthonous detritus ecosystem. *Journal of Arid Environments* 17, 37–48 (1989).

38. Seely, M.K. (ed.) *Namib Ecology: 25 Years of Research:* 83–98 (Transvaal Museum, 1990).

39. du Plessis, A., Kerley, G.I.H. & Winter, P.E.D. Dietary patterns of two herbivorous rodents: *Otomys unisulcatus* and *Parotomys brantsii* in the Karoo. *South African Journal of Zoology* 26(2), 51–54 (1991).

40. Ibid.

41. du Plessis, A. & Kerley, G.I.H. Refuge strategies and habitat segregation in two sympatric rodents *Otomys unisulcatus* and *Parotomys brantsii*. *Journal of Zoology, London* 224, 1–10 (1991).

42. du Plessis, A., Kerley, G.I.H. & Winter, P.E.D. Refuge microclimates of rodents: a surface nesting *Otomys unisulcatus* and a burrowing *Parotomys brantsii*. *Acta Theriologica* 37, 351–358 (1992).

43. Herbst, M. & Bennett, N.C. Burrow architecture and burrowing dynamics of the endangered Namaqua dune mole-rat (*Bathyergus janetta*) (Rodentia: Bathyergidae). *Journal of Zoology* 270, 420–428, doi:10.1111/j.1469-7998.2006.00151.x (2006).

44. Lovegrove, B.G. The cost of burrowing by the social mole-rats (Bathyergidae) *Cryptomys damarensis* and *Heterocephalus glaber*: the role of soil moisture. *Physiological Zoology* 62, 449–469 (1989).

45. Ibid.

46. Liversidge, R. Grasses grazed by springbok and sheep. *Proceedings of the Grasslands Society of Southern Africa* 7, 32–38 (1972).

47. Knight, M.H. Ecology of the gemsbok *Oryx gazella gazella* (Linnaeus) and blue wildebeest *Connochaetes taurinus* (Burchell) in the southern Kalahari. PhD thesis, University of Pretoria (1991).

48. Liversidge, *Proceedings of the Grasslands Society of Southern Africa* 7, 32–38.

49. Knight, M.H. Ecology of the gemsbok *Oryx gazella gazella* (Linnaeus) and blue wildebeest *Connochaetes taurinus*.

50. Loutit, B.D., Louw, G.N. & Seely, M.K. First approximation of food preferences and the chemical composition of the diet of the desert-dwelling black rhinoceros, *Diceros bicornis* L. *Madoqua* 15(1), 35–54 (1987).

51. Viljoen, P.J. & du P. Bothma, J. The influence of desert-dwelling elephants on vegetation in the northern Namib Desert, South West Africa/Namibia. *Journal of Arid Environments* 18, 85–96 (1990).

52. Louw, G.N. & Seely, M.K. *Ecology of Desert Organisms.* (Longman, 1982).

53. Lovegrove, *Symposia of the Zoological Society of London* 63, 183–198.

54. Perrin, M.R. & Curtis, B.A. Comparative morphology of the digestive system of 19 species of southern African myomorph rodents in relation to diet and evolution. *South African Journal of Zoology* 15, 22–33 (1980).

55. Watson, R.T. & Irish, J. An introduction to the Lepismatidae (Thysanura: Insecta) of the Namib Desert dunes. *Madoqua* 15(4), 285–293 (1988).

Chapter Five

1. Kellerman, T.S., Coetzer, J.A.W. & Naude, T.W. *Plant Poisonings and Mycotoxicoses of Livestock in Southern Africa.* (Cambridge University Press, 1988).

2. Stock, W., le Roux, D. & van der Heyden, F. Regrowth and tannin production in woody and succulent karoo shrubs in response to simulated browsing. *Oecologia* 96, 562–568 (1993).

3. Kemp, J.E. & Ellis, A.G. Cryptic petal coloration decreases floral apparency and herbivory in nocturnally closing daisies. *Functional Ecology* 33, 2130–2141, doi:10.1111/1365-2435.13423 (2019).

4. Miller, A.K., Maritz, B., McKay, S., Glaudas, X. & Alexander, G.J. An ambusher's arsenal: chemical crypsis in the puff adder (*Bitis arietans*). *Proceedings of the Royal Society of London B: Biological Sciences* 282, 20152182 (2015).

5. Charles-Dominique, T., Davies, T.J., Hempson, G.P., Bezeng, B.S., Daru, B.H., Kabongo, R.M., Maurin, O., Muasya, A.M., van der Bank, M. & Bond, W.J. Spiny plants, mammal browsers, and the origin of African savannas. *Proceedings of the National Academy of Sciences* 113, E5572-E5579 (2016).

6. Mills, M.G.L. *Kalahari Hyaenas: Comparative Behavioural Ecology of Two Species.* (Unwin Hyman, 1990).

7. Henschel, J.R. Spiders wheel to escape. *South African Journal of Science* 86, 151–152 (1990).

Chapter Six

1. Clutton-Brock, T. Breeding together: kin selection and mutualism in cooperative vertebrates. *Science* 296, 69–72 (2002).

2. Hamilton, W.D. The genetical evolution of social behaviour. *Journal of Theoretical Biology* 7, 1–16 (1964).

3. Harman, O. *The Price of Altruism: George Price and the Search for the Origins of Kindness.* (Vintage, 2010).

4. Legendre, F. & Condamine, F.L. When Darwin's special difficulty promotes diversification in insects. *Systematic Biology* 67, 873–887, doi:10.1093/sysbio/syy014 (2018).

5. Jarvis, J.U.M. & Bennett, N.C. Eusociality has evolved independently in two genera of bathyergid mole-rats – but occurs in no other subterranean mammal. *Behavioral Ecology and Sociobiology* 33, 253–260 (1993).

6. Visser, J.H., Bennett, N.C. & van Vuuren, B.J. Phylogeny and biogeography of the African Bathyergidae: a review of patterns and processes. *PeerJ* 7, e7730 (2019).

7. Jarvis, J.U.M. Eusociality in a mammal: cooperative breeding in naked mole-rat colonies. *Science* 212, 571–573 (1981).

8. Lovegrove, B.G. The energetics of sociality in the mole-rats (Bathyergidae). PhD thesis, University of Cape Town (1987).

9. Bennett, N.C. & Jarvis, J.U.M. The social structure and reproductive biology of colonies of the mole-rat, *Cryptomys damarensis* (Rodentia, Bathyergidae). *Journal of Mammalogy* 69, 293–302 (1988).

10. Jarvis, *Science* 212, 571–573.

11. Lovegrove, B.G. The evolution of eusociality in mole-rats (Bathyergidae): a question of risks, numbers, and costs. *Behavioral Ecology and Sociobiology* 28, 37–45 (1991).

12. Skinner, J.D. & Chimimba, C.T. *Mammals of the Southern African Sub-region.* (Cambridge University Press, 2005).

13. Visser, Bennett & van Vuuren, *PeerJ* 7, e7730.

14. Price, G.R. Extension of covariance selection mathematics. *Annals of Human Genetics* 35, 485–490, doi:10.1111/j.1469-1809.1957.tb01874.x (1972).

15. Price, G.R. Selection and covariance. *Nature* 227, 520–521, doi:10.1038/227520a0 (1970).

16. Lovegrove, *Behavioral Ecology and Sociobiology* 28, 37–45.

17. Lovegrove, B.G. & Knight-Eloff, A. Soil and burrow temperatures, and the resource characteristics of the social mole-rat *Cryptomys damarensis* (Bathyergidae) in the Kalahari Desert. *Journal of Zoology, London* 216, 403–416 (1988).

18. Lovegrove, *Behavioral Ecology and Sociobiology* 28, 37–45.

19. Ibid.

20. Reeve, H.K., Westneat, D.F., Noon, W.A., Sherman, P.W. & Aquadro, C.F. DNA 'fingerprinting' reveals high levels of inbreeding in colonies of the eusocial naked mole-rat. *Proceedings National Academy of Sciences (United States of America)* 87, 2496–2500 (1990).

21. Burland, T.M., Bennett, N.C., Jarvis, J.U. & Faulkes, C.G. Eusociality in African mole-rats: new insights from patterns of genetic relatedness in the Damaraland mole-rat (*Cryptomys damarensis*). *Proceedings of the Royal Society of London B: Biological Sciences* 269, 1025–1030 (2002).

22. Lovegrove, B.G. The cost of burrowing by the social mole-rats (Bathyergidae) *Cryptomys damarensis* and *Heterocephalus glaber*: the role of soil moisture. *Physiological Zoology* 62, 449–469 (1989).

23. White, F.N., Bartholomew, G.A. & Howell, T.R. The thermal significance of the nest of the sociable weaver. *National Geographic Society Research Reports* 13, 107–115 (1981).

24. Bartholomew, G.A., White, F.N. & Howell, T.R. The thermal significance of the nest of the sociable weaver *Philetairus socius*: summer observations. *Ibis* 118, 402–410 (1976).

25. White, F.N., Bartholomew, G.A. & Howell, T. The thermal significance of the nest of the sociable weaver *Philetairus socius*: winter observations. *Ibis* 117, 171–179 (1975).

26. Bartholomew, White & Howell, *Ibis* 118, 402–410.

27. White, Bartholomew & Howell, *Ibis* 117, 171–179.

28. Covas, R., du Plessis, M.A. & Doutrelant, C. Helpers in colonial cooperatively breeding sociable weavers *Philetairus*

socius contribute to buffer the effects of adverse breeding conditions. *Behavioral Ecology and Sociobiology* 63, 103–112 (2008).

29. Mills, M.G.L. *Kalahari Hyaenas: Comparative Behavioural Ecology of Two Species.* (Unwin Hyman, 1990).

30. Lewis, D.M. Cooperative breeding in a population of white-browed sparrow weavers *Plocepasser mahali. Ibis* 124, 511–522 (1982).

31. Nelson-Flower, M.J., Wiley, E.M., Flower, T.P. & Ridley, A.R. Individual dispersal delays in a cooperative breeder: ecological constraints, the benefits of philopatry and the social queue for dominance. *Journal of Animal Ecology* 87, 1227–1238 (2018).

32. Hill, D.L., Pillay, N. & Schradin, C. Alternative reproductive tactics in female striped mice: heavier females are more likely to breed solitarily than communally. *Journal of Animal Ecology* 84, 1497–1508, doi:10.1111/1365-2656.12431 (2015).

33. Schoepf, I. & Schradin, C. Better off alone! Reproductive competition and ecological constraints determine sociality in the African striped mouse (*Rhabdomys pumilio*). *Journal of Animal Ecology* 81, 649–656 (2012).

34. Schradin, C., Lindholm, A.K., Johannesen, J., Schoepf, I., Yuen, C-H., König, B. & Pillay, N. Social flexibility and social evolution in mammals: a case study of the African striped mouse (*Rhabdomys pumilio*). *Molecular Ecology* 21, 541–553, doi:10.1111/j.1365-294X.2011.05256.x (2012).

35. Schradin, C. & Pillay, N. Female striped mice (*Rhabdomys pumilio*) change their home ranges in response to seasonal variation in food availability. *Behavioral Ecology* 17, 452–458, doi:10.1093/beheco/arj047 (2006).

36. Schradin, C. When to live alone and when to live in groups: ecological determinants of sociality in the African striped mouse (*Rhabdomys pumilio*, Sparrman, 1784). *Belgian Journal of Zoology* 135, 77–82 (2005).

37. Schradin, C. & Pillay, N. Demography of the striped mouse (*Rhabdomys pumilio*) in the succulent karoo. *Mammalian Biology* 70, 84–92, doi:10.1016/j.mambio.2004.06.004 (2005).

38. Schradin, C. & Pillay, N. The striped mouse (*Rhabdomys pumilio*) from the succulent karoo, South Africa: a territorial group-living solitary forager with communal breeding and helpers at the nest. *Journal of Comparative Physiology* 118, 37–47, doi:10.1037/0735-7036.118.1.37 (2004).

39. Schradin, C., König, B. & Pillay, N. Reproductive competition favours solitary living while ecological constraints impose group-living in African striped mice. *Journal of Animal Ecology* 79, 515–521 (2010).

40. Schradin & Pillay, *Journal of Comparative Physiology* 118, 37–47.

41. Jackson, C. & Bernard, R.T. Variation in the timing of reproduction of the four-striped field mouse, *Rhabdomys pumilio*, in the Eastern Cape province, South Africa. *African Zoology* 41, 301–304 (2006).

42. Siegfried, W.R. & Underhill, L.G. Flocking as an anti-predator strategy in doves. *Animal Behaviour* 23, 504–508 (1975).

43. Ibid.

44. Lubbe, N., Czenze, Z.J., Noakes, M.J. & McKechnie, A.E. The energetic significance of communal roosting and insulated roost nests in a small arid-zone passerine. *Ostrich* 89, 347–354 (2018).

45. Siegfried, W.R. Vigilance and group size in springbok. *Madoqua* 12, 151–154 (1980).

46. Bertram, B.C.R. Vigilance and group size in ostriches. *Animal Behaviour* 28, 278–286 (1980).

47. Clutton-Brock, T.H., O'Riain, M.J., Brotherton, P.N.M., Gaynor, D., Kansky, R., Griffin, A.S. & Manser, M. Selfish sentinels in cooperative mammals. *Science* 284, 1640–1644 (1999).

48. Manser, M.B. The acoustic structure of suricates' alarm calls varies with predator type and the level of response urgency. *Proceedings of the Royal Society of London B: Biological Sciences* 268, 2315–2324 (2001).

49. Manser, M.B., Bell, M.B. & Fletcher, L.B. The information that receivers extract from alarm calls in suricates. *Proceedings of the Royal Society of London B: Biological Sciences* 268, 2485–2491 (2001).

50. Waterman, J.M. & Roth, J.D. Interspecific associations of Cape ground squirrels with two mongoose species: benefit or cost? *Behavioral Ecology and Sociobiology* 61, 1675–1683 (2007).

51. Ibid.

52. Clutton-Brock, T.H., Gaynor, D., Kansky, R., MacColl, A.D., McIlrath, G., Chadwick, P.N., Brotherton, P.N.M., O'Riain, M.J., Manser, M. & Skinner, J.D. Costs of cooperative behaviour in suricates (*Suricata suricatta*). *Proceedings of the Royal Society of London B: Biological Sciences* 265, 185–190, doi:10.1098/rspb.1998.0281 (1998).

53. Clutton-Brock, T.H., Brotherton, P.N.M., O'Riain, M.J., Griffin, A.S., Gaynor, D., Kansky, R., Sharpe, L. & McIlrath, G. Contributions to cooperative rearing in meerkats. *Animal Behaviour* 61, 705–710 (2001).

54. Clutton-Brock, T., Russell, A.F., Sharpe, L.L., Brotherton, P.N., McIlrath, G.M., White, S. & Cameron, E.Z. Effects of helpers on juvenile development and survival in meerkats. *Science* 293, 2446–2449 (2001).

55. Jackson, T. The social organization and breeding system of Brants' whistling rat (*Parotomys brantsii*). *Journal of Zoology* 247, 323–331 (1999).

56. Bell, M.B., Radford, A.N., Rose, R., Wade, H. & Ridley, A.R. The value of constant surveillance in a risky environment. *Proceedings of the Royal Society of London B: Biological Sciences* 276, 2997–3005 (2009).

57. Mosser, A. & Packer, C. Group territoriality and the benefits of sociality in the African lion, *Panthera leo*. *Animal Behaviour* 78, 359–370 (2009).

58. Macdonald, D.W. The ecology of carnivore social behaviour. *Nature* 301, 379–383 (1983).

59. Turner, J.S. *The Extended Organism: The Physiology of Animal-built Structures*. (Harvard University Press, 2000).

60. Marsh, A.C. The foraging ecology of two Namib Desert harvester ant species. *South African Journal of Zoology* 22(2), 130–136 (1987).

61. Marsh, A.C. Checklist, biological notes and distribution of ants in the central Namib Desert. *Madoqua* 14(4), 333–344 (1986).

62. Marsh, A.C. Ant species richness along a climatic gradient in the Namib Desert. *Journal of Arid Environments* 11, 235–241 (1986).

63. Curtis, B.A. & Seely, M.K. Effect of an environmental gradient upon the distribution and abundance of the dune ant *Camponotus detritus*, in the central Namib Desert. *Journal of Arid Environments* 13, 259–266 (1987).

64. Lamb, T. A fatal agonistic interaction between ant and darkling beetle (Coleoptera: Tenebrionidae: Pimeliinae: Adesmiini) in the northern Namib Desert. *The Coleopterists Bulletin* 72, 314–317 (2018).

65. Curtis, B.A. Observations on the natural history and behaviour of the dune ant, *Camponotus detritus* Emery, in the central Namib Desert. *Madoqua* 14, 279–289 (1985).

66. Lowney, A.M., Flower, T.P. & Thomson, R.L. Kalahari skinks eavesdrop on sociable weavers to manage predation by pygmy falcons and expand their realized niche. *Behavioral Ecology* (2020).

Chapter Seven

1. Louw, G.N. & Seely, M.K. *Ecology of Desert Organisms*. (Longman, 1982).

2. Lovegrove, B.G. Obligatory nocturnalism in Triassic archaic mammals: preservation of sperm quality? *Physiological and Biochemical Zoology* 92, 544–553, doi:10.1086/705440 (2019).

3. Maor, R., Dayan, T., Ferguson-Gow, H. & Jones, K.E. Temporal niche expansion in mammals from a nocturnal ancestor after dinosaur extinction. *Nature Ecology & Evolution* 1, 1889 (2017).

4. Wharton, R.A. Colouration and diurnal activity patterns in some Namib Desert Zophosini (Coleoptera: Tenebrionidae). *Journal of Arid Environments* 3, 309–317 (1980).

5. Curtis, B.A. Activity of the Namib Desert dune ant, *Camponotus detritus*. *South African Journal of Zoology* 20, 41–48 (1985).

6. Watson, R.T. Niche separation in Namib Desert dune Lepismatidae (Thysanura: Insecta): detrivores in an allochthonous detritus ecosystem. *Journal of Arid Environments* 17, 37–48 (1989).

7. Perrin, M.R. Notes on the activity patterns of 12 species of southern African rodents and a new design of activity monitor. *South African Journal of Zoology* 16, 248–258 (1981).

8. Lovegrove, B.G. & Heldmaier, G. The amplitude of circadian body temperature rhythms in three rodents (*Aethomys namaquensis*, *Thallomys paedulcus* and *Cryptomys damarensis*) along an arboreal-subterranean gradient. *Australian Journal of Zoology* 42, 65–78 (1994).

9. Lovegrove, B.G., Heldmaier, G. & Knight, M. Seasonal and circadian energetic patterns in an arboreal rodent, *Thallomys paedulcus*, and a burrow-dwelling rodent, *Aethomys namaquensis*, from the Kalahari Desert. *Journal of Thermal Biology* 16, 199–209 (1991).

10. Lovegrove, B.G. The zoogeography of mammalian basal metabolic rate. *The American Naturalist*. 156, 201–219 (2000).

11. Fielden, L.J., Waggoner, J.P., Perrin, M.R. & Hickmann, G.C. Thermoregulation in the Namib Desert golden mole, *Eremitalpa granti namibensis* (Chrysochloridae). *Journal of Arid Environments* 18, 221–237 (1990).

12. Scantlebury, M., Lovegrove, B.G., Jackson, C.R., Bennett, N.C. & Lutermann, H. Hibernation and non-shivering thermogenesis in the Hottentot golden mole (*Amblysomus hottentottus longiceps*). *Journal of Comparative Physiology B* 178, 887–897 (2008).

13. Lovegrove, B.G., Lawes, M.J. & Roxburgh, L. Confirmation of pleisiomorphic daily torpor in mammals: the round-eared elephant shrew *Macroscelides proboscideus* (Macroscelidea). *Journal of Comparative Physiology B* 169, 453–460 (1999).

14. Lovegrove, B.G. *Fires of Life: Endothermy in Birds and Mammals*. (Yale University Press, 2019).

15. Boyles, J.G., Smit, B., Sole, C.L. & McKechnie, A.E. Body temperature patterns in two syntopic elephant shrew species during winter. *Comparative Biochemistry and Physiology A* 161, 89–94, doi:10.1016/j.cbpa2011.09.007 (2012).

16. Lovegrove, Lawes & Roxburgh, *Journal of Comparative Physiology B* 169, 453–460.

17. Dumbacher, J.P., Rathbun, G.B., Osborne, T.O., Griffin, M. & Eiseb, S.J. A new species of round-eared sengi (genus Macroscelides) from Namibia. *Journal of Mammalogy* 95, 443–454, doi:10.1644/13-mamm-a-159 (2014).

18. Hallam, S.L. & Mzilikazi, N. Heterothermy in the southern African hedgehog, *Atelerix frontalis*. *Journal of Comparative Physiology B* 181, 437–445, doi:10.1007/s00360-010-0531-5 (2011).

19. Lovegrove, *The American Naturalist*. 156, 201–219.

20. Lovegrove, *Fires of Life*.

21. Ibid.

22. Ibid.

23. van Rooyen, M.W., Grobbelaar, N., Theron, G.K. & van Rooyen, N. The ephemerals of Namaqualand: effects of photoperiod, temperature and moisture stress on the development and flowering of three species. *Journal of Arid Environments* 20, 15–29 (1991).

24. van Rooyen, M.W., Theron, G.K. & Grobbelaar, N. A phenology of the vegetation in the Hester Malan Nature Reserve in the Namaqualand Broken Veld: 2. The therophyte population. *South African Journal of Botany* 45, 433–452 (1979).

25. Day, J.A. Environmental correlates of aquatic faunal distribution in the Namib Desert in Seely, M.K. (ed.), *Namib Ecology: 25 Years of Research:* 99–108. (Transvaal Museum, 1990).

26. Ito, C., Goto, S.G. & Numata, H. Desiccation and heat tolerance of eggs of the Asian tadpole shrimp, *Triops granarius. Zoological Science* 30, 760–767 (2013).

27. Loveridge, J.P. & Withers, P.C. Metabolism and water balance of active and cocooned African bullfrogs *Pyxicephalus adspersus. Physiological Zoology* 54(2), 203–214 (1981).

28. Ibid.

29. Allan, D. The abundance and movements of Ludwig's bustard *Neotis ludwigii. Ostrich* 65, 95–105 (1994).

30. Curtin, N.A., Bartlam-Brooks, H.L.A., Hubel, T.Y., Lowe, J.C., Gardner-Medwin, A.R., Bennitt, E., Amos, S.J., Lorenc, M., West, T.G. & Wilson, A.M. Remarkable muscles, remarkable locomotion in desert-dwelling wildebeest. *Nature* 563, 393 (2018).

31. Naidoo, R., Chase, M.J., Beytell, P., du Preez, P., Landen, K., Stuart-Hill, G. & Taylor, R. A newly discovered wildlife migration in Namibia and Botswana is the longest in Africa. *Oryx* 50, 138–146 (2016).

32. Williamson, D.T. & Mbano, B. Wildebeest mortality during 1983 at Lake Xau, Botswana. *African Journal of Ecology* 26, 341–344 (1988).

33. Selebatso, M., Bennitt, E., Maude, G. & Fynn, R.W. Water provision alters wildebeest adaptive habitat selection and resilience in the Central Kalahari. *African Journal of Ecology* 56, 225–234 (2018).

34. Zidon, R., Garti, S., Getz, W.M. & Saltz, D. Zebra migration strategies and anthrax in Etosha National Park, Namibia. *Ecosphere* 8, e01925 (2017).

35. Kok, O. & Nel, J. The Kuiseb river as a linear oasis in the Namib Desert. *African Journal of Ecology* 34, 39–47 (1996).

36. Keeping, D., Burger, J.H., Keitsile, A.O., Gielen, M-C., Mudongo, E., Wallgren, M.,Skarpe, C. & Foot, L. Can trackers count free-ranging wildlife as effectively and efficiently as conventional aerial survey and distance sampling? Implications for citizen science in the Kalahari, Botswana. *Biological Conservation* 223, 156–169, doi:10.1016/j.biocon.2018.04.027 (2018).

37. Keeping, D., Keitsile, A.O. & Burger, J.H. Eland in Botswana's Kalahari. *Gnusletter* 35, 21–25 (2018).

38. Ibid.

39. Berry, H.H., Siegfried, W.R. & Remmert, H. Mosaic-like events in arid and semi-arid Namibia in Remmert, H. (ed.), *The Mosaic-Cycle Concept of Ecosystems*: 147–159. (Springer-Verlag, 1991).

40. Allan, R., Lindesay, J. & Parker, D. *El Niño Southern Oscillation and Climatic Variability.* (CSIRO Australia, 1996).

41. Fraser, J.G. *Episodes in My Life* (Juta, 1922).

42. Cronwright-Schreiner, S.C. *The Migratory Springbucks of South Africa.* (Fisher & Unwin, 1925).

43. Scully, W.C. *Between Sun and Sand: A Tale of an African Desert.* (Methuen, 1898).

44. Cronwright-Schreiner, *Migratory Springbucks.*

45. Davie, T.B. The trekbokke. *The Cornhill Magazine* 1921.

46. Fraser, *Episodes in My Life.*

47. Scully, *Between Sun and Sand.*

48. Skinner, J.D. Springbok (*Antidorcas marsupialus*) treks. *Transactions of the Royal Society of South Africa* 48, 291–305 (1993).

49. Roche, C.J. 'Ornaments of the desert' Springbok treks in the Cape Colony, 1774–1908. MA thesis, University of Cape Town (2004).

50. Skinner, J.D. & Louw, G.N. (eds). *The Springbok Antidorcas marsupialis* (Zimmermann, 1780). Transvaal Museum Monograph 10 (1996).

51. Couper-Johnson, R. *El Niño: The Weather Phenomenon that Changed the World.* (Hodder & Stoughton, 2000).

Chapter Eight

1. Dawkins, R. *The Selfish Gene.* (Oxford University Press, 1976).

2. Steiner, K.E. & Johnson, S.D. Specialized pollination systems in southern Africa. *South African Journal of Science* 99, 345–348 (2003).

3. Mayer, C., Soka, G. & Picker, M. The importance of monkey beetle (Scarabaeidae: Hopliini) pollination for Aizoaceae and Asteraceae in grazed and ungrazed areas at Paulshoek, Succulent Karoo, South Africa. *Journal of Insect Conservation* 10, 323 (2006).

4. van Rooyen, M.W., Theron, G.K. & Grobbelaar, N. A phenology of the vegetation in the Hester Malan Nature Reserve in the Namaqualand Broken Veld: 2. The therophyte population. *South African Journal of Botany* 45, 433–452 (1979).

5. Mucina, L. & Rutherford, M.C. (eds). *The Vegetation of South Africa, Lesotho and Swaziland.* (South African National Biodiversity Institute, 2006).

6. Gess, S.K. & Gess, F.W. Distributions of flower associations of pollen wasps (Vespidae: Masarinae) in southern Africa. *Journal of Arid Environments* 57, 17–44 (2004).

7. Gess, S.K. & Gess, F.W. Flower visiting by masarid in southern Africa (Hymenoptera: Vespoidea: Masaridae). *Annals of the Cape Provincial Museum* 18 (PT, 5), 95–134 (1989).

8. Gess, S.K. Biogeography of the masarine wasps (Hymenoptera: Vespidae: Masarinae), with particular emphasis on the southern African taxa and on correlations between masarine and forage plant distributions. *Journal of Biogeography* 19, 491–503 (1992).

9. Gess & Gess, *Journal of Arid Environments* 57, 17–44.

10. Klak, C., Reeves, G. & Hedderson, T. Unmatched tempo of evolution in southern African semi-desert ice plants. *Nature* 427, 63 (2004).

11. Hartmann, H.E.K. Mesenbryanthema. *Contributions from the Bolus Herbarium* 13, 75–157 (1991).

12. Dean, W.R.J., Milton, S.J. & Siegfried, W.R. Dispersal of seeds as nest material by birds in semiarid Karoo shrubland. *Ecology* 71(4), 1299–1306 (1990).

13. Rohwer, V.G., Pauw, A. & Martin, P.R. Fluff-thieving birds sabotage seed dispersal. *Royal Society Open Science* 4, doi:10.1098/rsos.160538 (2017).

14. Gunster, A. Aerial seed banks in the central Namib – distribution of serotinous plants in relation to climate and habitat. *Journal of Biogeography* 19, 563–572, doi:10.2307/2845775 (1992).

15. Wetschnig, W. & Depisch, B. Pollination biology of *Welwitschia mirabilis* HOOK. f. (Welwitschiaceae, Gnetopsida). *Phyton – Annales Rei Botanicae* 39, 167–183 (1999).

16. Hoffman, M.T., Cowling, R.M., Douie, C. & Pierce, S.M. Seed predation and germination of *Acacia erioloba* in the Kuiseb River Valley, Namib Desert. *South African Journal of Botany* 55(1), 103–106 (1989).

17. Barnard, W.S. Darwin and the Cape. *South African Journal of Science* 100, 243–248 (2004).

18. Thackeray, J.F. Darwin's interest in the natural history of the Cape: from beetles to antelope, plants and granite. *Transactions of the Royal Society of South Africa* 64, 79–81 (2009).

19. Barnard, *South African Journal of Science* 100, 243–248.

20. Darwin, C. *On the Various Contrivances by which British and Foreign Orchids are Fertilised by Insects, and on the Good Effects of Intercrossing.* (John Murray, 1862).

21. van der Niet, T., Peakall, R. & Johnson, S.D. Pollinator-driven ecological speciation in plants: new evidence and future perspectives. *Annals of Botany* 113, 199–211, doi:10.1093/aob/mct290 (2014).

22. van der Niet, T. & Johnson, S.D. Phylogenetic evidence for pollinator-driven diversification of angiosperms. *Trends in Ecology & Evolution* 27, 353–361, doi:10.1016/j.tree.2012.02.002 (2012).

23. Johnson, S.D. The pollination niche and its role in the diversification and maintenance of the southern African flora. *Philosophical Transactions of the Royal Society of London B: Biological Sciences* 365, 499–516, doi:10.1098/rstb.2009.0243 (2010).

24. Kahnt, B., Montgomery, G., Murray, E. & Kuhlmann, M. Playing with extremes: origins and evolution of exaggerated female forelegs in South African *Rediviva* bees. *Molecular Phylogenetics and Evolution* 115, 95–105 (2017).

25. Pauw, A., Kahnt, B., Kuhlmann, M., Michez, D., Montgomery, G., Murray, E. & Danforth, B.N. Long-legged bees make adaptive leaps: linking adaptation to coevolution in a plant-pollinator network. *Proceedings of the Royal Society of London B: Biological Sciences* 284, doi:10.1098/rspb.2017.1707 (2017).

26. Pauw, A. & Bond, W.J. Mutualisms matter: pollination rate limits the distribution of oil-secreting orchids. *Oikos* 120, 1531–1538, doi:10.1111/j.1600-0706.2011.19417.x (2011).

27. Pauw, A., Stofberg, J. & Waterman, R.J. Flies and flowers in Darwin's race. *Evolution* 63, 268–279, doi:10.1111/j.1558-5646.2008.00547.x (2009).

28. Steiner, K.E. & Whitehead, V.B. Pollinator adaptation to oil-secreting flowers: *Rediviva* and *Diascia*. *Evolution* 44(6), 1701–1707 (1990).

29. Whitehead, V.B., Schelpe, E. & Anthony, N.C. The bee *Rediviva longimanus* Michener (Apoidea, Melittidae), collecting pollen and oil from *Diascia longicornis* (Thunb) Druce (Scrophulariaceae). *South African Journal of Science* 80, 286–286 (1984).

30. Kuhlman, M. Nest architecture and use of floral oil in the oil-collecting South African solitary bee *Rediviva intermixta* (Cockerell) (Hymenoptera: Apoidea: Melittidae). *Journal of Natural History* 48, 2633–2644 (2014).

31. Kahnt, Montgomery, Murray & Kuhlmann, *Molecular Phylogenetics and Evolution* 115, 95–105).

32. Kahnt, B., Hattingh, W.N., Theodorou, P., Wieseke, N., Kuhlmann, M., Glennon, K.L., van der Niet, T., Paxton, R. & Cron, G.V. Should I stay or should I go? Pollinator shifts rather than cospeciation dominate the evolutionary history of South African *Rediviva* bees and their *Diascia* host plants. *Molecular Ecology* 28, 4118–4133 (2019).

33. van der Niet, Peakall & Johnson, *Annals of Botany* 113, 199–211.

34. Darwin, C. On the two forms, or dimorphic condition, in the species of *Primula* and on their remarkable sexual relations. *Botanical Journal of the Linnean Society* 6, 77–96 (1862).

35. Combs, J. & Pauw, A. Preliminary evidence that the long-proboscid fly, *Philoliche gulosa*, pollinates *Disa karooica* and

its proposed Batesian model *Pelargonium stipulaceum*. *South African Journal of Botany* 75, 757–761 (2009).

36. Goldblatt, P. & Manning, J.C. The long-proboscid fly pollination system in southern Africa. *Annals of the Missouri Botanical Garden* 87, 146–170 (2000).

37. Johnson, S.D. Carrion flowers. *Current Biology* 26, R556–R558, doi:10.1016/j.cub.2015.07.047 (2016).

38. van der Niet, T., Hansen, D.M. & Johnson, S.D. Carrion mimicry in a South African orchid: flowers attract a narrow subset of the fly assemblage on animal carcasses. *Annals of Botany* 107, 981–992, doi:10.1093/aob/mcr048 (2011).

39. Johnson, S.D., Pauw, A. & Midgley, J. Rodent pollination in the African lily *Massonia depressa* (Hyacinthaceae). *American Journal of Botany* 88, 1768–1773 (2001).

40. Kleizen, C., Midgley, J. & Johnson, S.D. Pollination systems of *Colchicum* (Colchicaceae) in southern Africa: evidence for rodent pollination. *Annals of Botany* 102, 747–755, doi:10.1093/aob/mcn157 (2008).

41. Wester, P. Nectar feeding by the Cape rock elephant-shrew *Elephantulus edwardii* (Macroscelidea) – A primarily insectivorous mammal pollinates the parasite *Hyobanche atropurpurea* (Orobanchaceae). *Flora – Morphology, Distribution, Functional Ecology of Plants* 206, 997–1001 (2011).

42. Flasch, L., von Elm, N. & Wester, P. Nectar-drinking *Elephantulus edwardii* as a potential pollinator of *Massonia echinata*, endemic to the Bokkeveld plateau in South Africa. *African Journal of Ecology* 55, 376–379 (2017).

43. Wester, P. Sticky snack for sengis: The Cape rock elephant-shrew, *Elephantulus edwardii* (Macroscelidea), as a pollinator of the pagoda lily, *Whiteheadia bifolia* (Hyacinthaceae). *Naturwissenschaften* 97, 1107–1112 (2010).

44. Johnson, S.D. & Midgley, J.J. Fly pollination of *Gorteria diffusa* (Asteraceae), and a possible mimetic function for dark spots on the capitulum. *American Journal of Botany* 84, 429–436, doi:10.2307/2446018 (1997).

45. Lea, A. Some major factors in the population dynamics of the brown locust *Locustana pardalina* (Walker) in Davis, D.H.S. (ed.). *Ecological Studies in Southern Africa:* 269–283 (1964).

46. Goldberg, S.R. & Robinson, M.D. Reproduction in 2 Namib Desert lacertid lizards (*Aporosaura anchietae* and *Meroles cuneirostris*). *Herpetologica* 35, 169–175 (1979).

47. Robinson, M.D. Summer field energetics of the Namib Desert dune lizard *Aporosaura anchietae* (Lacertidae) and its relation to reproduction. *Journal of Arid Environments* 18, 207–215 (1990).

48. Goldberg & Robinson, *Herpetologica* 35, 169–175.

49. Dietl, G.P., Kidwell, S.M., Brenner, M., Burney, D.A., Flessa, K.W., Jackson, S.T. & Koch, P.L. Conservation paleobiology: leveraging knowledge of the past to inform conservation and restoration. *Annual Review of Earth and Planetary Sciences* 43, 79–103 (2015).

50. Jackson, C. & Bernard, R.T. Variation in the timing of reproduction of the four-striped field mouse, *Rhabdomys pumilio*, in the Eastern Cape province, South Africa. *African Zoology*. 41, 301–304 (2006).

51. Maclean, G.L. The breeding seasons of birds in the south-western Kalahari. *Ostrich Supplement* 8, 179–192 (1970).

52. Maclean, G.L. The biology of the larks (Alaudidae) in the Kalahari Sandveld. *Zoologica Africana* 5, 7–39 (1970).

53. Maclean, G.L. Breeding behaviour of the larks in the Kalahari Sandveld. *Annals of the Natal Museum* 20, 381–401 (1970).

54. Maclean, *Ostrich Supplement* 8, 179–192.

55. Maclean, G.L. The sociable weaver, part 3: breeding biology and moult. *Ostrich* 44, 219–240 (1973).

56. Mills, M.G.L. *Kalahari Hyaenas: Comparative Behavioural Ecology of Two Species.* (Unwin Hyman, 1990).

57. Fairall, N., Jooste, J.F. & Conroy, A.M. Biological evaluation of a springbok-farming enterprise. *South African Journal of Wildlife Research* 20(2), 73–80 (1990).

58. Skinner, J.D., van Aarde, R.J. & van Jaarsveld, A.S. Adaptations in three species of large mammals (*Antidorcas marsupialis, Hystrix africaeaustralis, Hyaena brunnea*) to arid environments. *South African Journal of Zoology* 19, 82–86 (1984).

Chapter Nine

1. Smith, R.M. & Botha-Brink, J. Anatomy of a mass extinction: sedimentological and taphonomic evidence for drought-induced die-offs at the Permo–Triassic boundary in the main Karoo Basin, South Africa. *Palaeogeography, Palaeoclimatology, Palaeoecology* 396, 99–118 (2014).

2. Lovegrove, B.G. *Fires of Life: Endothermy in Birds and Mammals.* (Yale University Press, 2019).

3. Botha-Brink, J. & Modesto, S.P. A mixed-age classed 'pelycosaur' aggregation from South Africa: earliest evidence of parental care in amniotes? *Proceedings of the Royal Society of London B: Biological Sciences* 274, 2829–2834, doi:10.1098/rspb.2007.0803 (2007).

4. Wang, H.J., Sun, J., Chen, H. & Zhu, Y. Extreme climate in China: facts, simulation and projection. *Meteorologische Zeitschrift* 21, 279–304, doi:10.1127/0941-2948/2012/0330 (2012).

5. Smith & Botha-Brink, *Palaeogeography, Palaeoclimatology, Palaeoecology* 396, 99–118.

6. Botha-Brink, J., Codron, D., Huttenlocker, A.K., Angielczyk, K.D. & Ruta, M. Breeding young as a survival strategy during Earth's greatest mass extinction. *Scientific Reports* 6 (24053), doi:10.1038/srep24053 (2016).

7. Lovegrove, *Fires of Life*.

8. Lovegrove, B.G. A phenology of the evolution of endothermy in birds and mammals. *Biological Reviews of the Cambridge Philosophical Society* 92, 1213–1240 (2017).

9. Rey, K., Amiot, R., Fourel, F., Abdala, F., Fluteau, F., Jalil, N., Liu, J., Rubidge, B.S., Smith, R.M.H., Steyer, J.S., Viglietti, P.A., Wang, X. & Lécuyer, C. Oxygen isotopes suggest elevated thermometabolism within multiple Permo–Triassic therapsid clades. *eLife* 6 (e28559) (2017).

10. Levesque, D.L. & Lovegrove, B.G. Increased homeothermy during reproduction in a basal placental mammal. *Journal of Experimental Biology* 217, 1535–1542 (2014).

11. Lovegrove, B.G. & Génin, F. Torpor and hibernation in a basal placental mammal, the lesser hedgehog tenrec *Echinops telfairi. Journal of Comparative Physiology B* 178, 691–698 (2008).

12. Lovegrove, B.G., Lobban, K.D. & Levesque, D.L. Mammal survival at the Cretaceous–Paleogene boundary: metabolic homeostasis in prolonged tropical hibernation in tenrecs. *Proceedings of the Royal Society of London B: Biological Sciences* 281 (2014).

13. Fernandez, V. Abdala, F., Carlson, K.J., Cook, D.C., Rubidge, B.S., Yates, A. & Tafforeau, P. Synchrotron reveals Early Triassic odd couple: injured amphibian and aestivating therapsid share burrow. *PloS one* 8, e64978 (2013).

14. Botha-Brink, Codron, Huttenlocker, Angielczyk & Ruta, *Scientific Reports* 6 (24053).

15. Ruta, M., Botha-Brink, J., Mitchell, S.A. & Benton, M.J. The radiation of cynodonts and the ground plan of mammalian morphological diversity. *Proceedings of the Royal Society of London B: Biological Sciences* 280, 20131865 (2013).

16. Sulej, T. & Niedźwiedzki, G. An elephant-sized Late Triassic synapsid with erect limbs. *Science* 363, 78–80 (2019).

17. Romano, M. & Manucci, F. Resizing *Lisowicia bojani*: volumetric body mass estimate and 3D reconstruction of the giant Late Triassic dicynodont. *Historical Biology* 33, 474–479, doi:10.1080/08912963.2019.1631819.

18. Gower, D.J., Hancox, P.J., Botha-Brink, J., Sennikov, A.G. & Butler, R.J.A. A new species of *Garjainia* Ochev, 1958 (Diapsida: Archosauriformes: Erythrosuchidae) from the Early Triassic of South Africa. *PLoS One* 9, e111154 (2014).

19. Lovegrove, B. G. Obligatory nocturnalism in Triassic archaic mammals: preservation of sperm quality? *Physiological and Biochemical Zoology* 92, 544–553, doi:10.1086/705440 (2019).

20. McPhee, B.W., Benson, R.B., Botha-Brink, J., Bordy, E.M. & Choiniere, J.N. A giant dinosaur from the earliest Jurassic of South Africa and the transition to quadrupedality in early sauropodomorphs. *Current Biology* 28, 3143–3151, e3147 (2018).

21. McPhee, B.W. & Choiniere, J.N. A hyper-robust sauropodomorph dinosaur ilium from the Upper Triassic–Lower Jurassic Elliot Formation of South Africa: implications for the functional diversity of basal Sauropodomorpha. *Journal of African Earth Sciences* 123, 177–184 (2016).

22. McPhee, B.W., Bonnan, M.F., Yates, A.M., Neveling, J. & Choiniere, J.N. A new basal sauropod from the pre-Toarcian Jurassic of South Africa: evidence of niche-partitioning at the sauropodomorph–sauropod boundary? *Scientific Reports* 5, 13224 (2015).

23. McPhee, B.W., Choiniere, J.N., Yates, A.M. & Viglietti, P.A. A second species of *Eucnemesaurus* Van Hoepen, 1920 (Dinosauria, Sauropodomorpha): new information on the diversity and evolution of the sauropodomorph fauna of South Africa's lower Elliot Formation (latest Triassic). *Journal of Vertebrate Paleontology* 35, e980504 (2015).

24. McPhee, Benson, Botha-Brink, Bordy & Choiniere, *Current Biology* 28, 3143–3151.

Chapter Ten

1. Klak, C., Hanacek, P. & Bruyns, P.V. Out of southern Africa: origin, biogeography and age of the Aizooideae (Aizoaceae). *Molecular Phylogenetics and Evolution* 109, 203–216, doi:10.1016/j.ympev.2016.12.016 (2017).

2. Klak, C., Reeves, G. & Hedderson, T. Unmatched tempo of evolution in southern African semi-desert ice plants. *Nature* 427, 63 (2004).

3. Hilton-Taylor, C., le Roux, A. & Huntley, B.J. Conservation status of the fynbos and karoo biomes in Huntley, B.J. (ed.) *Biotic Diversity in Southern Africa: Concepts and Conservation*: 202–223. (Oxford University Press, 1989).

4. Integrated Rural Development and Nature Conservation (IRDNC). www.irdnc.org.na. [Accessed 6 May 2021].

5. Shackleton, R.T., le Maitre, D.C. & Richardson, D.M. *Prosopis* invasions in South Africa: population structures and impacts on native tree population stability. *Journal of Arid Environments* 114, 70–78, doi:10.1016/j.jaridenv.2014.11.006 (2015).

6. Shackleton, R.T., le Maitre, D.C., van Wilgen, B.W. & Richardson, D.M. The impact of invasive alien *Prosopis* species (mesquite) on native plants in different environments in South Africa. *South African Journal of Botany* 97, 25–31, doi:10.1016/j.sajb.2014.12.008 (2015).

7. Mucina, L. & Rutherford, M.C. (eds). *The Vegetation of South Africa, Lesotho and Swaziland*. (South African National Biodiversity Institute, 2006).

8. Webley, L. Archaeological evidence for pastoralist land-use and settlement in Namaqualand over the last 2000 years. *Journal of Arid Environments* 70, 629–640, doi:10.1016/j.jaridenv.2006.03.009 (2007).

9. Morris, D. Before the Anthropocene: human pasts in Karoo landscapes. *African Journal of Range & Forage Science* 35, 179–190 (2018).

10. Saaed, M.W., Jacobs, S.M., Masubelele, M.L., Samuels, I., Khomo, L. & El-Barasi, Y.M. The composition of the soil seedbank and its role in ecosystem dynamics and rehabilitation potential in the arid Tankwa Karoo region, South Africa. *African Journal of Range & Forage Science* 35, 351–361 (2018).

11. Hitchcock, R.K., Sapignoli, M. & Babchuk, W.A. What about our rights? Settlements, subsistence and livelihood security among Central Kalahari San and Bakgalagadi. *The International Journal of Human Rights* 15, 62–88 (2010).

12. Klak, Hanacek & Bruyns, *Molecular Phylogenetics and Evolution* 109, 203–216.

13. Klak, Reeves & Hedderson, *Nature* 427, 63.

14. Otto, F.E.L., Wolski, P., Lehner, F., Tebaldi, C., van Oldenborgh, G.J., Hogesteeger, S., Singh, R., Holden, P., Fučkar, N.S., Odoulami, R.C. & New, M. Anthropogenic influence on the drivers of the Western Cape drought 2015–2017. *Environmental Research Letters* 13, doi:10.1088/1748–9326/aae9f9 (2018).

15. Bengtsson, L., Hodges, K.I. & Roeckner, E. Storm tracks and climate change. *Journal of Climate* 19, 3518–3543, doi:10.1175/jcli3815.1 (2006).

16. Toggweiler, J.R., Russell, J.L. & Carson, S.R. Midlatitude westerlies, atmospheric CO_2, and climate change during the ice ages. *Paleoceanography* 21, doi:10.1029/2005pa001154 (2006).

17. Ganopolski, A., Winkelmann, R. & Schellnhuber, H.J. Critical insolation–CO_2 relation for diagnosing past and future glacial inception. *Nature* 529, 200 (2016).

18. Ibid.

19. Berger, A. *et al.* Interglacials of the last 800,000 years. *Reviews of Geophysics* 54, 162–219, doi:10.1002/2015rg000482 (2016).

20. Bengtsson, Hodges & Roeckner, *Journal of Climate* 19, 3518–3543.

21. Schuller, I., Belz, L., Wilkes, H. & Wehrmann, A. Late quaternary shift in southern African rainfall zones: sedimentary and geochemical data from Kalahari pans. *Zeitschrift für Geomorphologie* 61, 339–362 (2018).

22. Zhao, X., Dupont, L., Schefuß, E., Meadows, M.E., Hahn, A. & Wefer, G. Holocene vegetation and climate variability in the winter and summer rainfall zones of South Africa. *The Holocene* 26, 843–857 (2016).

23. Carr, A.S., Thomas, D.S., Bateman, M.D., Meadows, M.E. & Chase, B. Late Quaternary palaeoenvironments of the winter-rainfall zone of southern Africa: palynological and sedimentological evidence from the Agulhas Plain. *Palaeogeography, Palaeoclimatology, Palaeoecology* 239, 147–165 (2006).

24. Strobel, P., Kasper, T., Frenzel, P., Schittek, K., Quick, L.J., Meadows, M.E., Mäusbacher, R. & Haberzettl, T. Late Quaternary palaeoenvironmental change in the year-round rainfall zone of South Africa derived from peat sediments from Vankervelsvlei. *Quaternary Science Reviews* 218, 200–214, doi:10.1016/j.quascirev.2019.06.014 (2019).

25. Ward, J., Seely, M.K. & Lancaster, N. On the antiquity of the Namib. *South African Journal of Science* 79, 175–183 (1983).

26. Pickford, M., Senut, B., Mocke, H., Mourer-Chauviré, C., Rage, J. & Mein, P. Eocene aridity in southwestern Africa: timing of onset and biological consequences. *Transactions of the Royal Society of South Africa* 69, 139–144 (2014).

27. Weldeab, S., Stuut, J.B.W., Schneider, R.R. & Siebel, W. Holocene climate variability in the winter rainfall zone of South Africa. *Climate of the Past* 9, 2347–2364, doi:10.5194/cp-9-2347-2013 (2013).

28. Haensler, A., Cermak, J., Hagemann, S. & Jacob, D. Will the southern African west coast fog be affected by future climate change? *Erdkunde* 65, 261–275, doi:10.3112/erdkunde.2011.03.04 (2011).

29. Klak, Reeves & Hedderson, *Nature* 427, 63.

30. Klak, Hanacek & Bruyns, *Molecular Phylogenetics and Evolution* 109, 203–216.

31. Klak, Reeves & Hedderson, *Nature* 427, 63.

32. Valente, L.M., Britton, A.W., Powell, M.P., Papadopulos, A.S.T., Burgoyne, P.M. & Savolainen, V. Correlates of hyperdiversity in southern African ice plants (Aizoaceae). *Botanical Journal of the Linnean Society* 174, 110–129, doi:10.1111/boj.12117 (2014).

33. Klak, Reeves & Hedderson, *Nature* 427, 63.

34. Valente, Britton, Powell, Papadopulos, Burgoyne & Savolainen, *Botanical Journal of the Linnean Society* 174, 110–129.

35. Baines, P.G. Long-term variations in winter rainfall of southwest Australia and the African monsoon. *Australian Meteorological Magazine* 54, 91–102 (2005).

36. Young, A.J., Guo, D., Desmet, P.G. & Midgley, G.F. Biodiversity and climate change: risks to dwarf succulents in southern Africa. *Journal of Arid Environments* 129, 16–24 (2016).

37. Foden, W., Midgley, G.F., Hughes, G., Bond, W.J., Thuiller, W., Hoffman, M.T., Kaleme, P., Underhill, L.G., Rebelo, A. & Hannah, L. A changing climate is eroding the geographical range of the Namib Desert tree aloe through population declines and dispersal lags. *Diversity and Distributions* 13, 645–653 (2007).

38. Midgley, G.F. & Thuiller, W. Potential responses of terrestrial biodiversity in southern Africa to anthropogenic climate change. *Regional Environmental Change* 11, 127–135 (2011).

39. Valente, Britton, Powell, Papadopulos, Burgoyne & Savolainen, *Botanical Journal of the Linnean Society* 174, 110–129.

40. Linder, H.P. & Verboom, G.A. The evolution of regional species richness: the history of the southern African flora. *Annual Review of Ecology, Evolution, and Systematics* 46, 393–412 (2015).

41. Midgley, G.F. & Bond, W.J. Future of African terrestrial biodiversity and ecosystems under anthropogenic climate change. *Nature Climate Change* 5, 823 (2015).

42. Bond, W.J. & Midgley, G.F. Carbon dioxide and the uneasy interactions of trees and savannah grasses. *Philosophical Transactions of the Royal Society B: Biological Sciences* 367, 601–612 (2012).

43. Hoffman, M.T., Rohde, R.F. & Gillson, L. Rethinking catastrophe? Historical trajectories and modelled future vegetation change in southern Africa. *Anthropocene* 25, 100189 (2019).

44. Masubelele, M.L., Hoffman, M.T., Bond, W. & Gambiza, J.A. 50 year study shows grass cover has increased in shrublands of semi-arid South Africa. *Journal of Arid Environments* 104, 43–51 (2014).

45. du Toit, J.C., Ramaswiela, T., Pauw, M.J. & O'Connor, T.G. Interactions of grazing and rainfall on vegetation at Grootfontein in the eastern Karoo. *African Journal of Range & Forage Science* 35, 267–276 (2018).

46. Thomas, D.S., Knight, M. & Wiggs, G.F. Remobilization of southern African desert dune systems by twenty-first century global warming. *Nature* 435, 1218 (2005).

47. Rey, B., Fuller, A., Mitchell, D., Meyer, L.C. & Hetem, R.S. Drought-induced starvation of aardvarks in the Kalahari: an indirect effect of climate change. *Biology Letters* 13, 20170301 (2017).

48. Ibid.

49. Whittington-Jones, G.M., Bernard, R.T.F. & Park, D.M. Aardvark burrows: potential resources for animals in arid and semi-arid environments. *African Zoology* 46, 362–370 (2011).

50. Conradie, S.R., Woodborne, S.M., Cunningham, S.J. & McKechnie, A.E. Chronic, sublethal effects of high temperatures will cause severe declines in southern African arid-zone birds during the 21st century. *Proceedings of the National Academy of Sciences*, 201821312 (2019).

51. van de Ven, T., McKechnie, A.E. & Cunningham, S.J. The costs of keeping cool: behavioural trade-offs between foraging and thermoregulation are associated with significant mass losses in an arid-zone bird. *Oecologia* 191, 205–215, doi:10.1007/s00442-019-04486-x (2019).

52. Cunningham, S.J., Martin, R.O., Hojem, C.L. & Hockey, P.A.R. Temperatures in excess of critical thresholds threaten nestling growth and survival in a rapidly-warming arid savanna: a study of common fiscals. *Plos One* 8, doi:10.1371/journal.pone.0074613 (2013).

53. Conradie, Woodborne, Cunningham & McKechnie, *Proceedings of the National Academy of Sciences*, 201821312.

54. du Plessis, K.L., Martin, R.O., Hockey, P.A.R., Cunningham, S.J. & Ridley, A.R. The costs of keeping cool in a warming world: implications of high temperatures for foraging, thermoregulation and body condition of an arid-zone bird. *Global Change Biology* 18, 3063–3070 (2012).

55. Kinahan, J. *Pastoral Nomads of the Central Namib Desert: The People History Forgot.* (Namibia Archaeological Trust, 2001).

56. Hoffman, M.T., Walker, C. & Henschel, J.R. Reflections on the Karoo Special Issue: towards an interdisciplinary research agenda for South Africa's drylands. *African Journal of Range & Forage Science* 35, 387–393 (2018).

57. Henschel, J.R. Locust times – monitoring populations and outbreak controls in relation to Karoo natural capital. *Transactions of the Royal Society of South Africa* 70, 135–143 (2015).

58. Todd, M.C., Washington, R., Cheke, R.A. & Kniveton, D. Brown locust outbreaks and climate variability in southern Africa. *Journal of Applied Ecology* 39, 31–42 (2002).

59. Nailand, S. Modelling brown locust, *Locustana pardalina* (Walker), outbreaks in the Karoo. *South African Journal of Science* 89, 420–424 (1993).

60. Shackleton, R.T., le Maitre, D.C., van Wilgen, B.W. & Richardson, D.M. Towards a national strategy to optimise the management of a widespread invasive tree (*Prosopis* species; mesquite) in South Africa. *Ecosystem Services* 27, 242–252, doi:10.1016/j.ecoser.2016.11.022 (2017).

61. Shackleton, le Maitre & Richardson, *Journal of Arid Environments* 114, 70–78.

62. Shackleton, le Maitre, van Wilgen & Richardson, *South African Journal of Botany* 97, 25–31.

63. Shackleton, R.T., le Maitre, D.C., Pasiecznik, N.M. & Richardson, D.M. *Prosopis*: a global assessment of the biogeography, benefits, impacts and management of one of the world's worst woody invasive plant taxa. *Aob Plants* 6, doi:10.1093/aobpla/plu027 (2014).

64. Shackleton, le Maitre, van Wilgen & Richardson, *Ecosystem Services* 27, 242–252.

65. Carrick, P. & Krüger, R. Restoring degraded landscapes in lowland Namaqualand: lessons from the mining experience and from regional ecological dynamics. *Journal of Arid Environments* 70, 767–781 (2007).

66. Botha, M.S., Carrick, P.J. & Allsopp, N. Capturing lessons from land-users to aid the development of ecological restoration guidelines for lowland Namaqualand. *Biological Conservation* 141, 885–895 (2008).

67. Goudie, A.S. The drainage of Africa since the Cretaceous. *Geomorphology* 67, 437–456, doi:10.1016/j.geomorph.2004.11.008 (2005).

68. de Wit, M.C.J. Post-Gondwana drainage and the development of diamond placers in western South Africa. *Economic Geology and the Bulletin of the Society of Economic Geologists* 94, 721–740, doi:10.2113/gsecongeo.94.5.721 (1999).

69. Ibid.

70. Pauw, M.J., Esler, K.J. & le Maitre, D.C. Assessing the success of experimental rehabilitation on a coastal mineral sands mine in Namaqualand, South Africa. *African Journal of Range & Forage Science* 35, 363–373 (2018).

71. Botha, Carrick & Allsopp, *Biological Conservation* 141, 885–895.

72. Pauw, Esler & le Maitre, *African Journal of Range & Forage Science* 35, 363–373.

73. Todd, S.W., Hoffman, M.T., Henschel, J.R., Cardoso, A.W., Brooks, M. & Underhill, L.G. The potential impacts of fracking on biodiversity of the Karoo Basin, South Africa in Glazewski, J. and Esterhuyse, S. (eds), *Hydraulic Fracturing in the Karoo: Critical Legal and Environmental Perspectives*: 278–301 (Juta, 2016).

74. United Nations. *United Nations Conference on Desertfication, Round-Up, Plan of Action and Resolutions.* (United Nations, 1978).

75. du Toit, H.S. *Final Report of the Drought Investigation Commission: October 1923.* (Government Printer, 1923).

76. Acocks, J. Veld types of South Africa. *Memoirs of the Botanical Survey of South Africa* 28, 1–192 (1953).

77. Meadows, M.E. John Acocks and the expanding Karoo hypothesis. *South African Journal of Botany* 69, 62–67, doi:10.1016/s0254-6299(15)30360-4 (2003).

78. Roux, P.W. & Vorster, M. Vegetation change in the Karoo. *Proceedings of the Grassland Society of Southern Africa* 18, 25–29 (1983).

79. Hoffman, M.T. & Cowling, R.M. Vegetation change in the semi-arid eastern Karoo over the last 200 years: an expanding Karoo – fact or fiction? *South African Journal of Science* 86, 286–294 (1990).

80. Meadows, *South African Journal of Botany* 69, 62–67.

Index

Page numbers in **bold** refer to images such as photographs, paintings, drawings, graphs and maps.

global warming see global heating
Glossopteris **222**, 222, 223, 226
Gobabeb Namib Research Institute 23, **25**, 215
Goegap Nature Reserve **24**, 155, 179, 197, 243, **244**, 244
golden mole 37, 83, **115**, 173
golden wheel spider 140, **141**, 141
Gomphocarpus fruticosa see milkweed
Gondwana 36, 223
Gordon, Robert Jacob **204**, 266
gorgonopsids 224, 225, 226, 227
Gorteria diffusa 210, **211**
graminoid 19
granaatbos 204
Grant's golden mole 28, **83**, 83, 84, 143, 173
grass **24**, 25, 51, 52, **96**, 111, 183, 195, 223, 255, 257, 266, **267**, 267, 268
grasshoppers **115**, 130, 211
gravel plains 23, **25**, 55, 57, 98, 171, 188, 240, 258, 259
Gray's lark 29
greater kestrel **55**, 115
Greater Sossusvlei-Namib Landscape association 240
greenhouse gases 226, 254, 255
greening of aridlands 255, 256, 268
gregaria phase (locusts) 211, 212, 213
grey bietou 203
grey camel thorn tree 34
grey-backed sparrow-lark 186, 215, **216**
Grielum humifusum 177
Groen River 243, 264
ground agama 77, 77
ground pangolin **120**, **256**, 256, 257
Group Selection Theory 147
growth form 19, **20**, 24, 33, 34
gular fluttering 89, 90
Gymnosporia senegalensis see confetti spikethorn

H

Hadley cell 36, 250, **251**, 251, 252, 268
hairy-footed gerbil 82
halfmens (tree) **31**, 31, **74**, 74, 241
Hamilton, William Donald 60, **147**, 147
Hamilton's Rule 147, 148, 150
Harman, Oren 147
Hartley, Adrian 37
Hartmann's mountain zebra 63, **118**, 119, **188**, 188, 238
harvester ant **93**, **98**, 98, 163, 164, 197
harvester termite **100**, 102, **114**, 114, 115, 162, 172, 257
Haworthia 46, 47, 53, 72
    cooperi 47

heart 87, 123, 124, 126, 227
heat 59, 70, 76, 79, 80, **81**, 82, 83, 86, 87, 89, 151, 171
hedgehog lily 210
Heleosaurus **223**, 223
Heliophila lacteal **177**
    pendula 176
Heliophobius 149
Hologale parvula see common dwarf mongoose
Henschel, Joh 44, 140, 260
herb 19, **20**
herbivores 64, 94, 108, 109, 112, 114, 117, 119, 122, 123, 124, 126, 127, 128, 130, 137, 138, 206, 207, 222, 223, 224, 226, 227, 228, 230, 240, 245, 246, 255, 256, 260
Herero chat 246
Herschel 233
Hetem, Robyn 88
Heterocephalus glaber see naked mole-rat
Heterodontosaurus tucki **233**, **234**, 234
heuweltjies **100**, 100, **101**, 101, 102, 103, 116
hibernation 83, 168, 174, 175, 181, 227, 228
Hoanib River 92
Hoesch's pygmy toad **182**, 182
Hoffman, Timm 266
Hofmeyr (town) 266, 267
Hölldobler, Bert 95
Holocene **250**
Homeria 107, 178
honey badger 245
honeydew 99, 163
Hoodia 42, **43**, 50, 72
    gordonii **138**, **204**; see also ghobba
horned adder 155
horns 85, 122, 136, **140**, 140, 141
horsetails 223
hotspot see biodiversity hotspot
Hottentot golden mole 84, 174
houseflies 210
hunting (by humans) 189, 190, **191**, 191, 239, 244, 247
hunting (by carnivores) **161**, 161, 162
Hwange National Park 185
Hyaena brunnea see brown hyena
hydathodes 41, 58, **59**, 59
hyena 35, **115**
Hymenoptera 147, 148
Hyobanche atropurpurea 210, **211**
Hyperlepisma australis 105
Hypolimnas misippus see common diadem
hypoliths 57
Hyracoidea see hyrax
hyrax 37, 173
Hystrix africaeaustralis see Cape porcupine

I

Ice Ages 72, 102, 249, 250, 252, 253
ice plants **30**, 30, 252
Imitaria 201
impala 219
inbreeding 150, 154, 164
insecticides 260
insects 41, 47, 48, 53, 75, 126, 162, 164, 195, 211
Integrated Rural Development and Nature Conservation 239
Interglacial Periods 102, **250**, 250, 255
Intertropical Convergence Zone 252
invasive alien plants 260, 261
Iridaceae 31, 123, 178
Irish, John 119
Ixia 178

J

jackal buzzard 155
jackals **115**
Jacobsohn, Margaret 239
Jarvis, Jennifer 148
Jordaaniella spongiosa **253**
Ju/'hoan San 247
jumping spiders 136
Jurassic 148, 221, 233, 235

K

Kahnt, Belinda 209
Kalahari Desert 14, 16, **22**, 24, 33, 34, 70, 245, 256, 262
Kalahari duneveld 33, **35**
Kalahari Duneveld Bioregion 21, 34, 245
Kalahari gemsbok bean 66
Kalahari Gemsbok National Park 248
Kalahari grass 35
Kalahari research **248**, 248
Kalahari River 262, **263**
Kalahari sourgrass 35
Kalahari tree skink 165
Kamieskroon 176, 243, 254
Kanaan N/a'an ku sê Desert Retreat 62
Kannemeyeria **230**, 230
Kao River 262, **263**
Kaokoland **22**, 100, 112, 238, 239
kapokbossie 33, **95**, 95, **203**, 203, 204
Karoo 14, **22**, 23, 208, 213, **220**, **221**, 221
Karoo caterpillar 213
Karoo koppies **33**, 33
Karoo korhaan 216, **217**
Karoo National Park 245
Karoo num-num 136
Karoo prinia 204
Karoo River 262, **263**
Karoo Sea **221**
Karoo Shale Gas Ecology Project 264

viruses 57, 122
Vogel, Stephan 60
von Humboldt, Alexander 18
von Lindequist, Friedrich 245
von Willert, Dieter 58, 59
Vulpes chama see Cape fox
vygies 30, 197

W
Wahlenbergia 198
Walvis Bay **22**, 23, 27, 187, 257, 258
Warmbad (Namibia) 240, 241
wasps 140, 141, **198**, 198
water 39
 access to 65, **81**, 82, 96, 182, 185, 186
 artificial sources 63, **64**, **184**, 186
 ephemeral 34, **179**, 179, 180, 181, 187,
  233, 260
 foliar water uptake 59
 freestanding 63, 64, 65
 gain 40, **41**, 56
 groundwater 74, 97, 257, 258, 259
 loss **41**, 41, 42, 44, 46, 48, 53, 55, 72,
  81, 170
 storage 41, 43, 66, 67
 vapour pressure 15, 16, **17**, 41, **50**, 50,
  51, 53, 73
 waterholes **38**, 63, **64**, 94, 114, **155**,
  156, **157**, 157, **184**, **185**, 186, **246**

Waterberg Plateau 33
Watson, Rick 119, 171
weather fronts 250, 253
wedge-snouted sand lizard 77, **78**, 78, **142**,
 142
weevils **39**, **61**, 61, **115**
Wellwood farm 225, 229
Welwitsch, Friedrich 207
welwitschia 26, 44, **45**, 45, 51, 53, 62, 113,
 205, **206**, **207**, 207
Welwitschia 73, 74, 253; see also
 welwitschia
  mirabilis see *Welwitschia*
western keeled snake 28
western rock elephant shrew **173**, 174
white stork 213
white-browed sparrow-weaver **91**, 91, 155
Whiteheadia bifolia see pagoda lily
white-tailed shrike 246
wild tamarisk 26
wildebeest 208, 246
wildlife reintroductions 240, 245
Williamson, D.T. 66
Wilson, Edward O. 95, 99
wind circulation systems **251**
Windhoek **22**, 23
window plants **47**, 47, 73
wingless dune cricket **142**, 142
Wohlfahrtia pachytyli 205

wolf spider **76**, 76, **131**, 132
World Wide Fund for Nature 243

X
Xanthomaculina convoluta **27**, 27
Xanthoparmelia **56**, **27**, 27
Xanthoria **27**, **56**
Xerus inauris see Cape ground squirrel

Y
yellow mongoose 158, **159**
Young, Andrew 253

Z
zebra **38**, 208
Zeitgeber 214, 215, 216, 217, 219
Zophosini 170
Zophosis **48**, **171**
 moralesi 171
Zygophyllum stapfii see dollar bush